Praise for Marty Appel's

MUNSON

"A wonderful example of what's possible when you have a compelling subject and an author who not only has the insight to tell that subject's story but also the ability to tell it in a way that is affectionate without being fawning; that is honest without being voyeuristic; and that is eloquent without being purple."

—Mike Vaccaro, *The New York Post*

"A brilliant biography." —*The Boston Globe*

"Marty Appel's examination of Thurman Munson's traumatic life and controversial death is fascinating. The detail is amazing, and there's an anthology's worth of illuminating quotes. The glimpses of George Steinbrenner behind the scenes are priceless. An extraordinary book."

—Robert Creamer, author of *Babe: The Legend Comes to Life*

"Only Marty Appel could do justice to this fallen leader; a man who, a generation after his death, continues to inspire all who learn about him. Bravo, Marty, for every page!"

—Suzyn Waldman, New York Yankees Radio Broadcaster

"If the measure of a great biography is the amount of new, previously unmined material on the subject, then Marty Appel has hit a grand slam home run with this definitive portrait of Thurman Munson."

—Bill Madden, *New York Daily News*

"Appel's book is worth a read for fans looking for a behind-the-scenes look at a player and a baseball era that will forever remain compelling."　　　　　　　　　—Bill Littlefield, *Only a Game*, NPR

"Spectacular. . . . If you can get through this book without getting choked up, then you possess impressive resolve."
　　　　　　　　—Ken Davidoff's Baseball Insider, Newsday.com

"Thirty years after teaming with Munson on the Yankee catcher's autobiography, Appel comes back to finish the ultimately sad tale. No one else could have written this book. No one else could have written it better. Great stuff."
　　　　　—Leigh Montville, author of *The Big Bam* and *Ted Williams*

"Thurman Munson was the heart and soul of a team that transitioned from also-ran to champion. Marty Appel lived those years with the captain from the inside and now gives us a rare and intimate look at this remarkable, legendary Yankee. This is a must-read for any baseball fan."　　　—Michael Kay, YES Network, ESPN Radio

"A textured portrait of a flawed but likable individual, often angry and bitter, occasionally an ass, but ultimately worthy of our respect, on and off the field. The best biographies recount the public life, reveal the private life, and give readers a sense of the critical intersection between the two. Appel manages all three and deserves high praise for keeping one of baseball's most intriguing players in the forefront."　　　　　　　　—*Booklist* (starred review)

"Told through the voice of a friend and colleague for whom the death of the Yankee captain was a personal and a professional loss, Marty Appel's incisive and insightful biography of Thurman Munson is not just another sports book. It is a gift to baseball!"
　　　　　　　—Jane Leavy, author of *Sandy Koufax: A Lefty's Legacy*

Marty Appel

MUNSON

Following his years as the Yankees' PR director, Marty Appel became an Emmy Award–winning television producer and coauthored Munson's bestselling autobiography, as well as a number of other books. Appel lives in New York City and appears frequently on YES Network, ESPN, MLB, and HBO.

www.appelpr.com

ALSO BY MARTY APPEL

Now Pitching for the Yankees

Baseball: 100 Classic Moments in the History of the Game
   (with Joseph Wallace and Neil Hamilton)

Slide, Kelly, Slide

When You're from Brooklyn, Everything Else Is Tokyo (with Larry King)

Great Moments in Baseball (with Tom Seaver)

Yogi Berra

Working the Plate (with Eric Gregg)

Joe DiMaggio

My Nine Innings (with Lee MacPhail)

Yesterday's Heroes

The First Book of Baseball

Hardball: The Education of a Baseball Commissioner (with Bowie Kuhn)

Tom Seaver's All-Time Baseball Greats (with Tom Seaver)

Batting Secrets of the Major Leaguers

Thurman Munson: An Autobiography (with Thurman Munson)

Baseball's Best: The Hall of Fame Gallery (with Burt Goldblatt)

MUNSON

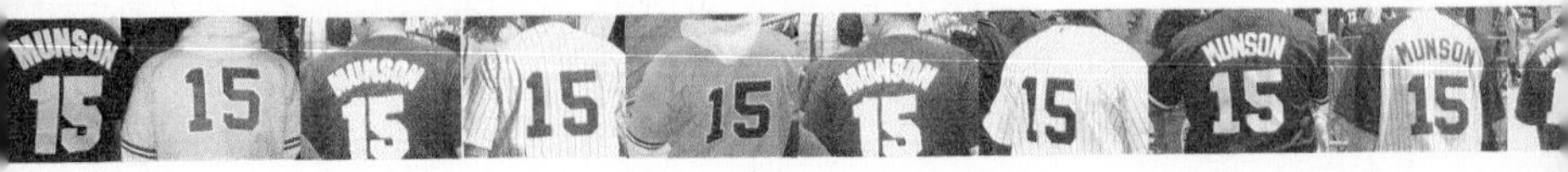

MUNSON

The Life and Death of a Yankee Captain

MARTY APPEL

ANCHOR BOOKS

A Division of Random House, Inc.

New York

FIRST ANCHOR BOOKS EDITION, JUNE 2010

Title page photographs courtesy of Marty Appel.

Permissions follow the bibliography.

The Library of Congress has cataloged the Doubleday edition as follows:
Appel, Martin.
Munson : the life and death of a Yankee captain / by Marty Appel.—1st ed.
p. cm.
1. Munson, Thurman, 1947–1979. 2. Baseball players—United States—
Biography. I. Title.
GV865.M78A67 2008
796.357092—dc22
2008026442

Anchor ISBN: 978-0-7679-2755-0

Author photograph © Raquel Lauren

www.anchorbooks.com

Printed in the United States of America
10 9 8 7 6 5 4 3

MUNSON

INTRODUCTION

At such a late hour, it took only twenty-five minutes for Bobby and Kay Murcer to drive Thurman Munson to Palwaukee Airport in Wheeling, Illinois, north of Chicago.

The Yankees had concluded their three-game series with the White Sox, and Munson, his knees hurting and unable to catch, had left that final game early, signaling to Billy Martin with a nod of the head that he needed to be replaced as first baseman. First base was supposed to ease the strain on his arthritic knees, but ever since he'd awkwardly fallen backward a few weeks earlier on a close pitch, he just wasn't the same.

The same, for him, meant a high level of proficiency, bordering on Hall of Fame greatness. But now, three straight seasons of championship play were coming to a close for the Yankees, and a great decade of performance was also winding down slowly for the thirty-two-year-old captain of the team.

Ah, but that was an hour ago. The Yanks had scored an easy victory, making the clubhouse loud and cheery on this getaway night,

August 1, 1979. The Murcers had agreed to drive Thurman to the airport, where they could see his new Cessna Citation jet up close. It was late at night—it was actually August 2 already—but baseball's schedule forces its participants to live late hours, and this didn't seem odd at all.

Except, of course, for Thurman leaving on his own plane and not flying on the big Delta charter out of O'Hare Airport with the rest of the Yankee team. Now *that* was pretty unusual.

Players just didn't do things like this. The great Bob Feller became a pilot after his playing career to get from one minor league park to another as he built a postplaying career out of personal appearances. His old Cleveland teammate Early Wynn had a pilot's license. So did Bob Turley, the former Yankee Cy Young Award winner, who used a private plane for business travel. For the most part, the older players simply couldn't afford such a hobby.

Ken Hubbs, a Chicago Cubs infielder, had died piloting his own plane fifteen months after winning the National League's 1962 Rookie of the Year Award.

"Thurman saw himself as more of an Arnold Palmer," says his older brother Duane, who for a time worked as a sky marshal. "He liked Palmer—his success at his field, his success in the business world, and the fact that he learned to pilot his own plane. I think Palmer was really his role model."

The Murcers, who had known Munson for a decade, had invited Thurman and Lou Piniella to stay with them in their Chicago apartment during the brief series. Bobby had been playing for the Cubs until just about a month before, and he still had his rented apartment there. It had been a great visit, all of them celebrating Bobby's return to the Yankees; one bright spot in an otherwise dismal 1979 season.

Murcer could be direct with Thurman, and he was on this night.

"Fly with you in that crazy thing? Not me, Tugboat," he said, calling Munson by one of his clubhouse nicknames.

Well, Thurman had at least extended the invitation. At the very least, the Murcers agreed to drive to the end of the runway and watch him take off. It was fun, in a way, late at night, the coolness of the summer evening, the temperature about sixty-seven degrees, Bobby and Kay feeling like teenagers somewhere in Middle America at an old-time airstrip, not just a half hour from a major city.

The Murcers agreed that the jet was beautiful. Thurman hadn't painted it in pinstripes, but he had put an identifying N15NY on the tail, and for those who thought he was hoping to get traded to Cleveland, there was a message in that. He was stamping his prized possession as "Yankee."

He ran his hand over the exterior, the shiny paint job not that old. He had gotten the $1.25 million twin-engine jet twenty-six days earlier, despite warnings by some that it was too much plane for him. But Munson, like most elite athletes, was not the conservative type when it came to risk-taking.

He said good night to the Murcers, who then drove to the end of the runway, and Munson climbed aboard his sleek prized possession, his aching knees settling into position. It was beautiful inside too. Sitting in the pilot's seat, the yoke in front of him, the airspeed indicator at eleven o'clock, the vertical speed indicator at three o'clock, the landing gear lever right there at his powerful right hand . . . it was all so magnificent! What a machine!

And so he went through his maneuvers and took off without delay, there being no other incoming or outgoing traffic at such a late hour. He slightly dipped his wings as he flew over the Murcers.

"The man's crazy," Bobby said, as they got in their car and headed home. "But that's Thurman."

The four-hundred-mile flight to Canton, Ohio, would be accomplished in just about an hour, with some bad weather keeping him on his toes. But this was the whole point of it all, wasn't it? If the jet could reduce the fly time over his Beechcraft King Air Model E-90, a prop plane, well, that was the goal. Get your own plane, take off when you're ready, and spend extra hours and extra days with the family—including four-year-old Michael Munson. ("That little guy, he's a handful," he acknowledged to friends.) Diana loved when he'd be home, because Michael would sleep through the night.

And of course she loved when he was home because theirs was one of the great love stories in baseball.

Up in the sky, passing over Lake Michigan, the lights of Fort Wayne, Indiana, in view, Thurman relaxed. He felt at home up there, although he'd only been flying for eighteen months. It was he and his plane and his wits.

During spring training, he had spoken to Tony Kubek, the old Yankee shortstop who now broadcast for NBC.

"I think it's great," he told Tony, "the feeling of being alone for an hour or two by yourself. You're up there, and nobody asks any questions. You don't have to put on any kind of an act. You just go up there and enjoy yourself. You have to be on your toes, but it's just a kind of relaxation when you spend a lot of time by yourself, and I need that. I also need to get home a lot, so I love to fly."

This was all so perfect. He was right where he wanted to be.

Some years earlier, a strapping truck driver who saw himself as more athlete than teamster would sit alone in the cab of his rig, perhaps thinking the same thoughts. Darrell Munson, Thurman's father, would think of the beauty of his independence, no one asking him questions, just on his toes, relaxing, putting America's highways behind him.

Maybe the two of them, long estranged, the father and his youngest son, had more in common than they realized.

1

Baseball wasn't cool in the 1960s.

During the "Summer of Love" not many young people were talking about Carl Yastrzemski. No one at Woodstock wondered whether the Mets could really go all the way. Few among my friends were particularly impressed when I took a summer job answering Mickey Mantle's fan mail for the Yankees in 1968. And it was the same when I was offered, and accepted, a full-time position in the public relations department midway through my senior year in 1970.

I was one of two people in my college who subscribed to *The Sporting News* (my roommate was the other)—but I couldn't watch baseball on Sundays in the fall when the one TV in the dorm was tuned to the NFL—even during the World Series!

As Mantle, Banks, Clemente, Mays, Aaron, Mathews, Maris, Killebrew, Koufax, Drysdale, and Colavito moved toward the twilight of their careers, few stars appeared to replace them. The mid- to late sixties gave us Reggie Jackson, Johnny Bench, and Tom Seaver, but not many other attention-getters.

But then, in the midst of this decidedly uncool period of baseball, the once proud Yankees, now mediocre and dull, found a player named Thurman Lee Munson to proudly take them to their tomorrows.

Thurman was a throwback; a lunch-bucket kind of guy who was all jock and no rock. He wasn't going to win over New York by being Joe Namath or Clyde Frazier. He liked Wayne Newton music and, in what was arguably the worst-dressed decade of the twentieth century, the 1970s, he was the worst of the worst. His wardrobe featured clashing plaids and checks made of the finest polyester. Socks were optional.

It was an everyman look that went with his regular-guy demeanor. He liked to pump his own gas, even in New Jersey, where you weren't allowed to, and even when he became famous. On occasion, thinking he was the attendant, someone would pull up next to him and say, "Fill 'er up"—and he would! He'd pump the guy's gas, collect payment, and hand it to the station manager. I was with him one day when he even washed a guy's windshield while filling up his gas tank. I suspect the guy drove away thinking, *That gas station guy looked a lot like Thurman Munson.*

No, cool wasn't his game. He was going to win them over the old-fashioned way—with gritty determination and a focus on respecting the game and playing it with heart. He would honor the tradition of the Yankees and wear the uniform dirty and proud, and would not tolerate mediocrity from his teammates. He would restore the Yankees to their prominence in the sports universe, the place they occupied when all seemed right in the world.

We would fall in love with his game and realize, watching him, that cool didn't have to count in baseball. Thurman Munson made it a virtue to be *uncool,* winning over the young and the hip with his decidedly unhip approach to his profession.

He wasn't Mickey Mantle—he wasn't born with those looks or that body, or that particular style that made "the Mick" a pinup boy for baby boomers. But he was Mantle's heir. Mickey retired in spring training of 1969. Munson made his debut later that season, giving the Yankees continuity in their ongoing parade of stars.

By 1970, my first year as assistant public relations director, New York had begun to latch on to his Ohio grit and guts. And since my career began along with his, he would become "my guy," the player I would grow up with in the Yankee organization, the one I'd write about and collaborate with.

I loved watching Thurman Munson play baseball. He just knew how to play the game, knew how to win the game, knew how to lead. He was grumpy but he had a great sense of humor and a magnificent sense of self. He was the kind of guy you wanted to be friends with.

As kids we had the same glove. His first glove was made by Hutch, as was mine. When I asked him whose model it was, the coincidence broadened—we both used the same model, a Billy Goodman infielder's glove. I remembered mine as a pancake that didn't really fold to trap the ball; he remembered his as a "good old mitt." Clearly, he made better use of his than I did of mine.

I was there when he made his first appearance at Yankee Stadium in August 1968, when the Yankees brought the Binghamton team to the stadium to play Waterbury, Connecticut. While some of his Binghamton Triplet teammates like Steve Kline and Frank Tepedino walked out to the monuments in center field for a look, Thurman was detained near the infield for some media interviews and photographs. He was clearly the guy everyone wanted to see.

At one point, he just decided to walk over to the Yankee clubhouse and say hello to Mickey Mantle. What the hell. The other guys could look at monuments to dead guys. Thurman would say hello to a future monument, still living.

Mantle, in the final weeks of his eighteen-year career, was seated on his stool by his corner locker, dressed in his baseball underwear, wrapping his legs in long Ace bandages, as was his custom.

"Mickey, I'm Thurman Munson," he said, his voice perhaps revealing that he was nervous but determined just the same. Since he was wearing his Binghamton uniform, he didn't think it was necessary to say who he was other than his name. Mick responded with a firm handshake and asked, "How ya doin'?"—hardly the stuff of highlight reels, but enough to make Munson's day.

Mantle had heard of him. Everyone in the organization had. He had been an elite high school athlete in three sports, and then went to Kent State, where he was the consensus All-American college catcher in his junior year. The Yankees felt fortunate that he was still available in the first round when they made him the overall fourth selection in the amateur draft. He was "fast-tracked" by the scouting department for a ticket to the majors.

Michael Grossbardt, a Kramer-like character in the Seinfeld vein, was the Yankee photographer. He was under orders from PR chief Bob Fishel to get some good "posed action" pictures of Thurman, which could be used as publicity stills. Grossbardt would go on to photograph most of Thurman's career, shooting thousands of pictures of him at bat and behind the plate, as well as baseball card photos for the Topps Company, family pictures for his personal use, and magazine covers.

I walked behind Fishel, his assistant Bill Guilfoile, and Michael, out to the area behind home plate for the photos. We took turns shaking his hand, and I was flattered that Bob took the trouble to introduce me. Munson had a chubby look, almost unathletic, and he wasn't much taller than I was, but he had those big forearms you always see on baseball players. His flannel hand-me-down Yankee uniform, converted to a Triplets uniform, was baggy and unflattering. The schedule called this a Waterbury home game, so he was in the drab gray road uniform. He seemed to know how to pose, and there was a confidence to him that I would seldom see among rookies, as it grew to be part of my job over the years to get them all photographed in spring training. Amazingly, you can always tell a rookie photo from a veteran photo by the poise or lack of poise on display. Thurman had some poise.

I had asked Bob if we were going to call him "Thurm" going forward in our press notices. Remembering that, he asked Munson if he went by any nicknames.

"None that you'd want to print," he laughed, a typical ballplayer answer. And indeed, he never really developed one that stuck with the public.

Howard Berk, our vice president for administration, had come down onto the field as well. "We really needed someone to capture the fans' imagination," he said later. "We were so hoping this would be the guy. And we liked him from the start. He was always very cooperative with me; always went on our *Winter Warm-Up* radio shows to help boost off-season ticket sales for us."

He did all that and more in the decade he played for the Yankees until his untimely death in 1979. By the time I wrote his autobiography in 1977, he had accomplished enough to fill up a plaque in Cooperstown. The book was a traditional baseball life story with little controversy, particularly given his place in the turmoil of the so-called Bronx Zoo. He offered an equally small amount of personal insight. "Does it have to get personal?" he asked, when I approached him with the idea.

What a strange question, I thought, from a man considering an autobiography.

The book sold a lot more copies after he died than before. I've received a lot of compliments on it over the years, particularly from Munson fans. His wife, Diana Munson, was especially admiring. "Thank you for writing it, thank God we have this," she said to me on the eve of his funeral in her home in Canton.

But as I have reread that book over the years, I've always felt that Thurman held back too much, skirting over personal matters, as was his right. The publisher was pleased with the final product, so I felt I had met my obligation to give them both the book they wanted. But I was never really satisfied with it.

I was also perplexed. Why were his comments so unenlightening? For example, there was the matter of his ancestry. I wrote he was of German stock. His sister told me later that the family was mostly English-Welsh, and only part German on both sides. Why didn't he correct me? Why didn't he care about getting his life right? Why did he have so little to say about his childhood?

Diana had asked me whether he brought up much about his childhood. She hadn't been in the room when we were doing the tapings. I told her I had brought up the subject but the conversation didn't go very far. I think she was just curious to know how much he had opened up.

Obviously, he hadn't. In the three decades since Thurman's death, I have wondered why a man who gave so much of himself on the field would withhold so much off of it. This book is an attempt to fill in the gaps that Thurman left in telling his own story to me in 1977–78. In the course of revisiting the details of his life and his death, of visiting his family and friends, I have thought back to the way he presented himself in the Yankee clubhouse in the last years of his career.

He had pretty much stopped talking to the media. Still, there were times when the glare of the Bronx Zoo fell squarely on his thickset body. Maybe it was something the Boss, George Steinbrenner, said. Maybe it was something Reggie Jackson said. Maybe it was something Billy Martin had done. Thurman was the captain, the go-to guy for the press, the steadying influence, the voice of reason. And so they had to ask him about it.

Munson would lower his gaze, refusing to make eye contact, walk through them all, and say, "I'm just happy to be here."

It was as though he were Mr. Magoo, walking blindly through the turmoil, oblivious to it all. Of course, Thurman wasn't oblivious at all. He was well aware that his home wasn't like the homes of his classmates and teammates. He didn't want his coach to drop him off at home and see it. He didn't want readers to see inside those walls. And he certainly wasn't going to reveal himself to the media. No, he would pretend everything was fine, and that life would go on—la de da—no matter what chaos surrounded him.

The story Munson didn't tell is how his childhood had in fact prepared him for the Bronx Zoo. I see him now walking through the tensions of the Munson home and saying, in his own way, "I'm just happy to be here."

2

Thurman Lee Munson was born on June 7, 1947, in Akron, Ohio, the tire and rubber capital of the United States.

He was the youngest of four children. Darla, the oldest, was born in 1941, and Janice came along eleven months later. Duane, the oldest son, was born fourteen months after Janice. After those three children in twenty-five months, there was a four-year gap between Duane and Thurman.

When Thurman was four, the Munsons moved as tenants to a farm in Randolph, a half hour east. When he was eight, they moved to the city of Canton, a half hour south. When Thurman was in second grade, the family moved to 2015 Frazer Avenue NW, between Nineteenth and Twenty-first streets. Canton, the state's eighth largest city, would always remain Thurman's hometown, even after fame and fortune would come his way. He was comfortable and well respected there, partly from his Yankee fame but also from his schoolboy fame, when he was one of the best athletes the town would ever see.

The Frazer Avenue home was a modest two-story home (plus an attic) with a gable roof and bevel siding, and a homey, brick-bordered front porch. There was a side entrance, and about thirty feet of front lawn along the modestly trafficked street. The houses on the block were set close to one another, and represented a comfortable standard of living for a working-class family.

"We moved around quite a bit," Duane Munson recalls. "Thurm was probably too young to remember much of those years, and sometimes they're pretty vague on me too. We were very active kids and got into our share of trouble, but nothing very serious. When Dad did find out that we were bad, he let us know it with his leather belt.

"We lived on Ido Avenue in Akron, and that would have been where Thurm was born. I vaguely remember my grandfather and my mother having polio or having had polio, but beyond that, Akron is a blur."

"When I finished my chores, I'd play ball mostly," said Thurman. "I loved to play and I'd come home at night where my collie, Fritzy, was waiting for me.

"I started playing as a kid and I was 'littler' than most. This may sound corny, but I remember seeing a lot of horses back in Ohio and baseball reminded me of a stallion just running free. There was a freedom to the game. No matter what your problems were and what you had on your mind, when you played baseball you forgot about it."

Denton T. "Cy" Young had gotten his nickname in Canton, when his warm-up throws against a fence (location long lost to history) prompted onlookers to think he was throwing like "a cyclone."

William McKinley, the nation's twenty-fifth president, was considered to be from Canton. He was certainly the most illustrious historical figure from that town (unless you count rocker Marilyn Manson), and as he was victim of an assassin's bullet, his memorial service was the biggest event the city had ever hosted. He was actually born in Niles, sixty-five miles northeast, and moved to Canton when he was twenty-six but, like Munson, he is associated with the town, birthplace notwithstanding. Like Munson, he is buried there.

The Pro Football Hall of Fame is located there, with the town coming alive each summer for the annual induction ceremony and Hall of Fame game. The American Professional Football Association, a forerunner of the NFL, was founded there in 1920. The Canton Bulldogs were an early powerhouse, and the great Jim Thorpe played for them.

There aren't many major league baseball players from Akron or Canton, but if you were raised in that northern Ohio region, sixty miles south of Cleveland, you had a bond, a commonality, an understanding of the sort of working-class, "tough it out" attitude that the people shared. It was a place where you had to speak up to correct an injustice or you'd be left behind.

Bill White, the former player, broadcaster, and National League president, although born in Florida, considered himself an Ohio guy. He lived in Warren and went to Warren Harding High School and then to Hiram College near Cleveland. Although older than Munson, and African-American, he and Munson understood the culture and understood each other. White was a Yankee broadcaster throughout Munson's career, and the two had a strong mutual respect.

"I think there is something about growing up in that industrial valley between, say, Steubenville and Cleveland, that just toughens you," White says. "We were all kids from the wrong side of the tracks, or at least no better than the middle. You had to fight for what you wanted; it made you tougher, maybe matured you a little quicker.

"If you were an athlete, you probably played all three sports, and that kept you disciplined and in training almost all year. And you played without an ego. You wouldn't find kids from this area developing 'style' on the field or on the court. You went out and played hard, and you could handle things when they went wrong. When the game was over, you shook hands, and you had a 'we'll get you next year' attitude. And you moved on. And that was the background Thurman and I came from.

"I once said on the air that he was the best clutch hitter in the game," White continues. "Later on he heard about it and called me over to his locker and thanked me. I told him he didn't have to thank me, it was true. If he was horseshit I would have said that too! He laughed, because we understood each other. We were both Buckeyes. There is an honesty to life there."

Thurman's father, Darrell Vernon Munson, a tough World War II veteran who said he was "in heavy equipment with the Marines in the Pacific," was a long-distance truck driver who spoke his mind and wound up in a lot of arguments with his employers over the years. He'd sometimes quit, sometimes get fired, but he knew the drill, and knew how to get another job right away. Sometimes the same people would hire him back.

"He couldn't get along with people," says Thurman's oldest sister, Darla. "He was always getting fired or laid off." He was good at what he did, temper aside. Driving trucks was perhaps the best career for him, because it didn't require a lot of human contact and thus minimized his chances of conflict during the week.

"He wasn't a drinker," his children agree. He could have a temper, and it wasn't pretty, but it wasn't fueled by alcohol. He'd have an occasional beer; that was all.

"He was friendly enough in the sense of inviting our friends in," recalls Duane. "Sometimes."

In the autobiography, Thurman said, "When Dad was around, everyone in the house, including Mom, was intimidated. It seemed as though her chief responsibility was to keep us out of trouble so that Dad wouldn't get mad at us."

That understated the issue.

"I hate to say it, but Mom was a bit of a snitch," sighs Darla, a soft smile poking fun at the childhood word. "She'd go and pick up Dad wherever he'd parked the truck. And on the drive home, she'd be like, 'This one didn't do his chores, this one didn't make her bed, this one didn't do this, didn't do that,' and so he'd come home after a week away and just start hitting us. A fist across the head. Scary. He'd throw things too, if that was convenient. And I remember Mom off to the side crying and saying, 'Stop! Enough!' "

Surely, the children were looking for more after a week's absence.

Duane joined the Air Force as Thurman was starting high school, leaving Thurm with no real family cheering section during his high school games, and removing his big brother from the household. His sisters had long ago left, as soon as they were of age. So in high school, it was pretty much just Thurman and his mom during the week.

"Thurm and I spent a lot of time playing Wiffle ball and we were both pretty good at it," adds Duane, who would go on to a career in government service, first with the National Security Agency and later with the Treasury Department as a sky marshal. He'd get a master's degree from the University of Maryland after the Air Force.

"I was a Yankee fan then as I am still today, and I always played as the Yankee lineup and Thurm played as the Indians' lineup. I remember him doing Rocky Colavito's famous stretches before he hit, and then pointing the bat at the pitcher. We had all the batting stances down pat and we could both switch-hit to make it authentic. We could imitate the pitching motions too. I was a huge Yankee fan starting in the mid-fifties, and Thurm was an Indians fan like our dad was. I think Thurm followed his lead on that.

"We saved baseball cards, but Mom threw them out, like all mothers eventually did.

"He always played baseball, basketball, and football, and we always played with kids my age or older, but rarely with any kids as young as Thurm, who was four years younger than me. I think that's where he got his skill from. He'd play with older kids and get knocked around in the process. He wasn't given any slack because he was younger or because he was my brother. By the time he got to high school, he was toughened up more than most kids his age.

"And what an athlete he was! Never mind that he was the youngest. He just made everything look so easy. He was a great pool player in college. He was a great golfer—that may have been his best sport. And he had such gifts for baseball that I think he may actually have underachieved in that game. Sometimes I think he didn't take it as seriously as people thought he did. I think he may have just done enough to make his money and get by.

"With Dad being a long-distance trucker, he wanted us to be at home a lot when he was off, especially during the weekends. But we got to play a lot and he liked the kids we played with, so it wasn't all that hard getting permission to go out and play. We always had to ask, though. We even took turns asking because we didn't know what the response was going to be. Dad could be mean. When he had a long-distance run, he would leave on a Sunday, a lot of the time in midmorning, so he could make Boston, New York, Philadelphia, or some other place the next morning. We couldn't wait for him to leave so we could go play. And we knew Mom was a softie, so she would say yes most every time.

"Dad had a very, very strict eleven p.m. curfew, and would lock the door at 11:01. I can still hear Mom inside yelling, 'Let him in, let him in!' but he would have none of it. There were nights when Thurman or I would sleep under newspapers in the car.

"During the summers, we'd spend most days playing baseball and softball or going to Stadium Park to get crawfish. Stadium Park is adjacent to where the Pro Football Hall of Fame is now. We rode our bikes everywhere. We had them stripped down to the bare frame and I was always surprised that Dad didn't say something about it and whip up on us in the process, but he didn't.

"Thurm was a star in high school in three sports and that probably helped to dilute the strictness and irrational behavior that Dad exhibited sometimes. I'm not sure what Thurm thought of Dad after he left home. He never wanted to talk about it but he knew I was the only family member that kept in touch with Dad, and I was really the only one of us kids that Dad kept in touch with."

By "us kids," Duane includes his sisters Janice and Darla, both of whom had their issues with family life in the Munson household.

"I try to get over things, but it hasn't been easy," says Darla. "I don't remember anything good about my childhood."

In 1987, Diana Munson told *Sports Illustrated*'s Armen Keteyian, "Thurman was basically an insecure person. It stems from his childhood. He had a tough one. His dad . . . was a real tough cookie. He was real hard. So Thurman had some real problems growing up, and I think he kept a lot of his insecurities inside. He had the kind of personality that he never wanted to talk about them, never wanted to show the hurt. He developed an exterior that was gruff, or whatever people wanted to call it."

"I used to take all my kids home from practice at one time or another," recalled Thurman's high school baseball coach, Don Eddins. "All except Thurman. It was almost as if he was ashamed of his house. And I guess Thurman was a very proud person and that house certainly wasn't much of a home. And by that I don't mean what the outside of the house looked like."

Thurman was the baby, so he had it easier than the older three. Both Duane and Darla agree on that much.

"He was my pet," Ruth Myrna Smylie Munson told the *Canton Repository* from her room in the senior citizens complex in Canton where she lived out her later years. This was Thurman's mother. She had suffered a stroke while in her fifties (she would eventually suffer five strokes). Thurman's father, Darrell, took her to Florida after the first, but then had had enough of caring for her and put her alone on a bus back to Canton, telling his children, "I'm done, you deal with her." The children placed her in a nursing home. Darrell Munson then took off for Arizona and a new life, seldom to be heard from again.

"Mom's mother died at eighteen," Darla says. "Her father, Howard, had trucks that Darrell drove for him. That's how he met Ruth. Howard remarried a woman named Mary. They despised my father; hence there was not much of a relationship with our only living grandparent, who died when I was about nine."

In 1977 Ruth was transferred to the senior citizens home by Janice, who furnished her room with a queen-size bed, a TV, portable shelving, a table, and three chairs. Among her possessions was a copy of Thurman's autobiography, published in 1978, signed "To my mother, with much love forever, Thurman Munson."

After Thurman's death, the *Repository* wrote, "Many in Munson's position have bought their parents castles."

"Sadly," says Darla, "Thurman rarely went to see her—maybe two or three times a year."

But Ruth said, "I'm happy with this place. All I ever wanted from my children was the chance to see them and the chance to see them turn out well. Anyway, I wouldn't know what to do with a big place."

Ruth "never missed a television game involving the Yankees," wrote the *Repository*. "Sometimes after the games her son would telephone her. 'I can hear him saying how much he loved me when he called,' said Mrs. Munson. 'He always said, "Mom, I love you." ' "

"She was so giving, such a matriarch," says Thurman's childhood friend Jerome Pruett of Ruth Munson. "Everyone admired her. But his father, oh he was tough. I remember there was this school dance and you had to have a sports jacket to go, but Thurman didn't have one. And his father wouldn't get one for him. Thurman was hurting from that."

In truth, Darrell Munson had a challenging upbringing himself, which may account partially for the spartan—almost merciless—attitude he would exhibit toward Thurman even later in life. Sometimes you have to go back a generation to understand what makes us who we are. People drew conclusions about Darrell being difficult without knowledge of his own troubled childhood. It began with his being moved into foster care at a young age. His father was an alcoholic, and his mother, Leola, ran off with another man. Soon after, she was dead. She might have been murdered or might have committed suicide; no one in the family is sure.

Darrell's father died when Darla, the eldest child, was two months old.

Still, the relationship between Darrell and Thurman was always, at best, strained.

Corky Simpson, writing for the *Tucson Citizen*, caught up with Darrell two months after Thurman's death, when he was working as a parking lot attendant in the Arizona town. He was sixty-four then, no longer driving trucks, far removed from his family, and he gave what turned out to be a startling interview:

> "Thurman was a tremendous athlete, could do anything he tried," recalled Darrell. "But he was not the best catcher I ever saw. He had two very pronounced weaknesses. I must have worked with him a thousand hours, but he'd invariably throw the ball wild to second base.
>
> "He could throw a hundred in a row perfectly, then—all of a sudden—one would go sailing on him. The other weakness was that he couldn't field a short bounce in front of him. I worked on that too, but he never overcame it.

"One time, when he was with Binghamton, before he went up to the Yanks, I went to see him play against Elmira. Thurman had two home runs and went 5-for-5 that day and after the game I walked up to him and said, 'Thurman, you were shitty.' It made him mad.

"I told him that because he made two wild throws and his team got beat. It made me furious. I figured this was an unpardonable mistake.

"You can do everything great on offense but if you lose a game on defense, well, that's something I can't tolerate.

"And you couldn't tell Thurman anything. He was pampered and babied 'til the cows came home by his mother. He thought he was so great he didn't need anybody.

"He figured he had a market on brains, too, but he didn't. Not outside sports.

"We were alienated a long time. He had nothing to do with me, his brother and one sister (Darla Jean). His other sister (Janice Marie) was sort of in the movement with Thurman and his wife, Diane.

"Thurman's trouble was he had too much natural ability. Some people, like myself, have to struggle to be good at something. It came natural to Thurman.

"He was a tremendous athlete—shot in the low 70s as a golfer, won a state handball championship in Ohio, was an all-city, all-county and all-state football player. Thirty-one football coaches came to our house recruiting him before he took a baseball scholarship to Kent State.

"I wanted him to play football, but he wouldn't do it. He went to Kent State on a baseball scholarship and the whole reason was to be near his sweetheart . . . not to be near his family.

"Thurman was an All-American baseball player and a varsity basketball player at Kent State. He never finished; he signed with the Yankees. And he wasn't going to sign if I had anything to do with it, but Gene Woodling and Lee MacPhail [of the Yankees] told him I had to be involved.

"Well, he got $70,000 from the Yankees—$45,000 in cash and $25,000 in benefits. They gave me $4,000.

"He got to be so important, he had a swell head. He couldn't be taught anything. He won a very prestigious sports award back in Ohio one time and didn't even show up to accept it. He had his father-in-law pick it up. I was in town but he didn't ask me.

"I remember getting mad at Thurman once and shouting 'Who do you think you are—Jesus Christ?'—and he said, 'Well, I'm not him, I just look like him.'

"I never had any folks," he told the reporter, getting into what may have been the most revealing portion of his troubled family relationships. "My mother and dad were divorced when I was six months old and I never lived with either one of them.

"My mother was either killed or committed suicide in 1928 in Detroit. I bounced around from one house to the other. I never got past eighth grade in school.

"I had to leave school when I was 13. It was the Depression and I was hired out as a farmhand for room, board and a pair of overalls. Thurman, on the other hand, had everything I never had, mainly a home.

"I had natural talent as a ballplayer. Even today, I have fast reflexes. I wish I could have made it to the big leagues because I think I could have outdone Thurman. I would have been better than him.

"When he died, he was worth several million dollars, but I have never heard anything about a will. I used to have a

bunch of scrapbooks, but his mother took them back to
Ohio when we got divorced.

"The only thing of his I have is a bunch of Banlon shirts
he got tired of wearing.

"Thurman resented me, but I did what I did the best I
could. What happened is hindsight.

"I just wasn't in his world. People used to say I criticized
him too much; maybe that's what I did wrong. But he resented me. He got carried away with his own self-importance.

"He hated me."

Simpson later said it was the only time in his career that he was
tempted just to close his reporter's notebook and walk away.

3

Thurman's interest in baseball—as a fan—was what you would expect from a lot of future professional players: minimal. They spend too much time playing to follow the big leagues the way most of us in my neighborhood did. He did tell me a story about getting Cleveland Indians pitcher Mike Garcia to sign a ball for him at Municipal Stadium one day in the fifties. It wasn't a moment that stayed with him and made him any more accommodating to fans once he became a Yankee. He was always a tough autograph.

"I can't even remember the Indians winning the pennant in 1954," he told me, "even though I was seven, and old enough to remember. It was really football, football, football in Ohio. I was a big Cleveland Browns fan, and I remember them winning year after year in the old American Conference."

Thurman went to elementary school at the Worley School on Twenty-third Street NW, and he and Duane got certificates of recognition in the sports programs.

Classmate Lenny May remembers Thurman in fourth grade,

climbing the fence after a baseball got loose, and then getting his leg caught climbing back in.

"Somehow in one of the few unathletic moves I ever saw from him, he caught his leg coming back over and landed on his arm. Because of the grotesque position of his arm we knew he was seriously hurt, but the thing I remember was that he shed no tears even though he was in terrible pain, as we later found out, from a compound fracture."

"We met in eighth grade," says Jerome Pruett, who was his high school battery mate and would go on to play pro baseball too. "I was playing tetherball in the playground and this guy comes peddling up on his bike, really cocky, like he could beat anybody there. Within a few minutes, he was playing the game as a blood sport. He was so talented at everything, and so egotistical—which is what you want to see in a competitive athlete."

"Thurm was like part of our family," recalls Susie Wilson. "He'd go down the alley by his house and show up at my grandmother's all the time just for her homemade cookies. And if there was a holiday, like Thanksgiving, there would be Thurman and Duane, sprawled out on the floor watching football with everyone else. They'd play sports trivia—Thurm always knew the answers."

His specialty was Big Ten Football. He knew everything.

"The cookies!" remembers Susie's uncle, Tom Wilson. "When he was famous and back home in Canton, he'd still come by for the cookies. Duane too. They loved my grandmother, who lived to be 102.

"Being boys, we got into fights now and then," says Tom. "Once we had a fight while playing baseball and my dad ran over to break it up. He said, 'Boys, boys, stop it, it's not like either of you will make it to the major leagues!' He was wrong.

"Another time we'd play this game in his basement with my brother Larry and with Duane and Thurman, where we'd turn off all the lights and just start beating each other up. And Thurman hit me so hard in the kidney that I peed blood for a week!

"When the Munsons moved here from Randolph, they really didn't have much. My family helped them move, and we actually gave them shoes to wear. But I was the one who saw what an athlete he was, and I took him with me to sign up for Mighty Mite baseball when he was nine. I wanted him on my team, but someone else got him first. I would have loved to have played Mighty Mite with Thurman."

"Thurman was the most regular guy you could imagine," adds Susie. "He wouldn't even call himself a jock if you asked him, even playing all the sports. He did it for fun. But he also would say, 'I'm gonna play for the New York Yankees one day.' And you sorta thought he was really going to do it. When I picture him now, he's walking down the hallways in school, in jeans and a T-shirt with an open shirt over it. Just a regular guy."

He would go on to Lehman High School. Built in 1920, it is today Lehman Middle School, with McKinley now the public high school in northwest Canton. (In 1976, Canton restructured its secondary schools, closing Lehman as a high school and expanding Canton McKinley.) The Lehman Polar Bears found in Thurman one of the greatest athletes the school had ever known. He was captain of the football, basketball, and baseball teams, earned nine letters, and was all-city and all-state in all three. He was a halfback, end, and a linebacker in football and a guard in basketball, where he averaged twenty points a game. Mostly he played shortstop on the baseball team, but eventually he caught, and occasionally even pitched.

"He'd strike out ten in a seven-inning game," recalls Pruett. "We played off each other. I'd be a better hitter because of him; he'd be a better pitcher because of me. And we'd play Wiffle ball by his house on Frazer and he'd hit the ball to the top level of his house; he'd cream it. When it got dark, we'd go over to the synagogue on Twenty-fifth Street and keep playing because the lighting was better there."

"He was very competitive and better than the rest of us in every sport other than golf," says his classmate Randy Board. "That bothered him a lot. He took up golf later than some of us and always wanted to beat the more experienced golfers."

"Even though he was a top-level athlete, he was fun to be on a team with," says Earl Rodd, who was a basketball teammate and considered himself the "last man" on the team. "If you were on the court with him in practice, he always did his best to run the plays and make things work for everyone. It didn't matter if you were the twelfth man on the roster."

Bob Henderson coached Thurman in basketball during Thurman's senior year. Henderson was only twenty-six and in his first year at Lehman. He also taught science. When he arrived he asked others, "Who do I have? What can I expect?" They pointed to Munson. "Five-nine and dumpy!" recalls Henderson. "This is my star?"

He was, by all accounts, a pleasure to coach. He was cocaptain of the basketball team, and Henderson remembers the final game of the Canton All-City Night, a round-robin tournament for the four city high schools, with five thousand seats packed. In this last game of the season, Lehman was down by a point with four or five seconds to play. Thurman stole the ball and headed for a layup. Naturally, he got clobbered and fouled.

Henderson called time and sat the kids down, looking for some words of wisdom. "I can still hear him now, it was an exact quote— he said, 'Don't worry about it coach, it's in the bag,' with that little smile of his. And of course he makes the two foul shots and we win.

"He was so coachable, and so honorable, he'd even call in if he was late getting home. We had a 10:30 curfew. He called me around 10:35 one night to say he had missed curfew and just got home."

"He was really gifted in football too," said Tom Albu, the cocaptain with Thurman in his senior year. "He liked the excitement of it; and football was a big event in Canton. Maybe he wasn't that big, but he could play the game. He had that great eye-hand thing—he was an end, and he could glance up, see the ball, and be where it was going to land. And he'd return punts on the dead run like something you'd see in an old Red Grange film. He had the moves of a professional wide receiver, and one time he bought a book by Raymond Berry of the Colts, and he'd study it over and over again. He always wanted to get better.

"He was just so good at everything. Once we went bowling. I clobbered him. It was so uncharacteristic. Then I thought, 'Maybe this was his first time . . .' A week or so later he called and invited me to bowl with him. And this time he clobbered me. He had obviously learned something or practiced a few times.

"He'd spend a lot of time at our house; he liked our family. Sometimes he just did it to get away from his own home. He'd sleep on our back porch. I remember one time when his mom was at our house, and she was just berating him and berating him in front of us, and he'd just keep repeating, 'Oh Mom, oh Mom.' It was so embarrassing."

"We'd draw twenty-two thousand people to high school football games," says Carl Santilli, who owned Thurman's favorite restaurant, Lucia's. "What other town this size does that? Kids come to play us from other schools; it scares the shit out of them, they've never seen such a crowd at a high school game. Thurman fed off that."

His baseball coach, Don Eddins, was a handsome, powerful man in his late thirties who never played college sports but learned how to run a disciplined sports team. Thurman described him as "a real driver and a hustler. He taught me a lot about the game, and I enjoyed playing for him."

He may in fact have been a father figure to Thurman, who never got positive reinforcement from Darrell. "Thurman was Coach Eddins's favorite," says Pruett. "And when Moose Paskert, the baseball coach at Kent State later came around, Eddins told him that Thurm was 'cocky and a winner.'

"What Thurman brought to the field was the ability to figure out how to beat you. If you had twenty-one outs in a seven-inning game, he'd figure out how to extend it to thirty-one, with walks, shots into the gap, whatever. He was so good at waiting on a pitch and then driving it into the gaps. He did all the little things. There were no easy outs to give away as he figured it. Nobody played the game like that. He'd do it in basketball too, where he'd save a ball from going out of bounds by slapping it at an opponent's leg. That stuff just wasn't done back then."

Munson hit .581 in 1965 and was the shortstop on the all-Ohio team. It was certainly during those years that he began to seriously think he could one day be a professional player.

"He started as a shortstop but was switched to catcher because no one else could handle Jerome Pruett," says Jim Lurie, who served as the Polar Bears statistician. Pruett would be a fifth-round draft pick by the Cardinals in 1965, but never made the majors, hurting his arm in 1967 when he was under a major league contract.

"Coach Eddins came to me and said, 'What would you think of Thurman catching you?'" says Pruett. "And I said, 'Fine!' Well, you never saw anything like it. He'd be calling for curveballs on three and two when all I really threw was heat. But he'd say, 'When I put down two fingers, I want you to throw the curve!' And he'd do it on three and two, which was really high risk!

"The first time he actually caught was our junior year [1964]. I threw ninety-plus as a junior, and a young man by the name of Terry Ripple couldn't handle my rising fastball, which sometimes rose from the dirt in front of home plate. We asked Thurm, and with his likable but take-charge personality, he and I became one, and he really did impart objectivity to my rogue talent. His favorite cartoon character was Huckleberry Hound; he'd imitate that character for fun, and it fit him; he had that cockiness.

"Thurman caught when I pitched, and then started catching some of the other pitchers. After I graduated and signed with the Cardinals, the gang said he really blossomed, got stronger, went to the pinnacle of confidence, and became known as *the* catcher, instead of the guy who could beat you with his head and his bat.

"No one really showed him how to do much; he just had a passion for being the best. So through watching others, like the Indians catcher John Romano at that time, and doing his own type of research, he just basically let his instincts take over."

"I just let my development as a catcher come naturally," Munson said. "Defense wasn't that important to me then. I just loved to hit, and it didn't matter to me where I played in the field."

In the summers Thurman would play in the Canton City Baseball League, and although he was the youngest player, he was the star. It was a terrific league for development of his skills; a well-run amateur league that played about forty games a summer. He played for the Huskies, which was coached by his sister Darla's first husband, Denny Gothot. Denny coached in that league for twenty-seven seasons.

Lenny May remembers, "Denny, who threw very hard, was throwing balls at Thurman's head and Thurman's role was to deflect the balls with the bat. It sticks in my memory because of the ease with which Thurman dealt with the pitches and the lack of interest the rest of us had in participating in that."

Moving up to the Junior Boys Baseball League, he played for the Seran Agency team. In his three midteenage summers, Thurman hit .369, .300, and .440, batting third in the lineup and playing shortstop. The team would regularly go to Battle Creek, Michigan, for the American Amateur Baseball Congress national tournament.

"In American Legion ball, we played for Post 44 back in 1963 and we had this little thing where we'd tip our caps to each other when one or the other of us got a hit," recalls Bob Beldon, who went on to play quarterback for Notre Dame and then spent two years with the Dallas Cowboys as a backup to Roger Staubach. "And we'd do it when we passed each other in town too; it just became our thing."

"He always had fun at sports," says Joe Gilhousen, who went to the Worley School with him and played with him in American Legion ball. "He was always the best player at whatever he did, but he did it all with fun. Later he recruited me to go to Kent State with him. I was like his little brother there; he looked after me."

In 1964 Thurman drove with his father and Duane to a tryout run by the Pittsburgh Pirates, in Columbus, Ohio.

"It seemed like it was two hundred degrees that day and we sat around a lot waiting for Thurm's name to be called to take a few ground balls and bat," says Duane. "He was a shortstop then, and when he took those ground balls after sitting in the hot sun for what seemed like an eternity, he was less than spectacular. Then when it was his turn to bat, he swung at the first and only pitch he got and hit a one hopper back to the pitcher, and the rest is history. The Pirates didn't know what they had missed."

His classmates remember him as funny, mischievous, realistic, mature, and generally good to be around.

Recalls Joe Kociubes, "We shared a delivery route for the afternoon paper, the *Repository*. I think he was transitioning it over to me so he could spend more time at sports. One day he was talking about his grades, and he said, 'I could work hard and turn myself into a solid B or B-plus student. Or I could continue to put my energy into sports and try to become a professional ballplayer. Why doesn't it make sense for me to get C's and take a shot at the big leagues instead of putting my energy into getting B's?' "

"He was smart though," says Susie Wilson. "And he enjoyed himself. I remember biology lab the day we had to dissect frogs. I was at the table behind him with a guy on each side of me. Thurman leaned over and said, 'You ready for this?' He was laughing. But I was ready, and the two guys I was working with couldn't deal with it. No sooner did I cut open the frog than the guy on my left passed out and the one on my right started to get nauseous. Thurman was loving it. He called up front—'Mr. Mutchmore, Mr. Mutchmore, we've got one down here and another one on the way!' "

Perhaps the most important moment in Thurman's life came in 1959 when he spotted a pretty girl in the schoolyard.

Thurman was twelve when he met Diana Dominick at the Worley School. They had both served on the Junior Patrol, walking children across the street. Thurman considered her a "rich kid" because she got thirty cents a day in spending money from her parents, and he didn't get any. And she'd spend the money on potato chips and Coke for Thurman.

Neither of them was a rich kid.

"I was with him the day he met Diana," recalls Susie Wilson. "We were in the Worley School playground when this pretty girl appears, and Thurman said to me, 'Who's that? She looks nice.' And I said, 'Oh, that's Diana Dominick.' He liked her at first glance."

Thurman would always call her Diane, almost as though he hadn't heard the name right or just wanted to save a syllable. His friends and teammates would be introduced to her as Diane. But she called herself Diana. Eventually, after Thurman died, she was Diana to everyone. But she was always Diane to him, and to those who knew her through the Yankees.

She would follow him on his paper route, and Thurman remembered running a mile to her house, giving her a kiss, and then running back to his own home on Frazer Avenue. "Not a bad way to get my running in," he'd say.

Diane became a regular presence at Thurman's side, attending all his games, making her home open to him, where he felt very comfortable in the close family setting the Dominicks provided.

Thurman wrote poems to her. He was discovering his romantic side.

"He was never around any other girls," said Don Eddins. "It was always sports and Diane. He was the type of student who had enough smarts but used only just enough to get by. He saved his energy for the ball fields—and for Diane."

A few of their classmates recall another boy here, another girl there, whom they had dated, but basically, they were each other's only real boyfriend and girlfriend.

"Diane, her parents, my parents, my baseball coach, and I all agreed that college was the right move for me," said Thurman. "But I knew I could only go if I could get a scholarship, because there was no way my parents could afford it.

"I got about eighty letters from colleges expressing an interest in me for their football programs, including Kansas, Ohio State, Syracuse, and Michigan. But it was baseball that I wanted, and schools just aren't that interested in awarding baseball scholarships. I wound up with exactly three offers.

"Arizona State offered me one contingent on making the team. Ohio University offered me a half-scholarship contingent on making the starting team. I had no doubts I could accomplish that, but it was Kent State that offered me a full scholarship, no strings attached, and that was where I decided to go."

And so Thurman would become the first member of his family to go to college. His siblings had all left home as soon as they could, Janice and Darla just moving out, and Duane joining the Air Force. (He later went to college on the GI Bill.)

The fact that Diane would be close by—Kent is just thirty-four miles from Canton—was certainly a plus.

"We had the Ohio All-Star Game in our senior year of high school," recalls Steve Stone, the five-foot-nine pitcher who would go on to win a Cy Young Award with the Orioles. Stone lived in Lynd-hurst. "It was actually three games. The east squad was loaded—Munson, Larry Hisle, Gene Tenace—a lot of really good players. For a lot of us, it was our first exposure to Munson, and man, was he abrasive. Nobody liked him. In fact, a kid named Jimmy Redmond beat him out to play shortstop in the first game, and we were all happy about it because no one could stand him. Then the third game ends and he comes over to me and says, 'I'll see you in September! I'm going to Kent State with you. I'm gonna be your catcher.'

"I said, 'My catcher? I thought you were a shortstop.'

"He answered, 'Hell no, I just play short in high school. I'm really a catcher. You and I are gonna be battery mates.'

"You could have knocked me over. I hated him, but we wound up being roommates on road trips and I loved the guy."

4

Kent State University, founded in 1910, has a baseball program that dates back to 1915. Through the 2006 season, ninety-nine of its players have either been drafted or gone on to play pro baseball, despite the team's short season, a fact of life for Northeastern colleges. It is not a collegiate baseball powerhouse. While the Sunbelt schools played schedules reaching seventy or more games, Kent State, a member of the Mid-American "MAC" conference, played more like twenty to twenty-five games a year during Thurman's time there. It was a schedule that meant a player had to be hot to be touted; there was no room for prolonged slumps, or scouts wouldn't have much to go by.

Bob Nieman (1951–62), Rich Rollins (1961–70), and Gene Michael (1966–75) were the first major leaguers who came from Kent State. Drew Carey, Chrissie Hynde, Michael Keaton, Arsenio Hall, Jack Lambert, and Lou Holtz also went to Kent State, with Holtz, like Munson, a member of the Delta Upsilon fraternity.

Michael, who would become a close friend, teammate, roommate, and somewhat of a mentor to Thurman on the Yankees, played for the Golden Flashes and lettered in baseball in 1958 before going on to a pro career that also included managerial stops with the Yankees and Cubs. As general manager and then as a superscout, he is widely considered to be the man most responsible for the turnaround in the fortunes of the Yankees by the mid-1990s, when the team became a perennial contender and stopped trading prospects for quick-fix players. He was one of the most highly regarded baseball minds in the country. The baseball field at Kent State would be named for him until replaced by the current Schoonover Field in 2005.

Kent State became well known nationally during Thurman's rookie season with the Yankees when National Guardsmen killed four student demonstrators during the height of Vietnam war protests going on across the country. It was in many ways the lowest point of the antiwar campus protests: Americans firing on Americans.

Although his sympathies were surely "antihippie," Thurman was not drawn into the nation's great debate over Vietnam. He and his friends—teammates mostly—concentrated on getting into the Army Reserve as a way of avoiding the draft. None of his high school friends can recall anyone from Lehman being killed in Vietnam, and as the Class of 1965, they were out of school before the war issue became divisive. College, then, provided an escape from the draft during the late 1960s.

Just as there were few teams known as the Polar Bears—his high school team's nickname—at Kent State he played for the Golden Flashes, a unique college nickname. His sophomore and junior years, when he became a full-time catcher, saw him mature into a pro prospect.

Thurman lived in a dorm for all of his Kent State years, although he was a member of a fraternity. He started out as a business major but switched to health ed, with an eye toward teaching.

"Moose Paskert, our coach, was 'old school,' " says Steve Stone. "He was a believer in seniority. If you were there longer, you earned the captaincy. If you were a senior, you pitched the big MAC tournament games instead of the sophomores. He had his rules. He was big and gruff. And we'd get on him.

"He used to say to us, 'Boys, I can go anywhere in the country and within five minutes, someone will come by and say, "How ya doin', Moose?" ' So we go to Durham, North Carolina, to play Duke on this one trip, and the umpire comes to the dugout, leans in, and says, 'How ya' doin', Bruce?' Ha! He called him Bruce. So on the bus trip home, Thurman and I sat in the back and every twenty or thirty minutes, one of us would holler to the front of the bus, 'How you doin', Bruce?'

"We never had a budget to take a Southern trip like other schools. Lynchburg, Virginia, was our idea of a Southern trip. It would be thirty-three degrees in Canton, then we'd bus it to Lynchburg, we'd get off the bus, and it would be thirty-two.

"One time we stayed in a place that wasn't quite a motel. It had a gym on the third floor, a pool on the second floor, the boiler room on the first floor, and we stayed below that. The place was crawling with giant cockroaches. Moose probably got a deal and we stayed for free. Thurman kept a bat in his bed and kept swinging at the cockroaches, trying to kill them all as they crawled from the pipes. It was ugly. Finally Moose comes in and says, 'All right, cut the crap. Anyone who wants to can go sleep in the bus for all I care.'

"Well, guess what? We all got out of bed and started to head for the bus. Moose blocked the door and made us go back to our bunks."

On the field, Thurman was blossoming.

"Thurman already carried himself like a star," says Stone. "He had no doubt that he was going to be a major league star. None. Amazing self-confidence. He was so gifted; he had this phenomenal ability, a heart the size of Long Island, and all of it wrapped in the wrong body. He shouldn't have been squatty; he should have been six-three with the grace of an antelope, not five-eleven and 195. But you know what? He was the second-fastest runner on our team, despite that body he was trapped inside of. He could really run.

"I'll tell you this, you could not shake that confidence. He and I used to play pool all the time. I was better than he was. We played maybe twenty-five times. I beat him every single time. And yet, after every game, he swore that he'd beat me next time, and he meant it. He never lost that edge. And he was never a good loser.

"When he played in the Eastern League in 1968, he was hitting something like .360 through the first few months, and that has always been a real pitcher's league. It was amazing. I caught up with him one day and said, 'You're really doing well,' and he said, 'Wait until you see my stats at the end of the season.' Well, he didn't maintain it, but he led the league and he really believed the .360 was going to go up."

Playing freshman baseball in 1966, Thurman got into only three of the team's eleven games, the season shortened by terrible weather. He fared much better with playing time back in the Canton City Baseball League during that summer. He came to understand why the game's real prospects liked to play ball in the South, like Florida, Texas, Arizona, or Southern California.

In his sophomore baseball season, 1967, his first on varsity, the Golden Flashes were only 11–12, but Thurman hit .367 with 4 doubles, 5 triples, 3 homers, 16 RBIs, and 23 runs scored in his twenty-three games. He was named third team, all-district, and all-region.

"Oh, he was some catcher," recalls Stone. "He could throw you out from any point where he caught the ball, like a quarterback hurrying a pass. If he caught the pitch knee high and away, he could throw a guy out from there. Especially with a curveball pitcher like I was, you need to have confidence that your catcher is going to be able to catch the ones in the dirt. I had that total confidence in him.

"We had a trick play too, and with no advance scouting in the league, we pulled this off eight times in one year. It involved wasting two pitches, putting me in a 2–0 hole, but we'd get an out out of it. After the first one, a fastball away, the third baseman would back up and I'd work from a full windup. The runner would take a bigger lead and I'd throw the pitch high and tight, backing a right-handed hitter off the plate. Munson would fire to third and get the runner. Eight straight games we pulled this off. The scouts took notice of his arm with this play, that's for sure."

In the summer of 1967, he returned to the Canton City League and was working part-time as a house painter when someone asked if he'd like to play in the Cape Cod League, a rather fast league for college players. The Chatham A's needed a quick replacement for their injured catcher. Thurman went.

In his first game, he tugged on his mask (a sign) and fired to first baseman Glen Lautzenhiser for a neat pickoff. He was primed and ready.

This was a league of strong competition. He played for Joe "Skip" Lewis, who later managed in the Detroit Tigers organization, and also earned seventy-five dollars a week working for the Chatham parks department. ("I slept on the lawn while other guys cut it," Thurman told Bobby Valentine, who was playing for Yarmouth.) His baseball summer was a lot better than his parks department summer. "Oh, he got fired three or four times from that job," laughs Ed Baird, a Chatham pitcher. "The supervisor, a guy named Slippery Slade, had a glass eye. Thurman would always talk to him on the side he couldn't see, and then when he'd turn around, Thurman would circle around him so he'd stay on the glass side. Drove him nuts."

He wound up winning the league's MVP award with a .420 average, sixty-five points higher than the runner-up, Glenn Adams, who later played for the Twins.

"I was in center field for Yarmouth the first time I ever faced him," says Valentine. "They had a player from UConn named George

Greer (later the longtime Wake Forest baseball coach), and in the first inning, I ran down a long drive by Greer over my head and made a nice catch. When I came to bat, Thurman was catching. He was very talkative back there; I wasn't used to that. He said, 'That was a pretty good catch, kid,' and I thanked him. Then he said, 'When I come up next inning, you should stand by the fence, because I'm going to hit one over your head.'

"Well, I didn't stand by the fence, but he was the cleanup hitter and I was playing him deep. And sure enough, he not only hit one over my head, but it went over the fence for a home run. And I remember writing a letter home telling my family about this guy with a strange name and how he called that shot like Babe Ruth."

He wasn't chatty with everyone though. Steve Greenberg, the son of Hall of Famer Hank Greenberg and later himself the deputy commissioner of baseball, was an opponent that summer between semesters at Yale.

"He was a man among boys when it came to hitting," Greenberg recalls, "and the flat-out best hitter I ever saw. But he was a mean cuss. I must have batted against Chatham twenty times that summer, and I couldn't get Munson to even acknowledge me, let alone have a conversation with me. I'd say hello, and Thurman would just spit tobacco juice, and put down the signs. He didn't even grunt. He was one great but grumpy hitter."

John Frobose, who pitched against Thurman in the MAC conference for Bowling Green, was a teammate on the A's and remained a friend through adulthood.

"A bunch of us called him 'Nate' for some reason, I never knew why," says Frobose. "But he was such a kick to have around. One day we were driving in my Chevy convertible to a road game in Cape Cod. We approach this overpass, and Thurman throws a ball over the overpass from about a hundred feet back. Steve Saradnik and Ed Baird were in the car too. One of them says, 'Speed up! Let's try to catch it on the other end!' And we race through the underpass and damned if Nate doesn't catch the ball on the other side! You couldn't do that again in a hundred years."

His cocky confidence in evidence, he would take infield practice with the A's wearing his catcher's mitt at shortstop, according to Billy Bor, who joined the team late and lived with Thurman in the final weeks.

And he could indeed be a magician with a baseball. Or baseballs! Later on with the Yankees, warming up before the game, he could throw two balls with one motion, both with accuracy. Roy White remembers himself and Graig Nettles being on the receiving end. "We'd be about five feet apart; it's really not that difficult," says Nettles. "But his accuracy was the thing; it was amazing. And of course, you needed hands big enough to hold two baseballs firmly."

"His most memorable game for the A's was definitely the 'crutch' game," says Frobose. "He had sprained his ankle on that home run against Bobby Valentine's team, and he was on crutches. It was an embarrassing injury; he had twisted it hitting home plate funny. Now we're tied in the ninth inning, one man on, and Skip sends Thurman up to pinch-hit. He goes to the plate with his crutches, tosses them aside, hits a game-winning single, hobbles to first base on the crutches, and that was all that was needed."

Chatham won the championship and a lot of big-league scouts watched Thurman play there. One of them was Harry Hesse of the Yankees.

Hesse, like Al Cuccinello, was a New York area scout. The two likable ol' baseball guys would seldom produce a prospect because the Northeast just wasn't turning out many good ballplayers anymore. (Cuccinello had played for the 1935 New York Giants with Mel Ott and Bill Terry.) So despite what might have seemed like "pressure" on Hesse and "Cooch" to occasionally come up with some names, they were both cautious and would rather not recommend failures than throw out names just to possibly look good one day if they got lucky.

The Yankees trusted them.

"I like this catcher at Chatham, the one from Kent State," Hesse told Johnny Johnson, the Yankees farm director and later president of the minor leagues. "You might want to make sure we watch him during his senior year. He could go high in the draft."

In his junior year, 1968, the team jumped to 16–9, and Thurman hit .413 with 3 homers and 30 RBIs. He set school records with 38 hits, 10 doubles, and 6 triples, and was named first-team All-American by the American Baseball Coaches Association and first-team All-District IV. He was also all-region. He was not the team captain (that was Ron Macks—a seniority thing for Moose). He would be the only player in school history to have his number (15) retired. His lifetime college average was .390.

"Being named All-American first-team catcher was, if you think about it, maybe a bigger honor than being named Rookie of the Year or MVP in the American League," Thurman would later say. "There are so many more players you are competing against, especially for the rookie award. I mean, think of how many college catchers there are every year. And I was first team!"

He was All-MAC-conference in both 1967 and 1968, joined in the latter year by his battery mate, Steve Stone, who also lettered twice and went on to have a sterling career in the major leagues.

Today the team plays nearly sixty games a year. It switched to metal bats in 1974, so many of Thurman's marks are small by school standards, but at the time he held a number of school records for a season and a career, and was named to the Kent State Varsity "K" Alumni Association's Hall of Fame in 1979.

Major league scouts were a fixture at Kent State games by Thurman's junior year. The Yankees assigned Gene Woodling, who lived in nearby Medina, to watch him. Woodling had been one of Casey

Stengel's platoon outfielders in the late 1940s and early '50s, alternating with Hank Bauer in right. He was one of the twelve players
who were part of the five consecutive world championship teams of
1949–53, Stengel's first five seasons. Woodling was a practical man,
one of the few who didn't spend his life living off his Yankee fame.
He gave his all wherever he played and was happily employed as a
Yankee scout and spring training instructor, but was a guy you could
rely on, like Hesse, for an honest assessment.

Moose Paskert would point him out to Munson and Stone when
he was at their games.

"Woodling really used to frustrate me," Thurman said. "I'm a talkative guy. I would have enjoyed having a conversation with him, but
I never could get one going. When the day finally came where he introduced himself, I acted as if I hadn't been aware of his presence
all along."

The Cleveland Indians, the "hometown team," also scouted Thurman, but their scouting report said he couldn't run well, and although he was a catcher, the team never showed much interest.
They had a promising catcher coming along named Ray Fosse.

When the 1968 season ended, Thurman returned to Cape Cod,
departing on June 6, the day of the baseball draft, the day before
his twenty-first birthday. "There was no reason not to go," he said.
"Even if I was drafted I could play there all summer and sign later.
We'd just watch and see what happened."

Thurman knew he would be a high draft pick, but of course had
no idea who would get to select him. After all, he was rated the number one catcher in the nation. Any suspense was over which team
more than when picked. He was pretty calm about the whole
process.

The Chatham team of the summer of 1968 was going to be one
of the great Cape Cod League teams ever. In addition to Munson,
they had future major leaguers in John Curtis, a left-handed starting

pitcher, Bobby Valentine at short, Rich McKinney at third, and Stone on the mound. Munson, Curtis, Valentine, and McKinney would all get drafted high and leave the team. Stone got mononucleosis and hepatitis and spent the summer in bed. So much for the great Chatham team of '68.

Munson was there only a few hours when his sister Darla called him. She had received a call from Lee MacPhail asking if she could have Thurman call him. She told Thurman that he'd been selected fourth in the nation.

"I reached him and told him to call the Yankees right away," she said. "I was very excited. I was a big Yankees fan!"

Woodling's final scouting report was reduced to two words: "Get him!"

Bad as the 1967 Yankees had been, leave it to their crosstown rivals, the Mets, to have been even worse. The Mets had the first pick in the draft and took infielder Tim Foli.

The Oakland A's had the second pick. Leaving Kansas City for Oakland didn't change their position, and with the first pick ever made by Oakland, the team took pitcher Pete Broberg. They never signed him, though; he eventually signed with the Washington Senators.

Third pick went to the Houston Astros, and they selected a catcher named Marty Cott over Munson. Cott was a high school kid out of Buffalo, where winters were long and baseball seasons were short. He never made it to the majors.

Bobby Valentine, Thurman's Cape Cod teammate, was picked fifth, right after Thurman.

"We tried out Cott in Buffalo with Pat Gillick pitching to him," recalls Tal Smith, then the Houston farm director, later the Yankees' general manager, and one of the most respected baseball executives of modern times. "Our reports were good and he put on an awesome display of power. I guess it wasn't the best draft pick we ever made. We'd gotten John Mayberry the year before and J. R. Richard the year after. But picking Cott over Munson, well, we sure paid a price for that."

"I remember that Cott was a bust, and our mistake was more in signing him than in drafting him," says Gillick, who, like Smith, also went on to become one of the best general managers in baseball. "That was forty years ago. My thinking has really come full circle since then. Back then I looked at a player's physical attributes much more than his mental. Today I know it's about the mental attitude and about his heart. Munson had that. He absolutely overachieved on the abilities his body might have given him because he had that heart of a winner."

And so Johnny Johnson, at a ballroom microphone in New York's Americana Hotel, announced, "The Yankees take catcher Thurman Munson, Kent State University, twenty-one years old tomorrow." Johnson told the press, "He was our first choice all the way."

Not too long after Darla's call, MacPhail, the Yankees' gentlemanly general manager, was on the phone with Munson, and it was obvious that there was not going to be a Cape Cod League season for Thurman. He was going to sign with the Yanks. Quickly.

Without unpacking, he turned around and drove back to Canton.

The next day, June 7, Thurman's birthday, MacPhail and Gene Woodling were in the Munson home on Twenty-second Avenue NE for the formality of signing him to a pro contract. MacPhail made the trip because he wanted to emphasize the importance of Thurman to the organization; to show that even the general manager of the team cared about signing their number one pick in person. He also wanted to explain the value of leaving college after his junior year to get his career going, with the Yankees pledging to finance his remaining education if he wanted. It wasn't necessary to push the point; Thurman was ready to sign.

While everyone in the house was buzzing with excitement over this great day, Darrell Munson was unmoved. Said MacPhail, "It was the strangest thing. There was his father, on what should have been a joyous day, lying on the couch in the living room. He barely said hello and didn't join us at all for the signing. At one point he just hollered into us, 'He ain't too good on pop fouls, you know.' It was really a bizarre moment. I think he might have even been in his underwear."

Duane accepts the story except for the underwear part. "That part doesn't sound like Dad," he says, and Darla agrees.

5

Before beginning his pro career, Thurman was sent to veteran coach Cloyd Boyer, the brother of big-league all-stars Ken and Clete. Cloyd was a solid baseball man who was managing the Yankee farm team in Binghamton, New York. Usually he served as roving minor league pitching coach, but this summer he had a managerial assignment. Johnny Johnson asked "C.B." to work Munson out at Binghamton and recommend what level he should start out in the minor league system.

"A week later Johnny called me and asked where I thought he ought to be playing," said Boyer. "I said, 'Yankee Stadium.' He thought I was kidding, but I wasn't."

The Yanks decided to keep him at Binghamton, where the Triplets belonged to the Eastern League. These were the final weeks of a franchise that dated back to 1923. Thurman thought the clubhouse, with holes in the floor, had to be the worst in all of baseball. Whereas the number four national pick in college football would be dressing in style in an NFL clubhouse, in baseball the minor leagues were the starting point for pretty much everyone. (Five-time all-pro Russ Washington out of Missouri, who played fifteen years for San Diego, was Thurman's number four counterpart in the NFL draft that year.)

What Thurman did have in Binghamton was Cloyd Boyer as manager.

Boyer told Munson, "You're probably going to be in the big leagues next year."

"I pitched the first game he caught," says Mickey Scott, who wound up with a brief career for Baltimore, Montreal, and California. "He arrived in a very impressive new Corvette, and we called him 'Stump' that year. I remember pitching a four-hit shutout in Elmira, New York, the day he made his debut. He was the top draft pick, so everyone noticed him."

The Corvette, purchased with a portion of his $70,000 bonus money, was a harbinger of a love for exciting and expensive new toys that would one day, it could be argued, lead to his decisions to purchase not just an airplane, but then bigger and faster ones.

Thurman wasn't at Binghamton long when the matter of the Army and the draft came up, and the Yanks, using what they hoped were special connections, dispatched Thurman to Fort Lauderdale, where an Army Reserve unit was based right next to Fort Lauderdale Stadium, their spring training home. Reserve duty would require occasional weekend absences plus a week or two of active duty during the season, but it loomed as a far more inviting alternative than being called up and sent to Vietnam.

The Yankees did their best to court recruitment officers to help their players, but not always with success. A notable failure was certainly Bobby Murcer. They tried Reserve duty but instead lost Bobby to military service for the 1967 and 1968 seasons, a genuine setback to his career and to Yankee fortunes.

In Munson's case, an extra bone spur in his right ankle, something he hadn't even been aware of, led to his being declared unfit for service, and back he went to Binghamton. Ironically, the absence cost him a few games, and he would wind up ten plate appearances short of qualifying for the batting championship. At .301, he was actually the Eastern League's only .300 hitter that year—a season known to baseball fans as "the year of the pitcher." Carl Yastrzemski, also at .301, had been the only *American* Leaguer to hit .300 that year.

The league featured Larry Bowa on his way up the ladder to the big leagues, and Jim Palmer, the Orioles star, working his arm back into shape on what would later be known as a rehab assignment. Al Downing, a Yankee star, also "rehabbed," pitching to Munson while wearing a Triplets uniform.

On July 20, the Yankees brought the Triplets down to Yankee Stadium to play that regular-season game against Waterbury in Yankee Stadium. For Munson, it would not only be his first visit to the stadium, it would also be his first visit to New York City. Fran Healy, a future Yankee teammate, was the catcher for Waterbury.

"Well, we didn't really see New York City at all," Munson said later. "We bused it to Yankee Stadium and then bused it right out after the game."

The game itself was played in a nearly empty stadium, with MacPhail and Ralph Houk watching from high above, looking at their future first-string catcher. The only other player Thurman spoke to that day, apart from Mantle, was Gene "Stick" Michael, his fellow Kent State alum.

That same month, Diana came up to Binghamton from Canton for a weekend visit, accompanied by her mother. Thurman and Diana decided to get engaged that weekend. Again, the Army was looming over their lives. Although the Reserve unit had declared him unfit, the possibility of being drafted still loomed, which would require another physical, and no guarantees with it.

Since Thurm and Diane had been talking about marriage since they were about thirteen, this inevitable date was set for September 21, right after the Eastern League season ended. A minor league teammate, first baseman Tim O'Connell, attended the Canton ceremony, held at St. Paul's Parish, with the Reverend J. Robert Coleman presiding. Darla and her husband were there; their daughter was in the wedding party. Neither Duane nor Janice, by now scattered, attended. Thurman's parents were at his side.

The couple would live upstairs in the Dominicks' home on Twenty-fifth Street when they returned from their honeymoon in Hawaii.

The marriage to Diana pretty much sealed Thurman's departure from the Munson family as he embraced the Dominicks as his own. He had found a much happier home there. Lou Piniella says that Thurman never talked about his family; Lou knew nothing about them. When I told Bobby Murcer that I had been in touch with Thurman's brother, Bobby said, "Thurman had a brother?"

In the meantime, Thurman did have a second physical, this time in Cleveland, and this time, alas, he passed and awaited a formal notice to report to military duty.

"We all felt fortunate to be in the Reserve," recalls high school classmate Gregg Schorsten, who went on to Kent State with Thurman. "I think all of us looked at the protesters as a group that didn't really affect us. They were doing their thing and we coexisted. The draft motivated us to keep our student deferment and the Reserve was the next best thing. It was an attitude of life goes on. Yes, it was a turbulent time, and maybe because we were so young, we just coped with everything."

But the call didn't come, at least not immediately, and as 1969 spring training approached, Thurman was assigned to the Syracuse

Chiefs, the Yanks' Triple-A farm club in the International League. Initially, he would begin spring training in the major league camp, where extra catchers were needed. He wore number 28. Once the roster began to shrink and the need passed, he'd head a few miles south to the minor league camp in Hollywood, Florida. In the meantime, he played in each of the Yankees' first six exhibition games that year, two of them complete games. He caught Stan Bahnsen and Al Downing, Mel Stottlemyre and Fritz Peterson, and veterans like Fred Talbot, Don Nottebart, Lindy McDaniel, and Steve Hamilton.

As the season was about to begin, the Army Reserve finally called; the Yankees had managed to get him in. Thurman was assigned to a four-month hitch at Fort Dix in New Jersey, where he worked as a desk clerk. Bahnsen, the American League Rookie of the Year with the Yankees in 1968, would do weekend Reserve duty at Fort Dix, so the two got to catch up on Yankee news whenever Bahnsen would arrive.

When Munson got a weekend pass, he'd fly to Syracuse and get some playing time in. If the Chiefs were on the road, he'd go to Yankee Stadium and take batting practice. It was pretty much a lost year professionally. He played only seventeen games for the Chiefs. But in August, Yankee catcher Frank Fernandez went off for weekend Reserve duty himself and Munson was available. The Yanks activated him on August 8 and he was on the roster, in time to catch the second game of a doubleheader. With Tom Tresh having recently been traded to Detroit, his number 15 was available and the size was correct. Pete Sheehy gave Thurman number 15—the number he had worn at Kent State.

"I had to go digging to find a pair of pants to fit him," said Pete. "His rear end was too big. I always kidded him about that."

The Oakland A's were in town for the weekend, and Munson not only caught the second game of the twi-nighter but got his first major league hit, a single to center off Catfish Hunter, his future battery mate and close friend. First base coach Elston Howard retrieved the ball as a keepsake. The newcomer drove in two runs and caught Al Downing's complete game, a 5–0 shutout, giving the *New York Times* a subheadline the next morning that read "MUNSON PACES ATTACK IN 2d GAME."

Thurman stayed at Gene Michael's house that first Friday night. On Saturday, which was Old-Timers' Day, he posed for photos with Gene Woodling, an invited guest. On Sunday, before he had to return to Fort Dix, he hit his first big-league homer—sandwiched between homers by Murcer and Michael. Never mind that Maris and Mantle had retired—here was a bit of M&M&M power, consecutive homers by Murcer, Munson, and Michael. Munson's shot came off Lew Krausse.

For the weekend, Thurman was 3 for 6 with a homer, 3 RBIs, and 2 runs scored. It was a very nice start.

His Reserve duty ended on August 30. The Yanks had him go to Syracuse, where the Chiefs were in the playoffs and on their way to the International League championship. He caught two games but then rejoined the Yankees on September 5, never again to wear a minor league uniform. He played only ninety-nine minor league games, plus four postseason games.

The recall on September 5 essentially began his career as a regular, and he never looked back. The Yanks were in fifth place, twenty-four games out of first. The Mets were on their way to winning the World Series. It was as low a point as the Yankee franchise could be.

He caught both ends of a twi-night doubleheader in Cleveland, with a contingent of friends and relatives on hand. A personal highlight was working with first baseman Joe Pepitone on a successful pickoff play at first. He loved that, as he would always enjoy the challenge of showing off his strong arm and quick release. In that final month, he threw out seven of twelve runners attempting to steal, a remarkable percentage. It established his reputation early.

In twenty-six games for the Yankees in 1969, Thurman hit .256, with that homer off Krausse and 9 RBIs. He started twenty-two of the final twenty-seven games of the season, as Jake Gibbs prepared to turn over the catching job to him in 1970.

In the winter of 1969–70, the Yankees arranged for Thurman to play for San Juan in the Puerto Rican League. As he had missed so much playing time during the 1969 season, it was important that he get the experience under his belt and make up for the lost time.

In San Juan, Thurman found himself a teammate of the great Roberto Clemente. Clemente did not need winter ball at that stage of his life, but it would have been a national scandal had he sat out the winter. The Puerto Rican players were expected to play before their hometown fans.

Thurman remembered little about his relationship with Clemente when we talked about it for his autobiography. Obviously I would have loved to have written of a close friendship, or learned some personal things about Roberto for the book. But there wasn't much there; I didn't get a sense they hung out at all. After all, Clemente would go home to his family each evening. Thurman did speak of standing and watching Clemente hit during batting practice. I couldn't get more out of him, although he said Clemente told him that if he ever hit .280 he should consider it a bad season.

Munson finished second in the league in hitting that winter with a .333 mark. There was little doubt as to who would be the Yanks' starting catcher in 1970. And ultimately, that 1969–70 San Juan Crabbers team would be remembered for having two elite players, both of whom would lose their lives prematurely in aviation accidents.

6

By spring training of 1970, I became Bob Fishel's assistant in the Yankees' PR department, with Bill Guilfoile having moved on to the top job in Pittsburgh. One of my assignments was to set up yearbook photos in the first week so we could rush them off to the printer in time for opening day.

That year, instead of a spring training team photo, we decided to take "mini-team photos" by grouping the players by position. We had three catchers: the incumbent regular of the past two seasons, Jake Gibbs; the first-round draft pick, Munson; and a strong boy from New London, Connecticut, John Ellis, a rookie who could also play first base. Fishel told me to position them with Gibbs the most prominent, out of respect to the veteran who was about to lose his job. Jake knew he was passing the torch but appreciated the gesture.

Thurman was not the most productive rookie in camp that spring—that honor went to Ellis, winner of the James P. Dawson Award as the spring's top Yankee rookie. John did in fact move to first base in time to be the opening day first baseman and to receive a letter cheering him on from Eleanor Gehrig, Lou's widow. No one from the Yankees arranged that—no one called her and asked, "Could you send a letter?" She acted on her own, and wrote something about "waiting all these years for Lou's true successor." Very flattering, but she wasn't much of a scout.

The attention to Ellis (who hit an inside-the-park homer on opening day) was helpful in taking some of the focus off Thurman, who was handed the catching job and started off with an absolutely miserable slump.

In his first nine games, he managed a single and seven walks in thirty-seven trips to the plate. By going 1 for 30, he was the owner of an .033 batting average, and naturally, talk was afloat that perhaps more seasoning in the minors was necessary. He had, after all, played only twenty-eight games at Syracuse the year before.

"It shook him," says his roommate Gene Michael. "I remember him sitting on the bed in our room at the Shoreham Hotel in Washington, really despondent. He didn't even want to go to eat. I was trying to encourage him. At the end of the year he outhit me by eighty points."

Ralph Houk knew better, and not only that, he knew how to deal with such a situation.

"Thurman, don't give a thought to your hitting. You're my catcher, you're going to win a lot more games for me catching than hitting, and the hits will come. Don't worry about it. Just relax and go out there and play the way we both know you can."

He managed to maintain both his confidence and his normally cocky personality.

"Thurman was 'cocky' in the good sense, very confident," says pitcher Fritz Peterson. "He was so talented he could get away with it. He also had quite a sense of humor. All the players liked him from the beginning. And he was such a team man. He did all the things a Yankee of old would have done to win games. Run, hit, throw, and break up double plays."

Maybe there were other things on his mind. Diana gave birth to their first child, Tracy Lynn Munson, on Friday, April 10, 1970, and Thurman was not able to be in Canton for the birth, being of course at Yankee Stadium. He was just twenty-two, a married father, a regular on the fabled New York Yankees, and seemingly holding on to more responsibility than one might throw at such a young man.

He was also courteous and responsive to fans, something the vast public and media couldn't see. After Tracy was born, a fan sent a homemade knit vest and skirt as a baby gift to him at Yankee Stadium. Thurman wrote a thank-you note on Yankee stationery.

> *Tracy and her mother and I all thank you for knitting the little vest and skirt. Some time during the season we'll take a picture of her in the outfit and send it to you.*
>
> *It's nice to know that fans still think of you and your family, especially when you're not having a particularly good year. I just hope I can make you as happy on the field as people like you make me feel off.*
>
> *Thanks again,*
> *Thurman Munson*

After the Sunday doubleheader in which he went zero for seven, he flew home to see Tracy and Diana, and later said, "I was about the happiest I'd ever been."

Thurman didn't have to rejoin the team until Tuesday night in Boston. So, in the first week of his rookie season, he got that little break in the schedule that allowed him a quick trip home—the same circumstances that would allow him to go home in that fateful, final week of his career.

The real problem with going 1 for 30 at the start of the season is that you spend the rest of the year digging out of it. A lot of players will have slumps during the season, maybe not 1 for 30, but when you're hitting .288 and you have your slump in July and drop to .272, it's just not as glaring as starting off hitting .033.

On April 20, Munson went 3 for 4 with a double and two singles, and he never had another slump all season. He didn't hit a home run until June 28, but no one questioned his hitting from April 20 on through for the rest of his career.

The 1970 Yankees had only two players remaining from their last World Series in 1964—Mel Stottlemyre and Steve Hamilton. There were a few players who had been teammates on the Mantle-era Yankees, notably Roy White and Bobby Murcer. But essentially, the rise of Thurman Munson in 1970 was the first building block toward the three championships that awaited the team later in the decade. Each year, one or two new additions would enhance the roster, until the team was ready to return to an elite status.

Munson wasn't especially patient with that plan. A battler, a winner, a guy who took every game as a challenge, he appreciated that the 1970 Yanks were having a good year, but he wanted a pennant, not just a good year. He took little pleasure in the team doing well so long as the Orioles were doing better. He wanted to be those guys, and he'd pump his fist at the pitchers in key situations and want more.

"Even as a rookie, he had a confidence and a maturity back there," says Stottlemyre. "We in turn had confidence in him. He was a kid, but he was very mature as a major league player. We loved pitching to him."

The fans felt that spirit and liked to see a guy come along who didn't give in to complacency and mediocrity. The fans were in love with Munson early on, embracing him as New York fans can do— quickly.

A prime example of this came in August 1970, when he was on Reserve duty at Fort Dix and not expected back in time to play at all on Sunday in a doubleheader against Baltimore. However, he drove impetuously and made it to Yankee Stadium—eighty-six miles—in a little over an hour, in time for the sixth inning of the second game. He listened to the game on WMCA radio as he rushed up the Jersey Turnpike. He went straight to the clubhouse and got into his uniform, emerging into the dugout, where Houk and his teammates greeted him warmly. "Grab a bat and pinch-hit," said Houk.

Out of the dugout popped Munson. In the press box, Bob Fishel tapped me on the arm with his pencil and pointed toward the on-deck circle. He was smiling. The fans did not expect to see him and his appearance on the field brought a tremendous roar from the crowd. To have been there at that moment was to see Thurman appreciated at a new level—our guy, and our hero.

He lined out to Brooks Robinson at third, but that wasn't the point. The response to his arrival signaled a bond between him and the fans that would never fade. If you could define the moment the fans fell in love with the future captain of this franchise, that was it.

Munson had arrived with a flourish, very much a part of the team, already emerging as a leader, and surely as "one of the guys."

"Thurm wanted so much to be included in the little 'side trips' that I would arrange on off days," recalls Fritz Peterson. "The routine was 'okay Tugs,' or 'okay, Beer Can' (nicknames I'd given him), 'you just wait out in the hallway [of the hotel] and we'll pick you up when we get up and you can come along,' when we would go to a lake or motorbiking, or whatever. He was great to have along.

"Once we went riding motorized trail bikes—Stottlemyre, Bahnsen, Munson, and me. All of a sudden he made a sharp curve and we all followed. He was going too fast. He missed the curve, went straight, and disappeared. He had driven right off the road into a deep ravine. The bike turned over twice, the headlights and taillights were smashed, and Thurman was cut and bruised all over. He had so much pride in not getting hurt that when we reached him and saw that he was alive, he just said, 'Let's go.' "

Munson kept lifting his average day by day until, on September 17, he went two for five against the Red Sox and reached the .300 mark. He never looked back and finished at .302 for the season, tops on the team. After the 1-for-30 start, he hit .322. After July 21, he hit .370. And he led all the league's catchers with 80 assists, half of them nailing would-be base stealers.

The line drives kept coming off his bat, and the team was playing very well. The Yankees had moved into second place on August 1— rarefied air for this team—and never relinquished it. The Orioles were so good that their ultimate margin was fourteen and a half games over New York, but the Yanks won ninety-three games, certainly their best season since 1964, with Lindy McDaniel recording 29 saves and Peterson winning 20. Although it was embarrassing to those who remembered the Yankees winning pennants every year, the team celebrated the clinching of second place with a modest champagne celebration in the clubhouse.

"I know old Yankee purists must have been thinking that celebrating second place was really bush," said Munson, "but we enjoyed it."

The Baseball Writers' Association named him first on twenty-three of twenty-four ballots as he easily won the Rookie of the Year Award. The only strange thing about it was that The Sporting News Rookie of the Year Award, voted on by players, somehow went to Cleveland outfielder Roy Foster, who hit 23 homers to Munson's 6. (Foster would hit 45 in a three-season career.)

Players always like to think they are the best judges of other players, and while it is hard to dispute that intellectually, they have occasionally cast some really dumb votes when given the opportunity. Most notably, they awarded a Gold Glove for fielding prowess to Rafael Palmeiro in 1999 when he only played twenty-eight games at first base all season.

Thurman was the first catcher to win Rookie of the Year honors in the American League since the award was created in 1947, and the sixth Yankee to win the honor in that time. The only other catcher to win the award was Johnny Bench of the Reds, who had won it in the National League two years earlier. Here, then, you had the beginnings of a decade in which Munson and Bench would be the two premier catchers in their respective leagues, perennial all-stars, World Series rivals, and admirers of each other.

Bench would ultimately come to be thought of as perhaps the greatest catcher in the game's history. Prior to him, there had been no clear-cut winner. The debate would include Gabby Hartnett, Mickey Cochrane, Bill Dickey, Yogi Berra, and Roy Campanella, with a nod to Josh Gibson of the Negro Leagues. Although Bench's life-time batting average would be only .267, he had a great highlight reel and revolutionized defensive play at the position. Thurman was honored to be compared to him.

Oh yes, but then there was Carlton Fisk.

Fisk was the anti-Munson. If Affirmed needed Alydar, if Ali needed Frazier, and if Evert needed Navratilova, Munson and Fisk needed each other.

Fisk first tasted the big leagues on September 18, 1969, about a month after Thurman did. It was enough to eventually make him a four-decade player.

He played a little bit in 1971, and then won the Rookie of the Year Award in 1972, making him the *second* AL catcher to nab the honor.

In many ways, he was everything Munson was not—tall, hand-some, graceful, maybe even a little delicate in his movements and body language. The players would sometimes tease him about the latter as only players can. His famous "coaxing" of his walk-off homer in the 1975 World Series was an example of what opposing players saw as the delicate movements.

People think there was always a Yankee–Red Sox rivalry, going back to 1903, when the Highlanders (the original Yankees) were formed, and certainly heightened by the sale of Babe Ruth to the Yankees in 1920, and later by Joe DiMaggio and Ted Williams being opposing players.

In fact, there really wasn't much of a rivalry at all after the Sox fell onto hard times after the Ruth sale. A rivalry can only be strong when both teams are strong. And for a long, long time, leading to the Munson-Fisk years, tickets to Fenway Park or Yankee Stadium for Yankee–Red Sox games were not that hard to get.

The Red Sox "Impossible Dream" pennant of 1967 turned a moribund team into a good one, something that, remarkably, is still going on. Not since Ruth helped the Yankees win the 1921 pennant—their first—has a single season so turned around the fortunes of a franchise.

But the Yankees didn't catch up right away. While the Red Sox remained strong after 1967, the Yankees were still down, save for the surprising 1970 finish. It wasn't until the mid-seventies that both teams peaked, and Munson and Fisk seemed to be the symbols of both.

Fisk was the New England lumberjack, Munson the Ohio blue-collar worker who led their teams to the top of the American League East.

Munson genuinely hated Fisk. And it was pretty much mutual.

"I know they were aware of each other's presence," said Bill Lee, the Red Sox pitcher. "Munson was always checking Fisk's stats, and Carlton would go nuts any time a reporter mentioned Munson's name."

It was partly due to his competitive nature, and of course it was fueled by the rising rivalry between the two glamour franchises, but Munson was also jealous and resentful of the attention Fisk was getting, and the All-Star elections he was winning.

"It's Curt Gowdy on the Game of the Week always playing him

up," said Munson. "He used to be the Red Sox announcer, he loves them, and now he's on the national games and he's always talking about Fisk this and Fisk that. And you know what? Fisk is always getting hurt, and I'm always playing through injuries, and he's getting credit for things he might do if he was healthy. Gowdy has this thing for him."

True or not, it was what Munson believed. (Gowdy had earlier been a Yankees announcer.) Thurman thought you played hurt. "Whenever someone was complaining about anything, Thurman would look at him and say, 'So, retire!' " says Brian Doyle, later a teammate. "It was a wake-up call to remember how lucky we all were to be playing big-league baseball."

And the Fisk attention on NBC did tend to reflect itself in the annual All-Star Game fan voting, which had begun in 1969 by edict of Commissioner Bowie Kuhn.

Players always have an arm's-length regard for announcers anyway. They don't hear the broadcasts unless they are in the clubhouse for a bathroom break or a change of jersey. Much of what they know about announcers is fueled by secondhand interpretations. One of my biggest problems when I was doing the Yankees' PR was trying to tame what the players' wives were telling their husbands that the announcers said about them. They often got it wrong, or misunderstood the context, and it invariably caused problems.

Munson's point about Fisk's injuries, though, was not off the mark. From 1972 through 1976, Fisk caught 516 games and was on the disabled list four times. In the same span, Thurman caught 728 games and was never on the disabled list. In fact, Munson would play his entire career without ever going on the DL.

Those were the years in which Munson formed his opinion about the brittle Fisk.

Of course, Fisk turned out to be one durable son of a gun. He would go on to be a four-decade player who would catch 2,226 games, including twenty-five games when he was forty-five years old. He played more games at the position than any man in history.

Munson would have come around and saluted his rival. He had a respect for durability because it was how he played the game, and he would have come around on Fisk, as he eventually came around on Reggie Jackson when they were teammates.

But for those early years of the rivalry, it was real and it was bitter. The two would take some shots at each other in the papers (when Thurman was choosing to talk to the press). And Munson told me that he'd speak to Fisk about things he didn't like seeing when Fisk came to bat. He'd call him by his last name.

"Listen, Fisk, I saw what you said in the paper this morning and it's bullshit," he might say as Carlton settled in at bat. Stuff like that.

Of course, his Yankee teammates loved to tease him about Fisk. Gene Michael, who roomed with Thurman for five years, used to tear out good Fisk stories or handsome pictures from magazines about Carlton and put them in Thurman's locker just to get his reaction when he arrived in the clubhouse. Michael says he's sure that Thurman never knew who was putting them there.

7

Off their big 1970 finish, with Houk getting Manager of the Year and Munson being so lauded, there were grand expectations for 1971. The front office, however, made no major additions, and the Orioles were still quite formidable, having polished off the Reds in the World Series. Nineteen seventy-one would be the only season during the Yankees' rebuilding in which not a single major new face joined the roster, save for aging but reliable Felipe Alou and a couple of midseason Rons—Blomberg and Swoboda.

Blomberg had been the Yankees'—and the nation's—number one draft pick in 1967, the year before Thurman. He was a remarkably gifted high school athlete with basketball scholarship offers as well. His minor league development was notable for the decision to have him hit only against right-handers. True to his high school reputation, he positively creamed fastballs delivered by right-handers. It baffled fans why he wouldn't bat against lefties in the minors, but his Syracuse manager, Frank Verdi, told the Yankees' front office, "When I play him against a lefty, it screws him up against righties for a week!"

He arrived in midseason to much ballyhoo and became an immediate fan favorite for his zany and sometimes nonsensical interviews, his "Li'l Abner" folksy charm, and his embrace of his religion (he was Jewish) without apologies. Fans waited outside the stadium to give him bagels. He spoke of his parents' wanting him to be "a doctor and a lawyer," and he was a regular at the Stage Deli. His batting practice sessions were not to be missed. On at least one occasion, he hit the facade in upper right field, famous as the place where Mantle had twice come close to hitting the only fair balls out of Yankee Stadium.

Blomberg didn't drink and liked to go to dinner with sportswriters. If the social occasion demanded it, he would order a vodka gimlet but never take a sip. (I used to tell him to order tap water with an olive in a martini glass.)

Munson was twenty-four when Blomberg, twenty-three, came up. Already behaving like a poised veteran, he became something of a mentor to Blomberg. Not much of a drinker himself (he was, after all, always in training while in high school and college), Munson was amused by Ron's innocence and liked his honesty. The two roomed together on occasion. Munson would get on Blomberg if he didn't think he was taking winning seriously enough, or if he detected that Bloomie was taking the easy way out of conditioning. There was a sense of mentoring going on that would foretell the time when Thurman would become team captain.

The two also had a common friend, a charismatic record company executive named Nat Tarnopol.

Nat was a huge fan, loving his association with the players, and able to get access to them in part by providing an unlimited supply of records and eight-tracks (players always loved free stuff) and by holding a coveted season box next to the Yankee dugout, which got him up close and personal in a hurry.

Nat, who was raised in a Detroit orphanage, was a figure of enormous charm: handsome, gregarious, generous, and a deal maker with a trophy wife. (Oddly, the couple had been photographed by Diane Arbus, who specialized in disturbing images, often freakish in nature, in her captivating and later famous black-and-white photography. Nat and June had posed for her in their expansive backyard, looking like an ordinary couple, but perhaps demonstrating for Arbus the loneliness of suburban wealth.)

Nat's fondness for Blomberg had a lot to do with Ron being Jewish, like Nat. He made a big thing out of it. He wasn't limited to the religious bond—he formed close friendships with Oakland manager Dick Williams, Yankee infielder Jerry Kenney, and others. His label, Brunswick, mostly recorded black rhythm-and-blues artists (the Chi-Lites and Tyrone Davis being his biggest), and he had a lot of friends in the black community.

He was seen by the Yankee front office as a bit of a meddler, but Gabe Paul, who would join the team in 1973, also foresaw the value of his connections, which would in fact one day bear fruit. Nat spoke brashly of one day buying the team. He organized the batboys to raise their pay in accordance with New York state labor laws. (He hired one batboy, known as "Hamhock," as a Brunswick employee.)

He would later lobby Gabe Paul to have a Ron Blomberg Day at Yankee Stadium (it didn't happen), and he negotiated Blomberg's contract for him before free agency, arguing that he should be paid on his future contributions and his gate appeal, rather than on his past season. It was an argument that would be ahead of its time.

The bar mitzvah for his son Mark in 1973, held on the grounds of his estate in Purchase, New York, was one of the great social events of the year in Westchester County, complete with Lionel Hampton and his orchestra performing. I was there (yes, I got my share of eight-tracks along the way), as were the Blombergs and the Munsons, along with Roy White, Bill White, Phil Rizzuto, Elston Howard, Gabe Paul, and Broadway producer Jimmy Nederlander (who owned part of the Yankees).

"Thurman's nickname for me was Roman because my hair style reminded him of Roman Gabriel of the Rams," says Mark, a Dallas attorney today. "Thurman was about as big-time an athlete as there was in New York at the time, and he was willing to devote a ton of personal time to a fourteen- or fifteen-year-old kid, plus my brother and sister. When he took us to see *Jaws*, a throng of people circled him at the theater for his autograph. He handled every request as politely as he could, but the crowd never dissipated. Eventually he signed all of the autographs and we barely made it into the movie on time. He hated the idea that he could not go to a public place without being surrounded. What many people thought was surliness we always took as a defense mechanism intended to create boundaries and retain some level of privacy.

"We spent a lot of time with Thurman. We hung out by the pool, played tennis, basketball, Wiffle ball, and he'd take us out to eat. In the years when the Yankees played at Shea, he'd drive us to the game, and we'd hang out in the clubhouse for a short time afterward until he would drive us home with him.

"He went to my awards banquets in high school but never got in the way of the guest speaker, usually another pro athlete. It was never like the world revolved around him."

Since Nat drove a Rolls, perhaps it didn't seem like such a big deal to him when he gave Blomberg a Mercedes 450 SL as a flat-out present, while out buying one for himself in Westchester. And it wasn't long after that he gave Munson one too. All three would arrive at the stadium parking lot in their 450 SLs, which was a big kick to Nat.

The Munson friendship even grew to the point where, when Nat and his family moved to a larger house in Purchase (almost hard to imagine), the Munsons stayed at their old house one summer while it was up for sale. Thurman became part of the "family" at this point, becoming friends with Nat's friends, and enjoying the life of a wealthy man, even if his salary was well under $100,000. In the evenings, Nat and Thurman would relax, listen to Neil Diamond *(Hot August Night),* Sinatra, or Louis Armstrong records, "get mellow," talk about life, talk about families.

"Nat used to yell, 'Let's go, Einstein,' at Thurman from his seat near the dugout, a little inside joke relating to those evenings," says Paul Tarnopol, Nat's other son. He'd make Thurman laugh even during a game.

Nat's friend Bob Solomon, a physician, was especially taken with Thurman.

"You see this among athletes more than others," he said. "There is a maturity there that is advanced for their years. Munson had it. He didn't really behave like someone under twenty-five. The way he presented himself—the total package—was very much ahead of the maturity curve. You could see that while he was just a kid by standards we are familiar with, he could become a real estate investor, be a husband and a father, converse with businessmen, and probably could have been a player-manager at any point of his career."

Paul Tarnopol says, "While Thurman was living with us in Westchester, a lot of times Dad would be too tired to go to the ball games at night, so Mark and I would just drive in with Thurman and then meet him outside of the clubhouse after the game to go home. He would take us to a pizza restaurant in Rye. Since Mark and I were out of school during the summer, Thurman would swim, play basketball, and ride our Honda dirt bikes with us through the woods behind the Pepsi complex in Purchase. He was the closest thing we had to an uncle.

"They were building their house in Norwood, New Jersey, and I remember Thurman complaining about the type of wood they were using on the house. He said they were using a poor grade of wood and if the house were being built in Canton, this would never have happened. Diana really missed Canton, though, and they moved back there year-round because of that.

"I even remember when Thurman was trying to decide whether to name their third child Mark Anthony or Michael Anthony when he was born. He was so excited about having a boy. I never saw him so happy.

"By 1976, Diana had taken the kids back to Canton and Thurman spent the entire 1976 season in our upstairs guest room in our new house on Lincoln Avenue in Purchase. And later, when he was learning to fly, he'd start to fly back and forth to Canton from Westchester Airport, which was very near where our house was. Whenever he tried talking Dad into flying with him, Dad would laugh and say, 'Are you out of your fucking mind?' Thurman got a kick out of flying over our house when he was taking off or landing in Westchester.

"Dad thought it was a really bad idea for Thurman to fly and would tell him so every time Thurman brought up the subject."

Michael Grossbardt had taken up photography as a hobby. His family owned the landmark Colony Music Store in Times Square. He loved baseball and used to go to Yankee Stadium, when the average crowd was about 17,000, and take photos of the players in the mid-1960s. One day he brought a sampling of his pictures and worked up the courage to walk over to team president Michael Burke, who was seated near the Yankee dugout in the old Yankee Stadium. (A seat never once occupied by George Steinbrenner after he bought the team.)

"Mr. Burke, I thought you might like to see some pictures I've taken here," he said.

Burke was impressed. Color photography was not yet done much at baseball games, simply because there was little market for it. Printing costs and logistics still made black-and-white the photography of choice. Michael's photos captured the excitement of baseball, even with a lot of empty seats in the background. They also captured the grandeur of the original ballpark.

Burke, running the team for entertainment giant CBS, decided to hire Michael as the team's first ever full-time photographer. He would go to spring training and all home games and shoot away. Previously, the team had just used local freelancers like Bob Olen or Louis Requena, or purchased newspaper photos as needed. Michael was given the run of the place.

Some players liked him because he had an innocent charm. Some players didn't warm up to him because he looked and dressed so antibaseball, with more of a hippie style than a jock look. He was in fact a unique presence at the ballpark, especially when accompanied by his likable, flirty, and sexy blond wife, which made the players notch up their respect for him a bit more.

Grossbardt would produce some of the most memorable pictures of the late 1960s and '70s—Mickey Mantle Day, the Old-Timers' Day photos of Mantle and DiMaggio during the national anthem, Casey Stengel's uniform retirement, where he looked like the Old Man in the Mountain (a New Hampshire landmark), and most of Munson's career, beginning with the day he played for Binghamton in that Yankee Stadium debut game.

No player was photographed by Michael more than Munson was, since he trained his camera on home plate whenever there was a possible play at the plate. An action shot of Thurman making a tag became the first action photo used on a Topps card when they began to move from headshots and "posed action" in the early 1970s.

As team photographer, Michael also had the responsibility of asking Munson to pose from time to time, no easy task given his frequent grumpy moods and his ability to intimidate someone even if only kidding around.

"He could have a lot of different personalities," says Grossbardt, now in his early sixties, still Kramer-like, and still running the family business at Colony Music. He gave up photography long ago, but enjoys communicating with obscure old Yankees like Ken Johnson or Rich Hinton or Wade Blasingame, getting them to sign their rare color photos in Yankee uniforms.

"Munson was really very friendly when he first came up. You know how he used to say, 'I'm just happy to be here,' when he wanted to move on and ignore questions? Well, in those early days, he really *was* happy to be here.

"I *think* he liked me, although he never actually said so. But his way of showing it was that every time I needed a favor from him—well, not really a favor, but say a photo of him for the front office—he developed a ritual where he had to punch me in the ribs before I could take it. And he hit me hard! It was fun for him. It was a burden for me. To get the picture, I had to take a punch. Maybe it was his way of just being a jock around something artistic like photography. I suppose on some level it was a sign of affection.

"True to his reputation as a great family man, though, he was just terrific with family photos, which we did for the *Yankee Yearbook* until Peterson and Kekich swapped wives. That was the end of Family Day, and that was the end of family photos."

(In spring training of 1973, Fritz Peterson and Mike Kekich announced to a startled press corps and an equally startled front office and team that they had decided they loved each other's spouses, and would be trading wives, children, pets, homes, etc. For Fritz and Susan Kekich, the arrangement "took," and they remain together more than thirty years later. For Mike and Marilyn Peterson, it didn't really last out the month. As Yankee scandals went, this one was at the top of the list.)

"Thurman was always very cooperative with these family photo opportunities," adds Grossbardt. "He loved to help set up the shot. At the bar mitzvah for Nat Tarnopol's son, Thurman brought his whole family, and was a totally different person. He asked for certain shots to be set up with Diane and the kids, and couldn't have been more cooperative. I didn't get punched in the ribs that day. He wouldn't do that in front of Diane.

"The children of his teammates loved him. He was great fun with them, like a teddy bear. Jack Aker's little girls called him 'Uncle Dum Dum,' which he probably told them to do. He played around with the Alomar boys and the Bonds boys, let them try on his catching gear, showed them where the really unhealthy clubhouse snacks were. The kids all loved him. Plus, he was great with the Getty Good Kids promotion that the Yankees did. Getty Gas was a sponsor, they had some contest with lucky kids winning a visit to the field, and he was very cooperative with these kids. And if for some reason he couldn't go out, he'd always sign a baseball for them. Those balls would be valuable today because he wasn't a big signer.

"The other thing I remember is how interested he was in the photos. I'd show him pictures I was especially proud of. He liked the action shots; he liked the portraits, he always wanted to see more. I just wish he didn't have to punch me in the ribs."

Louis Requena, many years senior to Grossbardt and a fixture at Yankee home games, found Munson to be a polite and cooperative subject.

"Punched in the ribs? Never happened to me!" says Requena.

Jack Danzis ran a trophy and gift business in New Jersey and provided the Yankees' Old-Timers' Day gifts for years.

"I first met Thurman on Old-Timers' Day in the clubhouse at the old Yankee Stadium in 1970, the year we gave all the old-timers Longines watches," he recalls. "I was supposed to get Bobby Murcer to pose for a promotional picture for Longines. For this he was supposed to receive a gold watch with some diamonds. While waiting for Bobby I met this little round young guy—Thurman—and we started talking about Canton, Ohio, where I would sometimes travel for business. He had been a golf caddie at the Brookside Country Club, where I went for lunch with my client.

"When I told him what I was doing at the stadium he told me he could really use a new watch. After an hour of waiting for Murcer to take the picture I got a message that he could not do it as he was running late. The only one around was Munson so I said I would let him pose for the picture and gave him the watch. I figured the watch company would probably make me pay for the watch personally because the picture was of this lesser-known player rather than Murcer. After taking the picture Thurman said, 'Thanks for the watch! I'll be your best friend till I die.'

"The watch company used that picture after Thurman became well known in lots of their ads. Thurman told me that they got him cheap. He was right."

Off the field, Thurman was beginning to test the waters of real estate investment, and Diana was pregnant with their second daughter (Kelly would be born just before Christmas of 1971). The pregnancy was not an easy one.

"Diana and Thurman lived at the Holiday Inn in Paramus with Ronnie and me," says Mara Young, at the time Mara Blomberg. "She was so nice; quiet and easy to be with. But you could always tell that she was happiest back in Canton, where her family lived."

Toward the end of the summer, Ruth Munson, Thurman's mother, suffered her first stroke, which led to the ultimate departure of his father from the family.

While that was obviously on Thurman's mind, he had by this point "adopted" Diana's family as his own. He grew closer to her warm, giving Italian family and effectively turned away from the Munsons and became a Dominick.

Big Tony "Tote" Dominick, Diana's father, was a cigar-smoking, card-playing bull of a man, and he was frequently with Thurman, even on Yankee road trips. A lot of people assumed he was Thurman's father, because of his hefty build. He owned a little two-table pool hall in Canton. No one was ever quite sure whether this was his means of income, because frankly, the place wasn't that busy. Plus, of course, Tote seemed to have plenty of time to visit Yankee Stadium a lot and to make the occasional road trip. Put it this way: Big Tony Dominick didn't look like the sort of a guy you would question about his abundance of free time.

Munson's 1971 season started almost as miserably as his rookie year did. He started out 2 for 30, and was in an 0-for-27 slump beginning right after opening day. He was hitting .067, and he was going to have to repeat 1970, unable to bury it in the middle of the summer when few would see .067 posted. (In those days, before box scores and scoreboards carried averages, newspapers would run little side boxes showing the home team's batting averages, so there it would be, every day.)

When he finally went 2 for 4 on April 18 and then 2 for 3 the next day, Houk sat him down.

"I want you to think about these last two games and focus on what you were doing right," Houk told him.

A former catcher himself, Ralph was just a perfect manager for Munson—patient, professional, a man's man. Thurman often stopped in Houk's office before games to talk baseball. It was never really about the past—Houk had played with DiMaggio and Mantle, and had been a caddie to Yogi Berra—but about the current players and strategy and newspaper gossip. There were times you would find Thurman smoking a cigar with Houk in the office off to the left side of the clubhouse. It was all part of the learning process.

As for the 1971 Yankees, perhaps the less remembered the better. Despite optimism in the air, they never really got going. They were six games under .500 at the All-Star break, fourteen and a half behind the Orioles. Shortly after the break, they won nine of eleven and took three and a half games off that lead. In early September, now eighteen and a half games out, they managed to win eleven out of sixteen, but it was too little too late, and in the end they would finish twenty-one games out, mired in fourth place from July 2 to the end of the season.

They finished 82–80 instead of 81–81 when the last day of the season found them winning by forfeit, playing the Washington Senators in that franchise's final game at RFK Stadium. The 14,000 angry fans got hostile (okay, drunk and hostile) and stormed the field with two outs in the ninth, sending the Yankee players running for their lives. (The Senators were winning 7–5.) The umpires were unable to restore order and the Yanks were awarded a 9–0 victory. It was the first forfeit in the major leagues in seventeen years.

Munson's high-water mark of the year was only .266. He finished at .251, a fifty-one-point drop from his rookie season. In fact, he hit .256 in the first half and .246 in the second half. He did make his first All-Star team, going in to catch Mickey Lolich in the eighth inning and calling for whatever pitch it was that Roberto Clemente hit out of the ballpark.

Writers called his season the "sophomore jinx" and no one seemed concerned because he still hit the ball with authority, drove it into the alleys, and did not get into a rut trying to swing for the fences in cavernous Yankee Stadium. But Murcer had hit .331 and even Jerry Kenney outhit Munson. It was just a bad season for a good hitter.

Ron Swoboda, a local hero as part of the Miracle Mets of 1969, joined the team in midseason. "In Thurman I saw a pretty raw and unconventional catcher," he recalls. "On a steal he'd throw the ball as fast as he could from any arm slot he happened to find—mostly sidearm. The ball would head to second with this huge tail on it, like a meteor.

"He used an S-44 model bat. It had an uncommonly small barrel but he could center the ball on it. Nobody else liked his choice of bats but they worked for him. Murcer was a better hitter with more pop and more polish. But you would see things from Munson that made you believe he could be something special. He could run for a little fat catcher. He was a better hitter every year I was with him from 1971 to 1973 and he wore out the Twins' outstanding right-hander Bert Blyleven. Blyleven could bring it with a very nasty curve-ball and Thurman hit everything he threw over the plate, hard and in all directions. He was amazing from my perspective.

"Thurman was a pretty sensitive guy and loved to talk, but we used to joke that no matter where the discussion started he always brought the conversation back around to himself and what was going on with him as a player. The guys liked him, though. I know he had a bumpy relationship with the media. I think he was basically shy and very sensitive."

Despite his lowly batting average, Munson enjoyed a remarkable season behind the plate. He caught 117 games in 1971, covering 1,019 innings, with 614 chances—and one error. One! And re-member, the catching position is one with the potential for many more errors than the chances accepted would indicate, because of all the throws to second on base-stealing attempts and all the pick-off throws that could come at any time.

The one error came on June 18 in a game at Memorial Stadium in Baltimore. Andy Etchebarren, the Orioles' barrel-chested re-ceiver, was on first when Paul Blair doubled. Etchebarren had little speed, but Billy Hunter waved him around third and toward home. Murcer had run down the double; now he threw to Gene Michael as the cutoff man, and Michael fired home. Munson had his left leg out to block the plate. The ball and Etchebarren arrived together. Both Munson and his counterpart knew the collision was inevitable; it was the way the game was played.

Thurman took the impact, got knocked backward, blacked out, and dropped the ball. He was unconscious for five minutes before being taken off the field on a stretcher and driven by ambulance to nearby Union Memorial Hospital.

Art Franz, the home plate umpire, had never called Etchebarren safe. He simply waited and then saw the ball lying next to Thurman's head. At that point, he signaled "safe."

The official scorer called it an error.

"Even looking back on it almost forty years later, it's still an error—a tough one, but an error," says Bill Shannon, the principal scorer at Yankee Stadium and author of *Official Scoring in the Big Leagues*. "Some errors are heartless, but they are what they are. It wasn't an unusual call."

It was not a big deal at the time, although the Yankee players were pretty hot about it. No one could have anticipated that this would be the only error Munson would be charged with all season.

Munson suffered a concussion, but he was back in the Yankee clubhouse before the end of the game, munching on a doughnut.

"He was so mad," says Fritz Peterson. "He wanted John Ellis to go out and beat up the entire Orioles club (which John could have done!)."

In fact, he pinch-hit the next day and then caught and got three hits the day after. If he needed to enhance his gritty résumé, this was the play that did it.

The one error for the season gave him a .998 fielding percentage for the year. He threw out 23 of 38 base stealers—61 percent where 35 percent is more common. The 38 attempts were also remarkably few over the course of a season, indicative of the respect for Thurman's throwing arm and quick release. For his first two years, he had thrown out 63 in 107 attempts, or 59 percent. Here, his reputation was made.

"He had the quickest release of any catcher I had ever seen," says Peterson. "And Gene Michael really helped him when he was at short with his quick tags and good glove.

"I had an understanding with Thurman that whenever I saw a

runner break off first I would automatically switch what I was going to deliver to the hitter to a fastball so Thurman could gun him out at second. Most catchers couldn't react like he could to a quick change like that."

Because he caught only 117 games, and the record book cites 150 as the standard required for fielding percentage records, his "almost 1.000" season cannot be properly measured. But his .998 percentage tied Elston Howard's 1964 Yankee catching record.

"Nobody could call a game the way he could," said Mel Stottlemyre. "From the day he arrived it was as though he had been somehow studying the hitters throughout the league. He knew what to call, and we had immediate confidence in him."

When Tommy John later came to the Yankees, he made five spring training starts but never happened to pitch to Munson. Then in the opening series against Baltimore, Munson was finally behind the plate. "When we came back to the dugout after the first inning, Munson said, 'You didn't throw a lot of curveballs to these guys in the spring, so we're going to throw a lot of first-pitch curves.' "

John said, "How do you know? You didn't even catch me all spring!" And Munson responded, "What do you think, I wasn't watching?"

8

Sparky Lyle arrived on the scene in 1972, a tremendous addition to the team. While the term "closer" had not yet become part of the baseball lexicon, it came to mean the man whose bulldog determination and daily success over one inning of work could essentially shorten a game to eight innings, with the opponents knowing they had little chance in the ninth.

Lyle embodied the personality of a closer, although he would usually be asked to work two or three innings. He had the arm for it.

He was a fun-loving character with an infectious laugh, and he knew how to have a great time. If he hadn't been a baseball "fireman," he might have been a real-life fireman. He was a Pennsylvania guy with a blue-collar attitude and a wonderful approach to life.

"When I was with the Red Sox I always enjoyed playing against Munson," recalls Lyle. "It was because he was a *ballplayer*. And you like to compete against guys like that.

"He called the game based on who the batter and pitcher were, not what he might be looking for if he was the hitter.

"I loved to have him back there when I was pitching. He was like me in that we were successful because neither of us was afraid to fail. That was just who we were.

"I'd throw him a slider in the dirt on an 0–2 count with a runner on third and the guy would strike out. It would be a tough pitch to handle because the guy was swinging and the ball was bouncing, all at once. But he'd catch it. And he'd hold the ball and walk out to the mound with this shit-eating grin and say, 'You didn't think I was gonna catch that, did you!' And we'd laugh because we were competing at the highest level and we were also having fun."

When I worked for the Yankees during that time, I played a little role in the Sparky Lyle mystique. His entrance was always dramatic at Yankee Stadium. He'd arrive in the Datsun bullpen car (our sponsor), throw open the door, jump out of it with fire in his eyes, throw his warm-up jacket to the waiting batboy, and storm to the mound. A few quick warm-ups and then he'd stare in to Munson, waiting for the batter to dare to step up.

I thought, *This is great, this needs a theme song.*

So I asked a friend in the music business to suggest a song, and he said, " 'Pomp and Circumstance.' It's about the end, the culmination."

Also known as the "Graduation March," it worked. Toby Wright was our stadium organist and the drill was for me to look into the bullpen with binoculars to make sure Lyle was getting into the car, then phone Toby in the organist's booth over first base and say, "It's Lyle." And he'd hit that first chord as the gate from the bullpen opened. The fans picked up on this quickly and at the sound of the first note, they would begin cheering. By the time Lyle emerged from the car, the place was going crazy.

Today, every closer seems to have a theme song, and Lyle has told me on more than one occasion that my choreography of his entrance really made me the creator of "The Closer." It isn't true. Dick

Radatz had a great act in Boston in the 1960s. But I love it when he throws me that compliment, even if he did say, "Let's not do it" the following year.

"Too much pressure," he said, and this from the man who thrived on it. Oh well.

The 1972 season, when Lyle saved thirty-five games, many in highly dramatic fashion, was really great fun, although it began with the first players' strike in history. Although future strikes would be longer, this was very painful to all of us in the game. It was unimaginable that the industry could shut down. But it did. For those of us who lived through all the work stoppages baseball has thrown at us, 1972 was the worst because it was so unthinkable.

Although the Yankees were never in first place—not even for a day—the race was so tight that we had to prepare for a possible World Series, printing tickets, designing a program, setting up a postseason media operation. The team had not had to go through this exercise since 1964.

On September 1 the Yanks were tied for second, just one and a half games behind Baltimore. A Stottlemyre shutout that day over Chicago, and then a 2–1 win by Steve Kline the next day, put the deficit at just a half game. These were truly exciting days, and no one was enjoying them more than Munson, tasting his first pennant race and loving every aspect of the competition. Three-for-four on September 1, he was hitting .292 and enjoying his first season in which he didn't have to climb up from the depths in the batting department. He started the year with an eight-game hitting streak, was at .338 on May 12, and would wind up with a solid .280. He hit .292 from July 15 to the end of the season. His buddy Murcer had a monster year, belting 33 homers, driving in 96 runs, and leading the league in runs scored and total bases.

Sadly, the hopes and promises of the season went unfulfilled. Detroit wound up winning the Eastern Division over Boston, with Baltimore third and the Yankees once again fourth, six and a half games out, thanks to losses in their final five games, all at home. The Tigers didn't clinch until the next-to-last day of the season. They won by only a half game, the worst possible result of an uneven schedule, necessitated by the strike and unplayed games never made up.

The lost games cost the Yankees their four-game opening weekend against the Orioles, which included opening day and a Sunday Cap Day, easily 100,000 in total attendance. For the season, the Yankees would draw only 966,328—about 34,000 short of a million. It would be the first time since 1946 that the team failed to crack the million mark, a very unsettling stat.

The truth was, attendance was never great at Yankee Stadium—not for being the glorious Yankees in the nation's number one population center, playing in a beloved, historic ballpark. The team was capable of drawing two million, as it had done for five straight years after World War II. But then attendance sank toward the 1.5 million mark as people stopped going to the Bronx. When the Dodgers and Giants left for California in 1958, Yankee attendance actually dropped 70,000 for the year. And in 1961—a great team, a great pennant race, and the great home run race with Maris and Mantle—attendance was up only 120,000 from the year before, and still a paltry 1.7 million as the only team in town.

Mantle retired in 1968. The Yankees were prepared to give him another $100,000 to play another year, but he said he couldn't hit anymore. So they went out there without him—and drew only 57,000 fewer fans, including a full house on Mickey Mantle Day during the summer.

The 1972 attendance number was embarrassing, but in line with what had been going on. All fingers were pointing to the stadium itself.

Those of us who worked there knew the increasing crime numbers in New York made subway travel late at night precarious and trips to the South Bronx scary. We also knew that Yankee Stadium was literally falling down.

Bat Day in 1971, and again in 1972, had the young fans pounding their bats on the concrete to get a rally going. The action caused cracks, chips, and then chunks of the fifty-year-old concrete to fall. Nothing awful happened—no one was hit with debris, and there were no photo ops of the crumbling, but it was a strong message to us that the stadium needed an overhaul.

We also saw that new ballparks in Cincinnati, Philadelphia, St. Louis, Kansas City, and Pittsburgh had helped attendance spike in those towns.

So, armed with a small threat of considering the Superdome in New Orleans as a possible new home, Mike Burke, the Yankees' president (on behalf of CBS), and John Lindsay, the city's mayor, agreed on a plan that would condemn the current stadium, turn the land and the structure over to the city, and have the city pay for a complete remodeling. Lindsay was no baseball fan, but he knew he didn't want the Yankees leaving on his watch. The process would take two years; the Yankees would share Shea Stadium during those years, and 1973 would be the fiftieth anniversary and final year in the original Yankee Stadium.

Munson, the budding real estate baron, was interested in all of these proceedings and phoned me often in my stadium office with questions. "How long would the lease be for?" he wanted to know. "How did they come up with the $24 million cost? Seems low."

I had a feeling part of him wanted to be the Yankee catcher and part of him wanted to have a real role in the rebuilding process.

He was right about the $24 million being low. It wound up costing about four times that, prompting howls of protest from budget watchers. The figure had been the cost of Shea Stadium, from the ground up, a decade earlier. It was a number to work with, nothing more. And certainly nothing less.

We thought that celebrating the fiftieth anniversary would be our big focal point for the year, with the announcement that it would be the last season of the original "House that Ruth built." But right after New Year's came bigger news. The franchise was being sold.

CBS had presided over eight seasons of generally uninspired baseball. It hadn't been a good business acquisition for them, they hadn't leveraged the relationship in any meaningful way, and they were happy to get out. In fact, they sold the team at a loss—they paid $13.4 million and sold it for $10 million. It remains, at least as far as public records indicate, the only time a major league team has ever been sold at a loss.

Munson's attention focused on the Cleveland connection. The purchaser was George M. Steinbrenner III, whose father had started American Ship Building on the Great Lakes, and who was buying the team with Mike Burke as well as thirteen limited partners. Gabe Paul, a part owner of the Cleveland Indians and their general manager, had brokered the deal, introducing Burke to Steinbrenner, who he had known was interested in buying the Indians. Steinbrenner had owned the Cleveland Pipers of the American Basketball League in the 1960s when he was only thirty-one years old. Now, at forty-two, he owned the Yankees.

Steinbrenner rid himself of Burke before April ended, the dashing Burke departing when it was clear their styles could never mesh. Steinbrenner was military school, football discipline, short hair, no beards, win at all costs. Burke was hip New York, a longhair who drove a Datsun 240z, dated starlets, posed for formal pictures without a jacket (oh, did George Steinbrenner hate that in the yearbook photo), and liked poetry and rock music. That the relationship lasted until April was pretty amazing itself.

Still, Burke had pulled off the stadium modernization project, had forced the architects to preserve the stadium's facade as a design element, and turned over all the protests about cost overruns and the very decision to stay—to Steinbrenner.

In his early press encounters, George swore allegiance to the front office staff he inherited (a loud *whew* from the PR office, for sure), said he'd leave baseball to his baseball people (meaning mostly Lee MacPhail and Ralph Houk), and promised a return to the World Series within five years.

After finishing just a half game out of first in September 1972, the five-years promise seemed longer than fans wanted to hear, but realistic if you looked at the Yankee farm system. There was not much there.

That was where Gabe Paul came in. Before he left Cleveland, he swapped their star third baseman Graig Nettles (with backup catcher Gerry Moses) to New York in exchange for John Ellis, Charlie Spikes, Rusty Torres, and Jerry Kenney. All had won the James P. Dawson Award—a Longines watch—as the top rookie in spring training at one time or another, so between the four of them, it was expected that they would at least arrive at the ballpark on time.

With a left-handed swing designed for Yankee Stadium, Nettles reminded some of the Yankees' trade for Roger Maris prior to the 1960 season. In fact, with that very thing in mind, I persuaded Pete Sheehy to assign number 9 to Nettles: the only time I had a hand in a uniform number selection. (Nettles would then become the first Yankee since Maris to lead the league in home runs.) And boy, could he ever field third base.

Nettles had been a favorite in Cleveland, and was the favorite player of Darla Munson's husband, Denny, Thurman's brother-in-law, an Indians fan. When the Yanks and Indians played at Municipal Stadium, various members of the Munson family would be present.

One day when Nettles was still with the Indians, Thurman left tickets for his two sisters, his brother-in-law, and for Diana and her father.

In this particular game, the Yankees were leading and Nettles came up for Cleveland with the bases loaded. According to Darla,

Denny shouted, quite loudly, "Oh God, I hope he gets a home run." This enraged Diana, who found it in extremely bad taste, and afterward she and Thurman's sister Janice told Thurman about Denny's outburst.

Thurman was pissed. He had, after all, been the one who left the free tickets. And right then, he cut off tickets for Denny and damaged the precarious relationship with Darla, who was seen as Denny's enabler.

Now Nettles was a Yankee teammate, but the Denny-Darla marriage was ending anyway, and family matters were growing more complicated. Thurman further withdrew from the Munsons and drew even closer to the Dominicks.

"It wasn't long after that incident at Municipal Stadium," says Darla, "that we were driving to a game there when Thurman and Diana drove up right alongside of us. He was still mad at us and they flipped us off. Well, we went to the ballpark and went to the will-call window, and asked for the Munson tickets. He had left them for someone else, but we claimed them. Ha!"

An example of Thurman's curmudgeon-like personality is in a tale from Rob Franklin, who served a few years as the Yankees' traveling secretary early in Thurman's career.

"One day he opened a present from a fan, and it was a pair of cuff links," said Rob. "He took one look, grunted, and said, 'What the fuck would I want these for!' I was standing nearby, sorting out ticket requests, and he gave them to me. Not because he liked me, but it was the quickest way he could get rid of them. If the wastebasket was closer than I was, it would have won. I still have them; they are the only pair I own."

Although billing himself as an "absentee owner," Steinbrenner made his presence known early. He avoided comment on the tabloid-dream wife swap between Mike Kekich and Fritz Peterson, which was revealed during spring training (he hadn't been officially approved by the other American League owners yet), but by opening day he was on record as writing down the uniform numbers of the players whose hair was too long. Number 15 made the list. He had Ralph Houk read the list of numbers to the players, the first step toward an awkward relationship between the manager and the owner.

"He was developing his famous Yankee haircut policy," said Munson, "about ten years behind the times."

Steinbrenner, though, liked Munson. He saw him—correctly—as a gamer, a guy who played every day to win, just as his own philosophy dictated. And of course they were a couple of Cleveland-area guys, Thurman from the blue-collar background of Canton, and Steinbrenner born on a farm in Rocky River, where he was assigned an egg business as a child and would go on to run the family's shipping concerns. He had watched Yankees-Indians games at Municipal Stadium and witnessed Thurman's on-the-field qualities, and knew that the Yankee catching position was in good hands.

As the June 1973 trading deadline approached, the Yankees found themselves again in a pennant race. On June 7, Lee MacPhail engineered a pair of trades that brought two workhorse starting pitchers to pinstripes: Sam McDowell and Pat Dobson. These were unlike the moves that the CBS Yankees would have pulled off, and clearly reflected the new owner's philosophy of trading youth for veterans and going for the gold at once.

"If we don't win it all now, we only have ourselves to blame," said Bobby Murcer, excited that the team made such bold moves and was taking the pennant race seriously.

A win at Kansas City on June 9 moved the Yankees ahead of the Tigers and into first place. Although they were only five games over .500, Steinbrenner was gleeful about this first-year showing. It was the first time the team had been in first place since 1964. And the Yankees remained in first place all through June and all through July, eventually getting to twelve games over .500. Once again, the PR department was spinning into action with postseason publication plans, the ordering of World Series press pins, and a conference with the local Baseball Writers' Association about ticket allotments and press box seating. The ticket department began to plan for the printing of postseason tickets.

It was shaping up to be a glorious finale for the final year of old Yankee Stadium!

Munson was, of course, a big part of this success. He was hitting over .300, fielding sensationally, and taking charge of a strong pitching rotation with the great Lyle acting as closer. Blomberg was hitting over .400 as July 4 approached and shared a *Sports Illustrated* cover with Murcer.

The Yankee–Red Sox rivalry was really taking hold this year as both teams battled for the top, led by their tough catchers.

The Yankees went to Fenway Park for a four-game series July 30–August 2, one game up in the division as the series began. Just weeks earlier, Munson had finished second to Fisk in the All-Star voting. He wasn't happy about it.

The games were not sellouts, something hard to imagine today. But they were thrilling. The first three were all decided in the ninth inning. After splitting the first two, the Yanks were tied 2–2 in the ninth in game three. Munson was on third and his roommate Stick Michael was at bat.

Houk called for a suicide bunt, and Michael missed it. Here came Munson. Fisk, holding the ball tightly, had to first shove Michael out of the way and then tag the charging Munson. Munson went into him hard and flattened him, but Fisk held on to the ball. The Boston catcher then flipped Munson over to get himself free, causing Munson to retaliate with a punch. Michael then jumped over Munson and began hitting Fisk. Both dugouts and both bullpens emptied, and the fight lasted fifteen minutes before the umpires could restore order. Munson and Fisk were both ejected.

"There was no question I threw the first punch," said Thurman after the game. "But he started it and then my roomie got into it. Fisk was lucky he didn't get into a fight last night the way he blocked the plate on Roy White."

For the Yankees, it all collapsed in late August and September. The team just didn't have what it took to go the distance. From August 20 until the end of the season, the Yanks went 12–23, and fell back to their now familiar fourth place. While they had been leading the league on the morning of August 1, they managed to finish seventeen games out of first by season's end.

And the end was really ugly. The Mets were winning the National League East, and patience had worn out in the Bronx. The fans were very tough on Houk, who was loudly booed every time he went to the mound to change pitchers. Banners were displayed demanding his ouster. The promise of a pennant evaporated into an 80–82 season, embarrassing everyone associated with the team.

"The final month was one of the worst I've lived through," said Munson. "The fans were on us every day, especially on Ralph. They were never worse than they were during the last game. It pained me when Ralph was forced to come out and make a pitching change late in the game. He got a terrible booing and walked back to the dugout like a beaten man."

He was a beaten man, but a beaten man with a secret. He had informed MacPhail and Bob Fishel before the game that he would be resigning after the game. He told them he couldn't manage for Steinbrenner; couldn't deal with his meddling.

Of course, the team's collapse and the fan reaction made the meddling seem irrelevant. A change was needed, and perhaps Houk had become too complacent anyway, working for the benign leadership of Burke and MacPhail. Besides, he already had another job lined up, and would soon be announced as the Tigers' manager. Ralph was a good baseball politician and engineered his move perfectly.

Still, his resignation after the game, announced in the press room about two hundred feet from the Yankee clubhouse, was a shocker. It ended a thirty-five-year affiliation with the Yankee organization, including three World Series appearances as manager. And as a former catcher, he was a wonderful mentor to Munson, whom he had brought along rapidly by showing enormous confidence in him even when his first two seasons had started out so poorly.

The final game at the old stadium drew only 32,238, most determined to leave with their seats, no matter how much they had to twist them out of the concrete and break their iron legs in the process. Everyone in attendance got an LP of *The Sounds of 50 Years at Yankee Stadium* (which I had helped to produce), but since a family of four got four records, three would wind up being scaled onto the field, disrupting play on several occasions.

The wrecking ball would arrive the very next morning, with Mrs. Babe Ruth receiving home plate, Mrs. Lou Gehrig getting first base, and most of the active players heading home on Monday flights.

Thurman hit .301 for the season with 20 homers, which would be a career high. Thirteen of them were on the road, as old Yankee Stadium still proved too much for this right-handed hitter to conquer. The new stadium would have more reasonable distances and would do away with the so-called Death Valley of left-center. To his credit, Thurman worked with the ballpark, never tried to hit home runs, and never lost that smooth swing that sent line drives down the line or into the power alleys. He was a skilled hitter who accepted the geometry of his home park (he had no choice, of course), and worked within its limitations.

He hit only .261 in September, so he was as responsible as any of his teammates for the collapse, and he did not go home feeling very good about the season. But he did feel good about what he saw in the owner and in his will to win. It mirrored what Munson wanted to accomplish.

Thurman didn't play in the final "lost weekend" of the old stadium. Duke Sims, a journeyman acquired only on September 24, was not only the catcher but had the dubious distinction of hitting the last home run in the old park; Babe Ruth had hit the first. It said a lot about the 1923 Yankees and the 1973 Yankees.

A few weeks after the World Series, Steinbrenner would be placed on suspension by Commissioner Bowie Kuhn for his involvement in illegal campaign contributions to Richard Nixon's reelection campaign—a link to the overall scandal known as Watergate. For the franchise, it would be a major setback. Not only would they be heading to Shea Stadium for two years while Yankee Stadium was remodeled, but their new win-at-all-costs owner was going to be sidelined.

9

While the years spent at Shea weren't a physical burden on the players, the 1974 and 1975 seasons felt like a long road trip just the same.

The Yankee players used the New York Jets locker room, which was not the first-class facility a home team likes to use. It was so cramped it was hard to imagine a full roster of big football players in pads changing there. The incentive was to get dressed quickly and get on the field and out of there.

There were missteps en route. The Yankees tried to hire Dick Williams to manage the team, fresh from his world championships with Oakland. Although Steinbrenner was suspended, it was clearly an early "George move," going for the glamour of the man who had just won the 1973 Series, and who had then left Charley Finley's employ in a huff.

The intermediary in getting Williams to the table was Nat Tarnopol, Munson's friend and also a good friend of Williams. Gabe Paul, now running the Yankees with Steinbrenner's absence and Lee

MacPhail's departure for the American League presidency, had called on Nat to make the connection. And so Nat had emerged as an important outside power broker, a nice development for Thurman.

Outgoing AL president Joe Cronin, in his final act, vetoed the deal. He said that even though Williams had quit, he was still under contract to the Athletics, and compensation would be required to move him to New York. The proposed compensation from the wily Finley was pitcher Scott McGregor and outfielder Otto Velez, "our crown jewels," according to Paul.

And so although a press conference was held to introduce Williams to the New York media and photograph him in his Yankee jersey, the deal was off. It was a shame for Munson, because the Tarnopol connection had already made him feel like family with Williams.

"Plan B," which included a far less lavish press conference, was the strong silent type, Bill Virdon, best known as a Pittsburgh Pirates center fielder and later as the Pirates' manager. He had a lot going for him: he was available and he would work cheap. Tal Smith, the brilliant baseball man who now held the GM title but who reported to Paul, was a big Virdon advocate. Munson was out of the loop on that one.

So 1974 had all the earmarks of a loony season. The owner was suspended, the stadium was being remodeled, and the manager was a second choice.

The big new off-season acquisition was lovable Lou Piniella, obtained from Kansas City so that the Royals could break in the rather ordinary Jim Wohlford. Piniella, being both hot-tempered and a good sport all at once, would never hear the end of his new teammates' teasing him about "Jim Fucking Wohlford" taking his job away. Lou was a great baseball mind, had the best smile in the game, and could go from raving lunatic on the field after a bad umpire call to laughter and a smoke and a cold beer in the clubhouse three minutes later. No one who ever played with or for Piniella could ever forget him. Players always got on him about being a big guy and hitting few homers. Piniella and Munson hit it off and remained close to the end.

For Thurman, sadly, there would be a spring training injury in 1974 that never quite healed, and it ruined his reputation for throwing out runners. He would make 22 errors in 1974 while fielding .974 and then 23 errors with a .972 mark in 1975. These were the worst fielding stats for any catcher since World War II, and remained so more than three decades later. How ironic that the records would land on the back of the man who had tied the Yankee fielding percentage record by making only one error in 1971. Almost all the errors were on throws to second that wound up in center field. (Despite this, he won Gold Gloves in 1974 and 1975, a tribute to his reputation for signal calling and general handling of the game behind the plate.)

The injury went back to April 2, an exhibition game between the Yankees and the Mets in Columbia, South Carolina, where ex–Yankee second baseman Bobby Richardson was the head coach at the University of South Carolina, and had persuaded the team to play an exhibition there on their way north. Early in the game, a Mets outfielder named Dave Schneck, a left-handed hitter, swung through a pitch, and his backswing made contact with Munson's throwing hand, right where the thumb and the forefinger come together. Thurman dropped to his knees in pain, but played four more innings.

While at bat later in the game, he was jammed with a pitch and the very act of holding the bat hurt. X-rays failed to reveal anything at that time, and Thurman played opening day and then caught 144 games that season.

"He suffered a deep bruise of the thumb/forefinger junction in his hand and a deep bruise of his thumb's thenar eminence," said

Gene Monahan, the Yankees' athletic trainer. The thenar eminence is the large muscular base of the thumb on the palm side.

This would later be compounded by a wear-and-tear shoulder injury that eventually required surgery. According to Monahan, "He injured the distal end of his clavicle, the collarbone. It was injured at the end where it meets the acromion. The cartilage there was torn up and the actual tip of the clavicle deteriorated. He had to have it resected, shaved down. He ended up throwing sidearm for that reason."

"I wish I had rested more," Munson said. "I played every game in pain and pushed myself too hard. I definitely would have had better numbers in '74 if it wasn't for the hand. I'm not trying to make excuses, but I really couldn't grip the bat properly and my whole defensive game was hurting. It's disappointing to me because I felt I could have helped the club a lot more. Maybe if I didn't hurt the hand we would have come out on top."

Not until 1977 would he feel that he was back at full strength.

Pain or not, his pitchers wanted him out there.

Not everyone felt this way, of course. There was Rick Dempsey, a catcher who came to the Yankees in 1973 and stayed until 1976. He was what Houk was to Yogi—the backup. But he also had terrific defensive skills in his own right, including an accurate rifle of an arm.

Dempsey loved Munson as a teammate, but it would drive him crazy that his managers (Bill Virdon and Billy Martin) couldn't see the logic of having him catch and just finding another place for Munson. It killed him to see all those throws drift into the outfield, as they curved away from whoever was covering the base.

Despite this natural in-house rivalry, Dempsey and Munson had a special affinity for each other, even a special sign of friendship between them, where Munson would tuck in his three middle fingers and wiggle the thumb and pinky. In 1973 Munson told the rookie, "You're the kid who's gonna try to take my job, aren't you?"

Dempsey replied, "Yeah, if I can."

"Well, nice to have you around," said Thurman, and he put his arm around his shoulder.

"From that day on Thurman was my idol," Rick says. "He was always reassuring me, telling me that someday I would get my chance. He was never afraid to tell me how I could go about taking his job."

Later, when Dempsey was with Baltimore, he stole second and scored on a close play in the ninth. "Thurman was really mad 'cause he thought I was out," says Rick. "But in the bottom of the inning, he smiled at me from the dugout and flashed our sign, meaning, 'Nice going, kid.' "

"Rick did go on to be a first-rate big-league catcher," says Tippy Martinez, his Yankee teammate who wound up going with him to the Orioles in the big 1976 trade. "And if you're a big leaguer, you have to feel that you're good enough to be a regular, and he did. He loved Munson, like we all did, but sure, it would frustrate him to see all those errors, knowing he had such a great arm.

"But the part about calling the game and working the whole dynamics—Rick just wasn't there yet at that stage of his career. There is so much you have to learn about that. Like the way Thurman would work his pitchers with the umpires, how he'd quietly argue on their behalf with the umps when nobody but he and the batter and the umpire knew about it. We didn't even know about it on the mound sometimes. But he was always there pulling for us.

"The other thing he taught me was about respecting rookies. They were full teammates, he'd tell me, just like anyone else. Usually, rookies were kind of ignored. But he'd call me for breakfast or for coffee and he'd tell me what a great future I had and I never forgot that. In my fourteen-year career, I always thought about Thurman whenever a rookie would show up."

Rick Manning was a rookie outfielder with the Indians in 1975. "I was tagging up to try and score on a fly ball and I went into home headfirst," he recalls. "Thurman was waiting for me and knocked me silly. As I walked away he said, 'Hey Rook, don't do that again.'

"I told him not to worry; I wouldn't. But he was always playing mind games with you.

"He'd talk a lot behind the plate and tell me what pitch was coming. I wouldn't believe him, and sure enough, they'd throw that pitch. I'd take it and Thurman would shake his head and say, 'I told you it was going to be a fastball.' "

Even rookie umpires had their special Munson initiations.

"Steve Palermo had just broken into the big leagues as an umpire," recalls Rich Marazzi, baseball's rule-book expert, someone umpires call on for interpretations. He consults for several teams. "He told me that part of his 'initiation' to the big leagues was calling Thurman out on a pitch that was knee high on the outside corner, a good 'pitcher's pitch.' Munson raised a fuss and said, 'Rookie, they don't call that pitch a strike up here.' Undaunted, and meeting his rookie test, Palermo replied, 'That pitch is a strike in any league.'

"After Thurman returned to the playing field with his gear on to start the next inning, he complimented Palermo, granting that he had in fact made a great call. Palermo answered, 'Why don't you go over to the dugout and tell your Yankee buddies that I made a great call!'

" 'Oh, I can't do that,' Munson answered sheepishly. They never had another dispute."

The Yanks opened the 1974 season on April 6 with a three-game series at home with Cleveland, and then, after a pair at Detroit, played a four-game series at Cleveland, emerging from that with a 5–4 record. The team was working with a nine-man pitching staff, which seemed sufficient at the time: Stottlemyre, Dobson, McDowell, George Medich, Peterson, Steve Kline, Fred Beene, Tom Buskey, and Lyle.

Munson had once been closer to Peterson; they had been among the leaders in the lunatic hockey games that were played in the clubhouse. After the wife swap a lot of players were more ill at ease with Fritz, since this was something that was really over the top for them. People still liked him, but the relationship wasn't as free and easy.

Fritz had had his measure of fun with Munson over a mail-in order. Thurman, a gun collector, had purchased a .357 Magnum. While reading a gun magazine in the clubhouse, he saw an offer for a holster that seemed just right. He checked off thirty-six-inch waist, right-hander, and put it in the clubhouse "outbox" for mailing.

Peterson, an eternal prankster, retrieved the envelope and changed the order to a twenty-inch waist. It took more than a month to arrive, but when it did, Thurman went crazy when he opened it and saw the skimpy holster. Finally, Munson repackaged it and mailed it back.

And of course Peterson retrieved the package, hid it in his locker, waited a few weeks, and then mixed it in with the incoming mail. Yes, Thurman had his "replacement" and again it was only twenty inches long. It was probably a good thing that he didn't know Fritz was behind this.

On the subject of guns, and on a scarier note, some years later, after a game, Munson was with Catfish Hunter when they came upon Munson's free promotional Cadillac in the players' lot at Yankee Stadium. The windshield had been smashed in. Hunter told this to me after it happened, and repeated it to journalist Michael Paterniti for an *Esquire* story many years later. Thurman was furious and thought he spotted the vandals on the other side of the fence. He went to his trunk and pulled out a .44 Magnum revolver.

"I'm going to kill them," he said to Hunter.

Hunter, laughing, told him not to get carried away. But Munson was furious, and he raised the weapon and fired it at the shadowy figures behind the fence.

"Oh shit!" screamed Hunter.

Munson fired twice more, at which point Hunter grabbed Thurman from behind and wrestled the gun away from him. All the time Hunter was thinking two thoughts: that his fingerprints were now on the gun, and *Please, please, don't nobody get hit.*

"I didn't hit anybody," Munson told him, "but I'm going to run them over!" And with that he screeched out of the lot, leaving Hunter standing there. Hunter was never sure if Thurman was serious.

Early in the season, an ugly press incident took place between Thurman and Herschel Nissenson of the Associated Press.

Nissenson wouldn't take crap from a player just because he was, well, a player. And he could be provoked in that bad mixture that sometimes emerges from the heat of the clubhouse after a bad game.

There had been a game in Anaheim when Thurm had dropped a pop-up, but his instincts took over, he recovered the ball, and nailed a runner at the plate. Because the batter had reached first, he was charged with an error. It was a legitimate scoring decision.

A week or so later, the Yankees were back in New York and a similar play happened. It was a meaningless moment in the game, but again, he was charged with an error when he dropped a pop-up, even though the team managed to record an out on the play.

Ironically, Thurman had been presented with his 1973 Gold Glove award before the game, so it was hard for a journalist to resist the contradiction. After the game, Nissenson passed Munson in the cramped Yankee clubhouse. "So Thurman," he said, "what's the record for the most pop-ups dropped by a Gold Glove winner?"

This was exactly the kind of comment that could set Thurman off. After all, what in the world did a $%@#%$# sportswriter know about what happens down there on the field?

"What's the record for the most horseshit stories written by a sportswriter?" he answered.

Okay, it was a decent comeback to a provocative question, and it could have ended there. But Bill Sudakis, a provocateur himself who had recently joined the team as a backup catcher to Munson, egged him on.

"You gonna take that bullshit?" he said to Munson. "What the hell does he know about playing the game? Look at him! Don't take that crap."

The clubhouse, small to begin with, seemed to encourage a closing of ranks. If Munson and Nissenson were four feet apart, it may have felt like four inches.

"How far can a sportswriter travel across the room if I hit him?" Thurman said.

Now there was a silence, an anticipation that things might get ugly. There had been scattered cases over the years of players hitting writers—and a rare one now and then of writers hitting players—but this was not an area where either party wanted to go. The nastiness of "charges being brought" looms large over such moments.

Nissenson should have shaken his head and walked away. He didn't. He was feeling a rush of blood to his face.

"I've seen you hit a baseball," he said. "I'm not worried."

Oh boy.

Some teammates stepped back anticipating the worst. Some, to their credit, stepped forward, ready to break up the inevitable.

As the PR guy, on the other side of the clubhouse, near Bill Virdon's office, I was not aware of what was going on, but the shifting of bodies and Munson's raised voice had gotten my attention. Policemen are trained to go toward trouble, not away from it. That certainly wasn't part of my training, but it was instantly clear that I needed to move closer to the situation.

And the next thing I saw was Nissenson pinned against a corner, face-to-face with Munson. No one had any idea where this was going, but it was scary. *Why isn't a teammate or a coach stepping between them?* I thought, as I now moved toward them. *Is this going to fall on me?*

Munson had the good sense never to touch Herschel. Not with his hands, not with his chest. In the days to come, it was said across the league that Thurman had spit at Nissenson, which would have in itself been very damaging.

"It didn't happen," said Herschel later. "He never spit at me. We were so close that there might have been some flying spittle in the air, but it wasn't an overt act. And in the end, I had the feeling that if you growled back at him, he was okay."

And that's how it ended. No blows exchanged, no contact. No lawsuits.

Jim Ogle, the senior writer covering the team, made peace between the two of them a few days later. They shook hands.

The 1974 season got off nicely for the Yankees. On Friday night, April 26, Stottlemyre won his fourth start in a row and the team was 11–8 and just a half game behind Baltimore. That was when the PR director (that would be me) made it known that a trade would be announced at the conclusion of the game.

And so I disappeared from my seat for a few innings and prepared the necessary press release back in my office across the street from Shea. At the end of the game we announced a seven-player trade. We were getting rid of almost half the pitching staff—Peterson, Kline, Beene, and Buskey (another rookie award winner taking his wristwatch to Cleveland: that would be five if you're keeping score)—for the Indians' first baseman Chris Chambliss and pitchers Dick Tidrow and Cecil Upshaw.

Suddenly four guys in the winning clubhouse—ours—were gone. It was a very awkward moment, made all the more so by Gabe Paul, the trade's engineer, marching into the clubhouse, chest out with great pride, a big smile on his face, to hold court with the media in front of all the players.

The players were in shock. Trades are not usually announced in such an embarrassing way, with the "victims" right there, left to clean out their lockers in the middle of their friendships.

The feeling among the Yankee veterans was that Mike Hegan, the regular first baseman, was getting screwed out of his job, and that Fred Beene had become an effective relief pitcher who was well liked in the clubhouse. Peterson, despite his somewhat awkward relationship with his teammates following The Swap, was in his ninth year in the rotation.

No one was more outspoken, angry, and generally pissed off than Munson. In front of the writers he let his outrage be known. "Beenie! How can they trade Beenie!" he repeated several times. "We're turning into the Indians, is that what they want? Because Gabe Paul came here from Cleveland he has to bring all his players?"

It wasn't Thurman's finest hour. By the time the new guys arrived on Sunday, he was still in a hostile mood and happy to let everyone know it. The welcome mat was definitely not out for the new arrivals, a process usually led by the veterans on the club. In this case, everyone was still mad that Hegan was losing his job and that half the pitching staff was gone.

Chambliss, one of the nicest guys in the game, had been hitting .328 at Cleveland and thought he'd be better received. He had been Rookie of the Year the year after Munson. Instead he found himself just quietly going about his business in wonderment and hoping his new teammates would come around.

They did. They were professionals and they got back to playing, and they came to see that Chambliss and Tidrow could be good contributors and were consummate professionals.

But the Gabe Paul/Bill Virdon moves weren't done. The biggest move of the season came on May 26, when Virdon put Elliott Maddox in center and moved Murcer to right.

Maddox was thought to be a utility outfielder when he joined the team from Texas, but Virdon knew the value of a great defensive center fielder, having been one himself, and was down on Murcer. So he made the shift, something that further angered Munson and the veterans, who knew that center field had descended from Hall of Famers Earle Combs to Joe DiMaggio to Mickey Mantle, and then to Murcer. It was hallowed ground for this franchise. Elliott Maddox? What were they thinking?

Murcer was not happy about it, and was not playing well in Shea Stadium either. One would think that a subpar season from Murcer and a bad attitude from Munson would spell trouble for the team.

On the contrary, the Yankees overachieved—and got themselves well into a thrilling pennant race. And suddenly Paul was looking like the wise old baseball man he was supposed to be, and Virdon was looking like the Manager of the Year—which in fact he won.

The Yanks were in last place as late as July 14, and even lost seven of eight after the All-Star break. But then the pieces began to fall into place, and the fact that they were never more than seven and a half games out at any point began to have meaning. They went 15–3 from August 7 to Labor Day and found themselves just a game out of first. This, then, would be a third straight pennant race. Would this one have another bad finish?

Munson, now making $75,000 (plus $5,000 for PR participation and extra spring training expenses), was not having a great year. His average was under .250 for much of the season, he was crankier than usual, and the spring training injury had turned him from a 1973 Gold Glove winner into a fielding liability.

But with Medich and Dobson both winning 19, with Maddox unexpectedly hitting over .300, and with Sandy Alomar prying second base loose from Horace Clarke and improving the defense up the middle, the Yanks wouldn't go away. Baltimore was a far more talented team, but there were the Yanks, one game out of first with two games to go as they headed for Milwaukee on September 30. They had won four in a row, and were feeling really good about themselves, even with the Orioles in the driver's seat.

Arriving at the stately old Pfister Hotel in downtown Milwaukee after their flight, the team was a bit on the intoxicated side. The beer had flowed freely on the flight. Munson's two backup catchers had been getting on each other during the bus ride from the airport to the hotel. Rick Dempsey, always upset not to be playing more, was being teased about it by Bill Sudakis, a redneck third-stringer whose repetitious plays of "Band on the Run" on his boom box had become both a rallying cry during long road trips and a source of annoyance to those who weren't fans of Paul McCartney and Wings. (MP3 players have definitely contributed to greater team harmony.)

The teasing continued as the team entered the hotel lobby, a palace of aging Edwardian splendor. While waiting for the room keys to be sorted on the table near the registration desk, Dempsey heard one thing too many and lunged at Sudakis. Virdon made a move to stop them, but Murcer was closer and got in the middle. In the process, Murcer's hand was injured. He would not be available for game 161.

His absence surely mattered. The Yanks battled but lost 3–2 in ten innings. The Orioles won, took a two-game lead with one to play, and clinched the division title. There would be no postseason for the 1974 Yanks, and for the third straight year, the pennant race had failed to find them at the finish line. For the tenth year in a row, there would be no postseason baseball in the Bronx.

Munson hit .261 in 1974, a forty-point drop from 1973. He called it an off year and he was right, but the spring training injury had surely hurt him for the full season. The Yanks gave him a modest $5,000 raise, up to $80,000 for 1975.

One little piece of business that year went undetected by the media. It seemed that during the season, with Gabe Paul still working the phones and Cedric Tallis as the general manager in Kansas City, a deal was cooked up that would have sent Munson, Murcer, Tippy Martinez, Scott McGregor, and Jim Mason to the Royals for the league's hottest hitter, John Mayberry, and shortstop Fred Patek. All letter *M*'s plus Patek. Like other trades before and since, it didn't happen.

"It was close, I can tell you that," says Jack McKeon, the Royals' manager. "I told Cedric, 'If you make this deal, I'll win you the pennant.' I think Chris Chambliss was probably in it too, since we'd be getting rid of Mayberry and would need a first baseman. But Cedric backed off. He said they'd run him out of town if he traded Mayberry and Patek. We were this close."

Tantalizing as this story is to ponder, Tal Smith, the Yankees' general manager at the time, has no recollection of it. McKeon is sure of it. Take your pick.

Bobby Murcer had now experienced the excitement of three straight pennant races, but had never been to the promised land. He came up in 1965, still a boy of nineteen, but it was the year the Yankee dynasty collapsed. Now one could sense a new one on the way. But Bobby was not going to get there with them.

In a shocking trade announced shortly after the 1974 World Series, Gabe Paul traded Murcer to San Francisco even up for Bobby Bonds. Said Tal Smith, "When you can get one of the five best players in baseball, you do it."

George Steinbrenner had given assurances to Murcer that he would be a Yankee for life, and as Mickey Mantle's successor and the handsome heartthrob of the team since 1969, the idea of dealing Murcer was far-fetched. But Gabe Paul had a flair for the dramatic, and when Horace Stoneham of the Giants told him Bonds might be available, Gabe swung into action.

The phone call from Paul to Murcer early that Wednesday morning (I was in the room when Gabe called him) was a devastating one for Bobby. It also stunned his teammates. His great friend Munson seemed less stunned.

"It's a business," Thurman told friends. "Nothing should surprise any of us. We know Gabe Paul likes to make trades."

In 1973, Bonds had hit 39 homers and stolen 43 bases, falling one homer short of being the first 40/40 man in history. He was an enormously gifted athlete, and as Smith had said, one of the best players in the game. He had fallen to .256 with 21 homers and 71 RBIs in 1974, making himself vulnerable to a deal. The Yankees seized the moment.

So Bonds was a Yankee and Murcer wasn't. Thurman's closest friend on the team had moved on.

In Thurman's "real" family life, Darrell Munson reappeared on the scene. Just before Christmas in 1974, he went to Canton to see his grandchildren. He caught up with Thurman at the local Y. The next day they spoke on the phone.

It did not go well. Thurman had moved on. That relationship was over.

That would be the last communication the two of them would ever have.

I was busy in the PR office preparing our publications for the upcoming season with Bonds as our cover boy and new superstar when we got into the bidding for Catfish Hunter, the 1974 Cy Young Award winner with Oakland.

Charley Finley had failed to make certain payments to Hunter on time, breaching terms of his contract. Few thought such an infraction would lead an arbitrator to make Hunter a free agent, but that's what happened. And we found ourselves in the Hunter sweepstakes along with a lot of other clubs.

"Gabe," I said, facing my boss in his Flushing office. "Could this get up to a million dollars?"

"Damn right it could!" he said with what I thought was a measure of glee. "This is war! And we're gonna win it."

I sensed he had been given a blank check by the suspended Steinbrenner, with whom he was obviously in touch.

Finishing two games out of first place in 1974, then adding Bonds and Hunter, was thrilling to consider. Suspended or not, George Steinbrenner's willingness to spend what it took was now apparent.

We got Hunter, and it didn't hurt that Munson was calling him almost every day, trying to persuade him to play in New York. We announced the $3.5 million deal at a New Year's Eve press conference in the group sales office at the Parks Administration Building across the street from Shea on a snowy night.

We now had the Manager of the Year, an owner willing to spend, and had added Munson in 1970, Lyle in 1972, Nettles in 1973, Piniella and Chambliss in 1974, and Bonds and Hunter in 1975. You had to like the way this team was coming together.

Unfortunately, things didn't work out the way they were supposed to. That can happen in baseball. Usually teams find their own level over the course of six months, and only major injuries stand in the way of their finishing where they are supposed to finish.

That didn't happen for the 1975 Yanks. Things actually went right and they still didn't win.

First, trying hard to return to the starting rotation, Mel Stottlemyre just didn't have it and was released in spring training. ("Thurman was the only Yankee player to come to our car in the parking lot to say good-bye," recalls Jean Stottlemyre.) Having missed most of the 1974 season, and with all the roster turnovers, Mel's closeness to his teammates had faded.

Then Hunter lost his first three starts, and if you don't think that put a scare in the front office, you'd be wrong. We were all nervous. Pitchers are fragile. Bad seasons happen.

His 0–3 beginning set the team off poorly, and by Memorial Day we were still under .500. Then came a glorious June in which the team went 21–9 to go eight games over .500 and briefly touch first place for a few days.

It didn't hold up. Seven straight losses around the July Fourth weekend pretty much killed things off, as Boston, enjoying great rookie seasons from Fred Lynn and Jim Rice, was making its way to the front of the pack. In some ways, 1975 was the first real season of the Yankees–Red Sox rivalry that we know today; the first year in which both teams were really good, and began to pack their ballparks when they played each other.

On a road trip to Texas, when things were really going badly, Thurman took it upon himself to run a team meeting to try to get things righted. This was before he was captain, of course, and Phil Pepe of the *Daily News* learned about it and wrote it. Munson was pissed. It was supposed to be a secret meeting.

"He didn't talk to me for a full year," said Pepe. "And we had been friends!"

Hunter's 1975 season, by today's standards, was truly out of this world. He made 39 starts and hurled 30 complete games, going 23–14 and leading the league with 328 innings pitched. It was the most work a Yankee pitcher had had since 1921, when Carl Mays, the year after killing Ray Chapman with a pitch, threw 337 innings in the Yankees' first pennant-winning season. No American League pitcher since Bob Feller in 1946 had hurled 30 complete games.

Some would come to feel that the Yankees looked to get their full $3.5 million value in year one of the five-year contract, for indeed, his remaining four years did not measure up either in accomplishment or in durability. But he brought a lot more to the team than stats. Catfish was the sort of guy who just looked like a leader when he walked through the airport with his teammates. He had a stature about him that seemed to say "champion." He brought with him a record of championship play in Oakland and maintained that commanding presence through good times and bad.

"He taught us how to win" were the six words spoken by many in the Yankee organization as the years went on.

Hunter attributed much of his Yankee success to Munson.

"Thurman was like a hundred years old in baseball knowledge," he said. "He was amazing. I trusted him totally."

Munson and Hunter formed a close friendship. Thurman had called him almost every day when he was a free agent to try to persuade him to play for the Yankees. They had a similar maturity, which is not to say that they couldn't be prone to moments of boyish mischief, as happens with athletes. They loved their Burger King cheeseburgers and their fast food pizza on the run. But on the field they were all business. They would share an apartment after Hunter's family returned to North Carolina late in the summer.

"Thurman liked to sleep on the couch," said Catfish. "Next to the phone so he could make his business deals.

"He's the only player I've ever seen who busts his butt all the time. Of course, I like to get on him a lot by saying he was the only player in the league who never hit a home run off me. But he says it's because I was always knocked out before he had a chance to bat. When I played against him, I never knew he was this good a guy."

Bonds, the other superstar acquisition during the off-season, was indeed one of the most gifted athletes to ever wear a Yankee uniform. He could run like an antelope, hit for power, and field with flashes of brilliance. He had been a Gold Glove winner. He did strike out far too often, and broke Mickey Mantle's single-season team record in that department. (I sent Mickey the "record-breaking" baseball, signed by Bonds.) He respected the game and played through pain to contribute what he could, and while he was healthy before running into a wall in Comiskey Park, the team was peaking.

Alas, the Bonds injury, striking as it did the team's key power hitter, led to a slowdown by the club, and with that came a manager shift. One year after Virdon had been Manager of the Year, he was to pay the price for not taking the team to the pennant despite the arrival of Bonds and Hunter. It would be George Steinbrenner's first firing of a manager, Ralph Houk having resigned.

Virdon's demise was sealed when the Texas Rangers fired Billy Martin. With Martin available and extremely attractive to Steinbrenner as a turnaround artist, the lure of having this important Yankee player from the 1950s was irresistible.

Although he was technically still under suspension, there was little doubt that it was at Steinbrenner's urging that Gabe Paul and scout Birdie Tebbetts were secretly dispatched to Colorado to run down Martin days after his firing in Texas and bring him home as manager.

Days earlier, Virdon had been instructed to play a tape made by Steinbrenner during a clubhouse meeting, in which the voice of the owner said, "I'll be a sonovabitch if I'm going to sit up here and sign these paychecks and watch us get our asses kicked by a bunch of rummies." The players mostly reacted with amusement, although some felt it clearly undermined Virdon's role as the manager.

While the mission to Colorado was secret, the writers knew that Martin's availability made for a tempting confluence of bad timing for Virdon. The ownership that had sent Martin into exile in 1957 was long gone.

Munson and Virdon were never close. That was mostly Virdon's style; he was not one who got close to his players, even the leaders of the team. It would have been helpful. There even came a point late in the season when several of the Yankee veterans, including Nettles, Piniella, and Munson, began giving their own signals on the field during games.

"He hadn't said a word to me in weeks," Munson recalled. "Then I walked by his office at Shea and I hear him say, 'Thurman!' So I went in. And on his desk were a bunch of baseball cards someone had mailed in. He wanted me to sign mine. We never really had much to say to each other, unless it was a conference on the mound.

But even then, he'd often sent Whitey Ford to the mound, even to change pitchers." Ford was the Yankee pitching coach under Virdon that year.

It was something that nagged at Steinbrenner. Virdon had been sending Dick Howser to the plate for the exchange of lineups at the start of games, and Ford to the mound to talk to the pitchers. His old friend Mel Wright, a coach, was his principal contact with the players. The communication skills were not strong, and Steinbrenner certainly wanted a more fiery manager when the going got tough.

Indeed, times were tough enough by Old-Timers' Day that Virdon would get sacked on the Friday night before, and then Martin would be introduced on Saturday. It was a difficult weekend for me as PR man. Planning Old-Timers' Day was one thing; changing managers was quite another. I walked with Joe DiMaggio from the executive entrance at Shea to the Yankee clubhouse around ten in the morning and said, "You know we're naming Martin as manager today, right?" (It had been in the papers.)

DiMaggio sort of rolled his eyes and said, "Good luck." He knew this was going to be the start of some challenging times for the organization. Billy was not low-maintenance.

In fact, Billy Martin's new managing contract stated that he had to "personally conduct [himself] at all times so as to represent the best interest of the New York Yankees and to adhere to all club policies." So, built into the welcome was the clause designed to hasten his firing. It was a tinderbox.

From the day of his arrival, August 2, until the end of the season, Martin led the Yanks to a 30–26 record. They were in third place, ten games out when he arrived, and finished in third place, twelve games out on the final day. But there were positive signs. The team ran more, played with more abandon, and seemed to be enjoying themselves more.

Bonds became the team's first ever 30/30 player (30 homers, 30 steals), and Chambliss hit .304.

In a setback, a knee injury in the spongy Shea outfield effectively ended Elliott Maddox's promising career, and opened up center field for the taking.

By hitting about .330 after Martin arrived, Munson showed new fire after the managerial change. For the season, Thurman would hit .318 and would drive in 102 runs despite hitting only 12 homers. He was the first Yankee in eleven years to top 100 RBIs, and he led the American League with 151 singles in the process.

He may have been helped by the healthy birth of his son Michael on July 29.

"He was so happy at having a son," recalls Mara Young, Ron Blomberg's wife at the time. "I remember seeing him outside of an elevator at Shea Stadium, and he picked me up and said, 'I'm so excited! It's a boy!' "

For Thurman to hit triple figures in RBIs without a lofty home run total spoke a lot about how frequently he would come through in clutch situations with men on base. And this was indeed the beginning of a long run in which Munson would be this sort of hitter—a guy who was extremely dangerous with men on base.

From 1975 through 1977, three seasons, Thurman would hit over .300 and top 100 RBIs every year. He would be the first player in the major leagues to accomplish this feat since Bill White did it for the Cardinals from 1962 through 1964, and the first in the American League since Al Rosen did it for the Indians in 1952–54. SABRmaticians would have been all over this with today's fast computers, but back then I stumbled onto it accidentally while scanning White's records in preparing his bio for our media guide. (White was the Yankee's announcer by this time.) That sent me searching for the last American Leaguer, who would turn out to be the future president of the Yankees and a longtime pal of George Steinbrenner's.

The last catcher to accomplish the feat had been Bill Dickey, in 1936–39, when the Yanks won four straight world championships.

Martin, like Virdon before him, recognized the value of having Thurman call the games despite his propensity to commit errors on throws to second. It just went with the territory, and both managers knew they won more than they lost in the process.

"Wait till I have this team with a full spring training and can lop off guys from the roster that didn't show me much," said Martin as the 1975 season concluded. "I can't wait for '76."

The 1975 World Series between Cincinnati and Boston was thrilling and was largely credited for a resurgence of interest in baseball. A lot of people still claim that to be the case today. Those who do tend to overlook the value to the game of having a strong Yankee team in New York, particularly one that would be playing in a new stadium. And so it would be the combination of the 1975 Series and the emergence of the 1976 Yankees that would, in fact, revitalize the game and send it into its modern period of marketing success.

Martin as manager and Munson as team captain would have a lot to do with that.

10

The idea of naming a team captain first came to George Steinbrenner during the winter of 1975–76. It came from the football mentality he was always accused of being consumed with, and he knew he needed to "persuade" Martin to go along.

All along, he was going through the arrangements that would get Bowie Kuhn to lift his suspension as the new Yankee Stadium was being prepared for opening day. I was involved with both efforts, meeting with lawyers in the evenings to develop the PR reasons for the need to lift his suspension, while working with the excitement of a new stadium.

Meanwhile, Gabe Paul was shaking things up by making huge trades. The winter meetings of 1975 were quiet for a few days, and then we stole the headlines.

On December 11 came the news that after just one season, we were trading Bobby Bonds. He would not see the new Yankee Stadium in a home uniform. He would be a one-year Yankee whose Yankee career would be confined to Shea.

Bonds was traded to the California Angels for center fielder Mickey Rivers and starting pitcher Ed Figueroa. (It also meant, of course, that it was Murcer's trade that ultimately led to Rivers and Figueroa.)

And then that same day, George "Doc" Medich, the pitcher who was pursuing his medical degree while playing baseball, was traded to the Pittsburgh Pirates for Dock Ellis and Ken Brett, with a rookie second baseman named Willie Randolph included in the deal for good measure.

The team that had been a series of building blocks—Munson, Lyle, Nettles, Piniella, Chambliss, Hunter, et al.—would now have a terrific leadoff hitter in Rivers who could jump-start any game he appeared in, and Randolph a great fielder who would finally put to rest the so-called Horace Clarke era of Yankee baseball, under which no one ever seemed to come along to move the rather ordinary Clarke out of the lineup. (Sandy Alomar finally did in July 1974, but at thirty-two, he was considered a stopgap until someone like Randolph would emerge.)

In mid-January 1976, a large group of Yankee officials including Billy Martin gathered at the Carlyle Hotel in Manhattan to begin several days of planning meetings for the new stadium and new season. Steinbrenner had been granted permission to run the meetings, his suspension clearly coming to an early end. A court reporter was on hand to transcribe the discussions, and each of us later received a copy.

At one point the conversation turned toward making the players more fan-friendly, more responsive to autograph requests, and even encouraging them to toss free baseballs into the stands.

"We're going to have to be more accommodating to the fans," said Steinbrenner. "The Mets have a better reputation than us on that. I don't want them to have a better reputation on anything. And Munson especially, he's becoming more and more grumpy, not more and more accommodating, and that has to change."

Then, after another mention of Munson was made, Steinbrenner said:

> Speaking of Munson, that brings up something that I want you to give some thought to, not necessarily speaking in terms of Thurman Munson. But Billy [glancing at Martin]—and this should be your decision, your decision strictly—we have never had a leader per se on the ball club. We've never had a captain. If you've got the guy that can be a leader—I don't know how you feel about this, but that's something I want you to wrestle with and make up your mind whether you want to appoint a captain to the ball club. I hear pros and cons. I've seen it be great and I've seen it when it was a nothing. So that's something that I want you to address yourself to, okay?

Mine is the next voice that appears in the transcript.

"Lou Gehrig was a captain of the Yankees," I said. "When he became ill and subsequently died, Joe McCarthy said something like 'Lou will always remain the Yankee captain and there'll never be another one.' And for that reason, DiMaggio and Mantle were never officially called captain or anything like that, so it's always been a practice that existed."

Steinbrenner heard me out and then said:

> Well, I think that's fine. But I'm not . . . you know, as much as I respect him, and I don't think anybody's done any more to try to preserve the memory of those guys than we have since we took this team over—CBS certainly didn't—I'm out for what's best for this ball club.
>
> And the minute we win a pennant and win the World Series, you know that's . . . that's why I say it's your problem to wrestle with. If you decide not to, that's fine. And I don't say

it should always be the Mantle, the DiMaggio, the Gehrig, or the Ruth that's going to be your best leader out there. That sometimes can cause you more problems. Maybe it's got to be some other guy. But that's something for the manager.

I appreciate the history on it, Marty, and I'm not saying we have to do it. I'm just saying I wish you'd wrestle with that problem and give it some thought.

There was the birth of the idea. And we all knew whom he was talking about.

Munson spent the off-season back at his Fifty-second Street home in Canton, playing handball, hanging out with his buddies, reading aviation and gun magazines, going pheasant hunting, and getting more involved in real estate. He had invested in apartment buildings and commercial property, and was now part of a syndicate that would be developing 146 acres into a shopping center and office complex that would be called Belden Village.

"He started playing doubles in handball with me at the Y around that time," recalls Jerry Anderson, who was helping to get him into real estate development. "Jess Tucker was the developer, and I was sort of Thurm's counselor and consultant. We were just building our friendship."

Of course, he was also spending the kind of quality time with his family that he so loved. Tracy was now seven, Kelly five and a half, and Michael barely two.

"People remember Thurman as this gruff tough guy, but he had a wonderful soft side," says Diana. "When the girls needed their hair brushed, they wanted their daddy to do it. They said, 'You're too rough, Mommy; Daddy does it so gently!' In that little loving act, you could learn a lot about him."

As for Michael, Thurman would say to Anderson, "The little guy is a handful!" Anderson felt he said that not only to reflect his times with his son, but to show his awareness of what Diana was going through when he wasn't around.

Diana would later tell the *Springfield* (Mass.) *Union,* "When Thurman is around, you wouldn't know he is the same child. Usually, Michael gets up ten or eleven times a night and calls for me. But when Thurman is home, he says, 'Michael, I don't want you getting up at night and calling Mommy.' And he sleeps until morning. And then when he wakes up, he calls Thurman. When I see that, I know we need Thurman around. This little boy needs his dad."

The child care issue and the real estate developments were what made Munson think about the benefits of playing for the Indians. He could keep a close watch on his properties while enjoying being at home with his children. He was expanding his thinking and re-alizing that he wasn't only a baseball player.

"I'd be more than happy to play in Cleveland," he confided to Murray Chass of the *New York Times.* "I even told the Yankees that if we couldn't get together, instead of losing me as a free agent, they should get three or four players for me by trading me to Cleveland.

"There are a lot of factors to weigh—what I could get here or in Cleveland where I would be home, or maybe I could get twice as much from an expansion club if I was a free agent. You have to weigh all those things. I'm not going to sign until I know for sure that I'm not making a mistake."

With Andy Messersmith and Dave McNally having been judged to be free agents prior to the start of the 1976 season, Munson, along with hundreds of other players, was in a position to play through 1976 without signing a contract and to declare himself part of the first "free agent class" after the season. As a good businessman, Thurman seemed likely to consider this possibility. Sparky Lyle had almost done it in 1975, and might have been there with Messersmith and McNally, but he signed in the waning days of the season. No doubt he and Thurman talked it over.

Now spring training for the 1976 season had finally opened. The owners had locked the camps while a new Basic Agreement with the union was being negotiated. The commissioner, Bowie Kuhn, finally ordered the camps opened in late March.

Thinking about the benefits of playing for Cleveland versus a straightforward business decision to evaluate an offer from the Yankees, Thurman arrived at Fort Lauderdale Stadium on March 23.

Martin called Munson into his office at the ballpark.

"I want to make you captain," he said. "I've discussed it with George and the coaches, and you're a natural leader on this team and I want you to be the captain."

"What does it mean?" asked Munson. "Like, I take the lineup out every game?"

The thought of that seemed a bit off, given that he would be in his full catching gear for home games, and often would have been warming up the starting pitcher in the bullpen.

"No," Billy replied. "I'll do that. I need to do that. It gives me time to talk to the umpires, ask about their kids, get on their good side if we need a close call."

"Then what am I supposed to do?"

"Just be a leader by example," said Billy. "You already are. But with the title, even a new player will know that you're the guy carrying on Yankee tradition. It's a good idea, the more I think about it."

I suspect that at some level, Billy must have thought that had Casey Stengel lifted the ban, he, Billy Martin, might have liked being the team captain in the 1950s, more so than Mantle or Berra or Ford.

Thurman left Martin's office and walked out to right field with George Steinbrenner before the team's first workout. It was a beautiful time of day in Fort Lauderdale—not yet too hot, a gentle breeze in the air, empty stands being hosed down by the few stadium employees, and an occasional private jet taking off from Executive Airport next door. The newly restored general partner and his captain were engaged in business talk. The conversation lasted about twenty minutes.

An intrasquad game was played, with Munson driving in the winning run. Afterward he dressed in his best double-knit plaid pants, threw a Banlon shirt over his head, and walked to the manager's office, where he, Steinbrenner, and Gabe Paul renewed their discussions about a new contract.

George and Gabe considered Munson's signing a priority. He had been third in the league in hitting in 1975, and with everyone feeling a pennant in the air, a happy Munson could be a big contributor to a new time of good feeling.

The three talked for more than an hour. With a towel draped around his neck, Thurman went to the players' parking lot and into Paul's trailer. Another hour passed, with a few reporters lurking outside.

Finally he emerged, the towel still in place. He looked tired. He got into Gabe Paul's Toyota, put the towel on the passenger seat, and said, "I don't want to say anything at this time. I want to sit back and think about what I've done. It's a big load off my mind. I want to relax. It's been on my mind a long time."

Murray Chass, the best reporter at coming up with salary terms, reported that Thurman had signed a new two-year contract for a total of $275,000, which would make him the fifth Yankee in history to make $100,000 in a season, joining DiMaggio, Mantle, Murcer, Bonds, and Hunter. Of course salaries were about to change dramatically, and the milestone would be barely notable.

This, Munson acknowledged: "It was a fair thing to both sides, very fair. I knew what I wanted out of it. I knew what I needed. I love to play baseball. Money doesn't enter into it, although I want to get paid what I deserve. But I don't need the money I get from playing baseball to live on."

With that, he drove Gabe's Toyota back to the Fort Lauderdale Inn on Federal Highway to report the news to Diana. He was of the belief that he would be subject to a sliding scale, adjusted upward to assure his being the highest-salaried player on the team (except for Hunter) as new free agents might arrive. This was, for him, the key to signing the deal. He would maintain that that was agreed to in the trailer meeting.

Munson hit third and went 0 for 5 on the historic opening day of the newly renovated Yankee Stadium, April 15, 1976, the Yanks winning 11–4.

The news of his being named captain was not made official until two days later, prior to the Yankees' second game in their newly refurbished stadium. (And in his first at bat that day as captain, Munson homered, making him the first Yankee to homer in the new stadium.)

So much news was being made by the reopening of the park that it was thought to withhold it until game two. Many had known about it for weeks, but the official announcement came on the seventeenth.

"What about Joe McCarthy's pledge to retire the position with Lou Gehrig?" asked Phil Pepe of the *Daily News*.

"If Joe McCarthy knew Thurman Munson, he'd agree this was the right guy at the right time," Steinbrenner replied. It was a great answer. And it was probably true. Thurman did indeed have most of the characteristics that made a player a team leader. They didn't extend to media relations and fan relations, but among his peers, he was seen as the perfect man at the perfect time in the franchise's history.

The Yankees got off quickly and were enjoying a wonderful season under Martin. While it was true that he didn't have a full spring training to work with, the team won five of their first six to go right to first place, and never looked back. After twelve years without a pennant, the 1976 Yankees were making this look all too easy.

On May 20 in New York, as though the rivalry needed refueling, the Yankees and Red Sox engaged in a brawl, set off by a home plate collision between Piniella and Fisk. In the ensuing scuffle, pitcher Bill Lee's shoulder was seriously injured after a clobbering from Nettles. This time, Munson was off to the side in a role as peacemaker, perhaps attributable to his new captaincy, but knowing Munson, probably just owing to his arriving late to the party.

There was a momentary setback on June 5, when a wild throw by Munson, no strange occurrence by now, resulted in a loss to Oakland. The fans booed and Thurman flipped them off with the well-known "gesture." Another player might have been doomed forever by the Bronx faithful. But the Yankee fans loved it, cheered him the next time up, and never got on him again.

Of giving the fans the finger, Thurman would say, "I wouldn't suggest doing that every day to win friends and influence people, but at the time, I felt I got a bum rap and did what I had to, right or wrong. It came out right, I guess."

Thurman could also be funny, especially after a drink or two after a long airport delay. In the days when the Yankees still flew on commercial flights, he was once playing his tape deck too loud. Alerted to some passenger complaints, Billy Martin sent Elston Howard back to tell Thurman to turn the music down.

"What are you, the music coach?" he said to poor Ellie. It was one of the more memorable lines on a flight that was too delayed for everyone's good.

If being captain gave Thurman a new sense of responsibility, the only way I saw it demonstrated was when I needed a favor from him, as when I asked him to pose with a sponsor before the game, accept a pregame plaque, or meet some VIP visitors.

Before being named captain, he'd snarl and tell me what I could do with the request. So I'd get another player. "I don't do that," he would say to me.

Now, as captain, his sense of responsibility took over. He'd say, "What time do you need me to be there?" I'd tell him and he wouldn't show up. So I'd scramble to get another player at the last second. I liked it better the original way.

The best example of this would come on Old-Timers' Day in 1976, when we had Bill Dickey, Yogi Berra, Elston Howard, and Munson all present—a chance to take a picture of this great lineage of Yankee catching, going back to 1928. We were unable to accomplish this until now because Yogi had been coaching or managing the Mets, and hadn't been to an Old-Timers' game during Thurman's time with the Yankees. Not even in 1972, when they retired his number.

So I rounded up Dickey, Berra, and Howard with no problem. Dickey was a wonderful older gentleman. Berra and Howard, both coaches, were fine. And then I ran around looking for Thurman. He was in his underwear in the players' lounge, eating a doughnut, watching a rerun of *The Three Stooges* on Channel 11. I explained what we wanted to do and that he'd need to get fully dressed and meet us on the field.

"What time do you need me?" he asked.

I laughed. "No, I mean it this time," I said. "I've wanted to get this picture taken for years!"

He sighed, got up from the lounge chair, and walked to his locker to get dressed.

But he didn't appear on the field. I ran back into the clubhouse and Pete Sheehy told me to try the players' lounge. There he was, still in his underwear, watching TV again. It was the same Three Stooges show. I wanted to cry but I could only laugh. Dickey, Berra, and Howard were by the dugout with Michael Grossbardt, our photographer.

I finally got Munson out for the picture. I loved that picture. And when I went to Thurman's home in Canton three years later for his funeral, there was the photo, enlarged and framed, in his office. He liked it too.

Joe D'Ambrosio had been a batboy during 1976 and 1977 and later became the number three man in the Yankees PR department, working behind Mickey Morabito and Larry Wahl.

"As a batboy with the team," Joe recalls, "I knew Thurman well, but we weren't very close. In fact, during my first year as batboy the kids rotated from ballboy to batboy to lineboy over the course of the season. When I was the only kid asked back for the 1977 campaign, Thurman was the one who told Pete Sheehy that I should be batboy all year. He said he didn't want the other kids ' 'cause Joey knows what he's doing.' That meant the world to me.

"One Sunday in 1976, a getaway day, around ten a.m. or so, Thurman came to the park more gruff than usual and said he had a disagreement with Diana and left his road trip clothes in the hallway while he was leaving the house. He came to my locker and said, 'Keys.' One word. I said, 'Keys?' He said, 'Give me your car keys.' Not in an impolite way, but in an 'I'm Thurman Munson, you're Joey the batboy' kinda way. 'Okay,' I said. And I gave him my keys.

"About forty-five minutes later, he was back.

"Now, I drove a 1974 mustard-colored Opel Manta by Buick back then. It was tiny. Thurman, not being tiny, must have had trouble fitting in. He tossed me the keys, said, 'Thanks,' and started back over to his locker. Then he doubled back to me. I didn't know what went wrong. He said, 'Where was the music coming from?' I said, 'What music?' He said, 'I had to listen to the goddamned Allman Brothers the entire way and I couldn't shut off your radio. Where was the music coming from?'

"Well, eight-track tapes were the rage back then and I had custom-installed an eight-track player under my seat. When I started the car,

I'd 'kick' the cassette in and away you go. All controls for volume, track changing, etc., were in the player under my seat.

"When I explained it to him, he just rolled his eyes, gave me a c'mon-get-out-of-here kinda shove (his way of showing affection) and laughed all the way back to his locker."

The Yanks held a nine-game lead by July 4. Randolph, the rookie at second, was so good he made the All-Star team. Rivers was every bit the catalyst they had hoped he would be, and he became a favorite not only among his teammates but also among fans, especially young ones. Figueroa was indeed a quality starting pitcher.

The Yanks and division rival Baltimore spun a rare ten-player mid-season deal, but it changed neither team's fortunes. The Yankees kept rolling.

Munson hit .319 in the first half of the season and was the starting catcher in the All-Star Game, playing in Philadelphia for the nation's Bicentennial. It was his fifth All-Star selection in his seven years in the majors.

(The American League players, along with team and league officials like me, all stayed at the Bellevue Stratford Hotel in downtown Philadelphia, checking out on July 14. On July 27, members of the American Legion checked in for a convention, and contracted what came to be called Legionnaires' disease. Thirty-four people died, allegedly from some bacteria in the cooling tower of the hotel.)

Thurman did not change his batting style to adjust to the shorter left field wall in the new Yankee Stadium. He never succumbed to the temptation of trying to conquer it. In the original stadium, he hit only 16 home runs in 944 at bats; about 1 every 59 times up. Maybe one a month. In 1976 with the new stadium, he hit 5 in 297 at bats—1 every 59 at bats. It didn't change at all.

Furthermore, whether Munson being captain helped or not, the press was feeling the presence of a mature team leader guiding his team to victory. In *Sports Illustrated,* Larry Keith wrote:

> At 29 years of age and late in his seventh major league baseball season, Thurman Munson of the Yankees is finally learning to relax. He is still not Mr. Congeniality, but he is becoming less the cranky, what-the-hell-do-you-want misanthrope of earlier years. Just the other day Munson signed an autograph, gave a civil answer to a reporter's question and allowed as how he was not the only catcher in organized baseball. The best, he said, but certainly not the only one.
>
> And the truth is, Munson is the best and probably has been for the last two seasons. As if Munson's own mounting accomplishments were not proof enough, it should be pointed out that the Reds' sore-shouldered Johnny Bench appears to be in decline. Carlton Fisk of the Red Sox is constantly in disrepair and Cardinal Ted Simmons and Pirate Manny Sanguillen do not have Munson's all-round abilities. It is public acceptance of the notion that Munson is the No. 1 big league catcher—and perhaps even the Most Valuable Player in the American League—that has encouraged him to reveal a better side.

Of course, before we think Munson had reformed, the article later quoted Diana: "He wasn't always so grouchy. He'll growl and swear rather than dealing with a situation directly. He even scares me at times. He'll leave the house for a game and kiss all the kids, then when he comes home, he's completely different. Sometimes when we're in public I just cringe at the way he acts."

The champagne flowed on September 25 at Detroit when the Yanks, eight games ahead of the pack, clinched their first-ever Eastern Division title in the eighth year of division play. The season ended with a rainout (not made up) on October 3, leaving Thurman with a .302 average in 152 games, 121 of them behind the plate. He batted third in the lineup almost every game. He hit 17 homers, drove in 105 runs, hit 10 sacrifice flies, went 3 for 4 as a pinch hitter, stole 14 bases, struck out only 37 times in 665 plate appearances, and cut his errors to 14.

By Labor Day, it was generally written that he was on his way to the league's MVP award. The voting was done the day the regular season ended, but wouldn't be announced until November.

The 1976 Yankees drew 2,012,434 fans, the first time an American League team had passed two million since the 1950 Yankees—twenty-six years before. The new stadium, the active return of George Steinbrenner, the coming of free agency, the pennant-winning team, and the big year from Munson were all factors, and this proud franchise was clearly headed into a new era of excitement and success. Two million would become standard for the team, and then it became three million in 2001 and four million in 2005. The dormant years of CBS ownership were long past, and those of us who had spanned the two eras were especially proud of what we saw come to be. I often think of our annual September press release announcing our having reached a million in attendance. The team now hits a million by early May.

The 1976 American League Championship Series was the first of three in a row to be played between the Yankees and the Kansas City Royals. This would be Munson's first taste of the postseason (at least since the 1969 Syracuse Chiefs) and he caught every inning of the five-game series, batting .435 with ten hits—an ALCS record that was then broken when Chris Chambliss got his eleventh—a game-winning, pennant-winning homer off Mark Littell in the last of the ninth of game five.

The Chambliss blast sent the Yankees to their first World Series in a dozen years, and as Chris raised his arms in triumph, steps from home plate, Munson, in his chest protector and shin guards, could be seen leaping from the dugout with the shriek of youthful delight that you'd hope would go with such a historic moment. The losing years were over. The Yankees were American League champions and going to their thirtieth World Series.

The Series opened in Cincinnati, all too quickly. The Reds were better rested and had their rotation in order. The Yanks had to fight and claw to win the pennant late on Thursday evening, October 14. The celebration followed on into the morning, when the exhausted team got on the bus for the airport and flew to Cincinnati. On Saturday, October 16, it all began. The Yankees had to start Doyle Alexander because neither Hunter, Figueroa, nor Ellis was rested, and Martin had chosen to ignore Ken Holtzman for reasons that remain a mystery.

The Big Red Machine, one of the great dynasties in baseball history, was simply too strong for the Yankees. They won 5–1 and 4–3 over the weekend at Riverfront Stadium. Back in New York, the Yankees quietly went down 6–2 and 7–2 before home crowds that had little to cheer about. Seven runs in four quick games. The players were pressing, Martin was tense and frustrated, Steinbrenner was angry, and the joy of the pennant was quickly forgotten.

Munson, however, was having a great time. He was busy collecting nine hits in the four games, batting .529, chatting up the Reds players as they came to the plate, and totally in love with the experience of being in the World Series. Four of his hits came in the final game, tying a World Series record for hits in a game. He wasn't happy about losing, of course, but he was enjoying the competition and the thrill of being in the Fall Classic. At one point, when Reds manager Sparky Anderson went to the mound to confer with his pitcher, the official World Series film captured Pete Rose saying of Munson, "Man, he can flat out hit."

He had the highest batting average of any player on a losing World Series team. Ever. And then the experience turned bad.

In the postgame interview room down the right field line and under the stadium stands, Series MVP Johnny Bench, who twice homered in the final game, spoke to the press. His manager Sparky Anderson was there as well.

Bob Fishel, my old Yankee boss and now the American League's PR director, asked Munson to come to the interview room to represent the Yanks. Martin wouldn't come. Thurman took the responsibility to represent his teammates and went to the room.

As he entered, Anderson was speaking. He was talking about how the Reds had "the most class" of any team in sports.

Someone asked Sparky to compare the two great catchers who had just played in the Series.

"Munson is an outstanding ballplayer and he would hit .300 in the National League, but don't ever compare anybody to Johnny Bench, don't never embarrass nobody by comparing them to Johnny Bench," he said.

If you read the quote over and over, you could take the position that he was just lauding it on Bench and almost begging off the question of comparison. But Munson, in the room and hearing this, grew livid. Bench had batted .234 in the regular season with 16 homers and 74 RBIs. Thurman had a right to consider himself the best catcher in baseball, at least for 1976.

Anderson exited.

When Munson got to the mike, he was bitter.

"For me to be belittled after the season I had and after the game I had . . . it's bad enough to lose, but worse to be belittled like that. To win four in a row and rub it in, that's class. To rub it in my face."

Some writers were confused by this tirade by Thurman, which was not in answer to any question. One said, "Are you talking about what Sparky said?"

Munson responded, "No, I'm talking about Mickey Mouse. They're a good ball club, but I don't believe that stuff about how good their pitching is. They outplayed us in every way, but I'm a realistic person too. When you lose four in a row, any team's embarrassed. But to be belittled on top of the embarrassment is not nice to hear, especially when you're standing next to somebody. But I don't know if he knew I was standing there or not. I never compared myself to Johnny Bench, but if I played in the National League, I might be the best offensive player in the league."

Someone took the bait and asked him to compare Billy Martin to Sparky Anderson.

"I never played for Sparky, but they both talk a lot."

Bench was now in the room. Munson left the mike and shook hands with him. "Nice going, J.B.," he could be heard saying. "Super."

Billy Martin was crying in the training room and didn't attend the press conference, as a manager is expected to. He'd been ejected from the final game for rolling a ball in disgust and frustration at the home plate umpire. Steinbrenner entered the training room and let him have it for the way the Yankees played, accusing him of not having the team ready.

After the glory of the pennant just days before, this was one miserable night in the Bronx.

Three weeks later, Anderson sent a letter of apology to Munson, which was released to the press by the Reds. It said:

> *Dear Thurman:*
> *First or all, I hope you will accept my sincere apology. I had no intention of trying to belittle you or any other catcher. What I said about comparing Bench to another catcher, I have said not only this year, but in other years.*
>
> *Thurman, I might be at fault for speaking so strongly on*

*Bench, but that is the way I feel. I sure hope I will never purposely
try to belittle anyone.*

  I only hope you will know how sincere I am about this letter.

                              Sincerely,
                              Sparky

Thurman said he never got the letter. If it was sent through the PR
office, I never got it either. It may still be sitting somewhere in the
clubhouse.

The day before the 1976 American League MVP announcement
would be made, Steinbrenner sent off a letter to Munson, addressed
to his New Jersey home. This one reached him:

November 15, 1976
Mr. Thurman Munson
315 15th Street
Norwood, New Jersey

Dear Thurm:
*A short note to say that Whitey Ford has been lined up to receive
your award from Cue Magazine, but more importantly, to tell you
how proud I am of all the honors that you've accumulated this
year.*

  *While I know the Series was somewhat of a bitter pill, you
had a great Series and we did win the American League
Championship—our first Pennant in 12 years, so I think that's
plenty enough this year. I just know that you're going to win the
Most Valuable Player Award in the American League, but the fact
that in the Major League All Star Team you pulled more votes
than any player is indeed a tribute to the kind of year you had.*

  Sometimes in the haste of everyday business we don't take time

to say "Nice Going!" to others, and I just remembered after talking
to you the other day that I had failed to add that.

Best regards,
George

Munson felt he had earned the MVP award, but he wasn't sure he'd get it, since he often didn't speak to the media, and it was the writers who voted.

On November 16, Thurman was in New Jersey when his phone rang at three p.m. It was Jack Lang, secretary-treasurer of the Baseball Writers' Association of America (BBWAA). As a beat writer for the Mets, he was not well known by Munson, so the conversation was formal.

"You've been elected MVP in the American League," said Lang. "Congratulations."

Munson asked him about the voting. He had received eighteen of the twenty-four first-place votes for a huge margin of victory over George Brett, who had two. One each went to Rivers, Rod Carew, Amos Otis, and rookie pitching sensation Mark Fidrych. Thurman was the first Yankee to win the award since Elston Howard in 1963. He became the first catcher to win both the Rookie of the Year Award and the MVP in the American League.

A press conference would be held in a few hours at the Americana Hotel in New York (now the Sheraton Centre). Lang asked me to preside, claiming he had another commitment. It was rare for the BBWAA to pass on an opportunity like this, but of course I agreed.

The turnout on the short notice was small. Thurman, the king of polyester, wore a plaid sports jacket with a tie and sweater.

"I'm proud that I won," he said of the MVP. "I know it wasn't politics. I won this on my ability."

Both Steinbrenner and Paul were in the room. It caught them by surprise when Thurman made mention of "a new contract." With free agency looming, he was preparing for the Yankees' signing some big free agents—maybe Don Gullett and Bobby Grich—and for his salary to be adjusted to meet theirs, and to include a World Series adjustment. At least that was what he believed.

I was asked about this the next day by the press and said, "I'm sure it is something that Mr. Steinbrenner and Thurman will talk through." I was trying to diffuse what I thought would be a mild controversy that was interfering with the big news about the award.

Steinbrenner didn't like my response at all. Even in the afterglow of the MVP award, he was ready to issue a statement putting Thurman in his place in terms of a possible renegotiation.

This would not be a quiet off-season. Those days were gone.

11

As Thurman's—and the Yankees'—successes on the field grew, his relationship with the media kept getting worse. Those who covered him early in his career, like Vic Ziegel, remembered him as "always cooperative and friendly," but now a darkness was forming over those relationships, leading many to wonder what had gone wrong.

After the 1976 season, Hillerich & Bradsby, the Louisville Slugger bat people, asked Thurman if he would contribute an essay on hitting to their *Famous Slugger Yearbook* annual. Thurman was fine with it and asked Murray Chass of the *Times* to help him.

"If I could draw a line between good Thurman and bad Thurman with the media, it would be around there," recalls Chass, later inducted into the writers' wing of the Baseball Hall of Fame.

> *He was basically a good guy, and easygoing with the media. I remember him and me playing tennis together in Dallas in '75 after the All-Star Game. You could pal around with him; there wasn't a division between him and the writers. But over the next*

couple of years, that began to change, and I think he was edged
away from us by Nettles and maybe some others. They didn't like to
see him too close to the writers, and however they did it, they
pushed him so far that he'd have the batboy bring his clothes into
the training room after a game so he didn't have to spend time at
his locker with us.

Nettles could be funny and give us a sarcastic line, and even if
he hated us, we were still drawn to him and he was okay with us.
But when he pushed Thurman against us, Thurm didn't have
that light touch, couldn't deliver the one-liner, and just became a
grouchy guy. There were times I'd pull him back by just saying,
"Thurman, don't be a jerk," and maybe he'd pause and give me a
moment. But there was no single incident that set him off; nothing
that we ever wrote that caused him to say, "I'm through with you."
It was a shame because basically, he was just a good, regular guy
to be with.

I was sorry that I never had a long talk with him about the place
of the media in the industry of baseball. It might have shown him a
different side. Since the game had begun, baseball had enjoyed so
much free publicity in the sports pages of newspapers and in the
sports segments of TV and radio reports. That free advertising for
the product was really the lifeblood of the game. Without it, the
teams could never afford the kind of ad campaign that would give
the fans all they needed to know and keep them coming to the
games. Movies and TV shows get one review, and if they are really
huge, maybe one additional feature story. And that's it—the rest is
up to their advertising departments. Baseball has that flow of daily
coverage that simply makes the game work as a professional business. Players need to be told that.

Of course, baseball has helped to sell a lot of newspapers too. It's
a two-way street.

Maury Allen of the *New York Post* never warmed up to Thurman's personality. "He was sour by nature," says Maury. "There was no single incident that I can recall. When he first came up I walked over and introduced myself and congratulated him for becoming a member of the Yankees. He said, 'What took them so long?' "

It was probably just Thurman's attempt at humor, and some might have found it funny. His teammates always loved his needling sense of humor. He had said pretty much the same thing to Gene Michael when he came up for the Binghamton game in 1968.

Rick Gentile, later a sports executive for CBS, was a UPI reporter back then. "He was a very intimidating presence in the clubhouse for a young guy like me. My most vivid memory is of asking him about a game-winning double that he laced to right-center with two out and two on in the ninth. I asked him if he was looking for a particular pitch in that situation or just for something he could drive. His response: 'Fuck you.' I guess he was having a bad week with the press."

"When I was a rookie reporter in spring training, he saw me waiting forlornly at the ballpark for a taxi," says Marty Noble, then of the *Bergen Record*. "So he offered me a ride to my hotel, which was out of his way. He didn't make a big deal of it. It didn't matter that I was a writer. He had an inherently good side."

The infectiously likable Phil Pepe of the *Daily News* was covering the Yankees in Fort Lauderdale when Thurman casually asked him, "How's it going?" Pepe responded that he missed his family, but it was too costly to bring them all down, so it was just part of the spring training routine of a beat reporter.

Barely missing a beat, Thurman said, "I'll pay for them to come down." Pepe, in need of no charity, wouldn't hear of it but was blown away by the gesture. And Thurman stuck to it—he wouldn't let his ledger show that he'd made a generous offer and then got off the hook. He insisted.

"I know he never wanted me to tell anyone," admitted Pepe. "It would have ruined his image. But he really made that offer and I did tell it to people over the years. He deserved to be seen as not always cranky and cantankerous."

Pepe once asked Munson for his home number in Canton during the off-season in case something came up for which he needed comment. Most writers undertook this sort of exercise as September wound down. Few bothered to ask Munson. They wouldn't have gotten it.

And sure enough, Munson wouldn't give his number to Pepe. But he said to him, "Here, call Tote." That would have been his father-in-law, Tony Dominick. "Tell him who you are and why you're calling. He'll call me and if I feel like calling you back, I will. If I don't, I won't."

Fair enough.

And so one day, Pepe needed to call. He left his number at the *Daily News* with Tote, and said Thurman should call back, collect.

Collect calls were a big deal in the days before telephone deregulation, phone cards, and cell phones. People would go through a time-consuming process to follow the "collect" procedure to save a buck.

But Pepe's phone rang and it was Thurman's voice, not an operator asking if he'd accept a collect call.

"Why didn't you call me collect?" asked Pepe.

"If I do that, I get some operator or someone in your office, I have to give my name, and then they know I'm calling a sportswriter and it would ruin my image!"

Of course, Thurman restored his image by not talking to Pepe for a year after Phil wrote about the secret clubhouse meeting in 1975.

Maybe Sparky Lyle had it down best. "Thurman's not moody," he laughed. "Moody means sometimes you're nice."

The Yankees signed former Reds pitcher Don Gullett as their first-ever free agent (apart from Hunter) the day after Munson's MVP announcement, so with Munson still in town, he came to the press conference, again at the Americana, and helped welcome his new battery mate to the team. Then attention turned to signing Bobby Grich, who could play shortstop for them.

Reggie Jackson loomed large out there as the glamour star of the first free agent class. Some on the team wanted no part of him. "His ego was too large, he wasn't a team player, he wasn't that good in the field, and was no longer a great base runner," ran the comments.

And although he could hit the ball a mile, even there he was inconsistent throughout his career. People are amazed to discover that in his twenty-one-year, 563–home run career, he never hit 30 homers two years in a row. There was good Reggie and bad Reggie, on and off the field.

Munson was an advocate for getting Jackson. He knew in his heart that the team could use a big bat in the middle of the lineup. At a winter sports banquet in Syracuse that year, he encouraged Steinbrenner to sign him. "Go get the big man," he said to his absent boss. "The hell with what you hear about him. He's the only guy in baseball who can carry a club for a month. He hustles every minute on the field."

Perhaps spurred on by his captain's words, Steinbrenner became obsessed with getting Jackson. He knew stars were important in New York. He knew Reggie put "asses in the seats."

He seduced him with a big contract and talk of owning New York. And on the morning of November 29, 1976, he got Jackson to sign a five-year contract at the Americana, after which we all went to a press conference in the same room, the Versailles Terrace, that had served as the venue for Munson's MVP announcement earlier in the month.

Munson flew in from Ohio for this press conference, having been told the day before that it was likely. For him, it was more than a press conference; it was, he thought, a salary boost for himself. Roy White, the senior Yankee, was there, along with coach Elston Howard, the first African-American Yankee, and Yogi Berra, also a coach. Reggie's father, Martinez Jackson, a tailor, was present, as well as his mother. His parents were divorced.

At the mike, Thurman said, "I felt we needed a left-handed power hitter and an outfielder who could throw. Jackson fits the bill. I'm thinking of the team."

He was also thinking of his contract. At one point, Munson took Gabe Paul off to the side and said some alterations were needed. Not the kind Martinez Jackson could make in his tailor shop. He was under the impression that his contract would be rewritten if the team won the pennant. He also found himself unable to determine Reggie's exact salary, because the contract hadn't been filed with the league office. He called the Players Association office but couldn't get an answer. It was also his belief that his salary would be adjusted to match or exceed any higher-paid new arrivals.

"Let's put this into proper perspective," Munson told Joe O'Day of the *Daily News*. "It's business—business, that's all. I have even renegotiated my contract, and with my verbal agreement with George Steinbrenner, I'll still be the highest-paid player on the club. All this came about within the last three weeks and I was even consulted on the negotiating for him [Jackson]."

So he waited and pouted.

At the baseball banquet in Syracuse, Thurman said that he would be asking for a trade if he couldn't count on Steinbrenner's word about a salary adjustment. It didn't get any media attention. And he was looking for some.

He tried it again in Canada a few days later and this time the Associated Press picked it up. When Munson got back to Canton, an angry Steinbrenner called him at home and insisted he come to New York to sign a press release denying the quotes.

"He was growing increasingly angry over this," said Elliott Pollack, a lawyer for Thurm's friend Nat Tarnopol. "Once Nat went with him to see George, and Thurman was so mad that Nat had to restrain Thurman from hitting him. It was a good thing that he asked Nat to go with him."

He didn't come to New York, but the two came to an uneasy accommodation. Munson never believed he was getting the full story on the Jackson salary, believing instead that deferred payments were being hidden. And he remained convinced that he had Steinbrenner's word that he would be the highest-salaried player on the team, except for Hunter. But he signed a new deal and decided to live with it. He thought any trust between boss and captain was gone.

There would never be an easy peace between Munson and Steinbrenner, although they would spend more time together than most players would ever spend with the team owner. Basically, Thurman never felt he could trust Steinbrenner. He did, however, admire his wealth and success. Being an aspiring tycoon himself, Munson enjoyed talking with Steinbrenner, learning from him, picking his brain, and getting away from conversations about upcoming pitchers—focusing instead on growth industries to invest in. Thurman routinely used to trek up to the Boss's fourth-floor office in Yankee Stadium after batting practice to talk about the economy, investments, the business of baseball, and the state of the union.

He'd walk the long walk from the Yankee clubhouse to the press elevators that took him past the stadium lobby and the luxury suites and right to the doors leading to the Yankee offices with the help of elevator operators who knew how to bypass floors. Otherwise, of course, luxury box ticket holders would encounter the sight of a fully uniformed Munson riding the elevator with them.

Steinbrenner's office was thirty feet by thirty feet, overlooked the field, and had a round wooden desk in one sector, three inches thick, no drawers, just plush chairs surrounding it, the one with the highest back for the Boss. Munson would enter and plop his feet on the desk. As he was still wearing his spikes, clumps of Yankee Stadium clay would land on the desk. Thurman made no effort to remove the mess.

"Heh heh heh," he told me. "Oh does that piss him off. You can see the lines in his neck turning red. But he never says a word."

In spring training of 1977, Reggie Jackson held court each day with the media while his new teammates shook their heads and rolled their eyes, making fun of him behind his back. Or at least they thought it was behind his back. He knew it was going on.

Meanwhile, an effort by freelance reporter Robert Ward to do a major interview with Jackson for *Sport* magazine landed on my desk.

Sport at the time was still an important publication, and the mention of it would get Reggie's attention.

Ward asked me where I thought he might bring Reggie, and I suggested the Banana Boat, a popular spot among the players on Oakland Park Boulevard in Fort Lauderdale.

I was in my final weeks with the Yankees. I had decided, along with Joe Garagiola Jr., the future general manager of the Diamondbacks and the son of the legendary broadcaster, to resign and form a representation business. (Joe was our in-house attorney.) But I was still at my desk, preparing for spring training as always, working frantically on the yearbook and the scorecard and the media guide to have them on schedule for publication. Mickey Morabito, my able assistant, would succeed me.

When Ward called I told him I couldn't imagine Reggie *not* wanting to do an interview for *Sport,* and with Reggie's agent Matt Merola, worked out a way for them to contact each other and set up the meeting at the Banana Boat.

Reggie had some trepidation, it happened; he did not always feel *Sport* had done right by him. That was news to me. I remember one

year that they had given him the World Series MVP award—a
Corvette—when Bert Campaneris was more deserving. It was to
many a gesture that would get more people to attend the awards
luncheon.

Ward and Jackson met and an interview was conducted. Ward was
not out to "get" Reggie—it was supposed to be a "welcome to New
York" kind of story. But Reggie took over the conversation and
moved away from Ward's prepared questions.

On May 23, the magazine came out.

The original story did not particularly scream out with the "straw
that stirs the drink" comment, but *Sport* publicist Sy Preston knew a
big story when he saw one, sent out a press release highlighting that
quote, and the story took off from there.

Thurman was in the training room with his copy and he asked
Herman Schneider, the assistant trainer, to ask Fran Healy to
come in.

"Did you see this?" he asked.

He began to read aloud from the *Sport* interview.

" 'You know, this team, it all flows from me,' " Jackson was quoted
as saying. " 'I've got to keep it all going. I'm the straw that stirs the
drink. It all comes back to me. Maybe I should say me and Munson . . . but he really doesn't enter into it.' "

"Can you fuckin' believe this?" asked Munson, continuing to read:
" '[Thurman] is so insecure about the whole thing. I've overheard
him talking about me . . . I'll hear him telling some other writer that
he wants it to be known that he's the captain of the team, that he
knows what's best. Stuff like that. And when anybody knocks me, he
laughs real loud so I can hear.' "

Asked by Ward about just talking to Munson about it, Jackson
said, "He's not ready for it yet. He doesn't even know he feels that
way . . . He'd try to cover up, but he ought to know he can't cover up
anything from me. Man, there's no way. I can read these guys. No,

I'll wait and eventually he'll be whipped. There will come that moment when he really knows I won, and he'll wait to hear everything's all right, and then I'll go to him and we will get it right.

"Munson's tough too. He is a winner, but there is just nobody who can do for a club what I can do. There is nobody who can put meat in the seats the way I can. That's just the way it is. Munson thinks he can be the straw that stirs the drink, but he can only stir it bad."

"Maybe he was quoted out of context," suggested Healy the Healer.

"For three pages?" Munson replied.

This story has been quoted so many times over the years; one wonders why it wasn't enough to keep *Sport* magazine in business. (The magazine died in 2000 but lost its impact much earlier.) "I'm the straw that stirs the drink"—where in the world that inspired line came from, Reggie never said. And in fairness, if in his early days of spring training, he had actually seen Munson laughing about him to writers, one could understand his own insecurity and confusion over not being better accepted by the team captain. The irony is it was the team captain who had told Steinbrenner to get him in the first place.

But Reggie was a very bright man and, at thirty-one, a very sophisticated student of the media. This was a really dumb thing to do on a new team, with new teammates, in a publication that would come out in the regular season as the pennant race was on.

Reggie's published explanation came in his 1984 autobiography with Mike Lupica:

> To this day, I don't think I've lived down the things Ward had me saying in that story. When the story finally came out and I read it, I had two reactions: One, he shouldn't have been quoting me in the first place, and two, he quoted me incorrectly. I really had thought there were rules between athletes and writers about bar conversations. I never would've talked

to him if I thought those rules didn't apply. Now I understand sensationalism.

My ignorance about that was my fault. I never should have let my guard down. Hell, I never should have invited him to sit down in the first place.

All in all, it was the worst screwing I ever got from the press. And I've had a few in my day. The only good thing that came out of it was that I became a lot more careful after that. I've become more acutely aware of who to trust and who not to trust. There have been times in the past few years when I've wanted to say something to a writer, wanted to get something off my chest, and I've just stopped myself cold because I haven't forgotten the Banana Boat.

Call it maturity if you want to. I wish I'd had a couple of orders of maturity in front of me at the Banana Boat.

The severity of this personal "feud" would never reach a point where either Jackson or Munson had to be traded, but it was an enormous story in New York that wouldn't die. With the tabloid war between the *Daily News* and the *Post* growing, this was made to order for them. Reggie was good copy; he sold a lot of newspapers. It was all Yankee fans could talk about, with few siding with Jackson. Munson was "their guy."

But they were both pro athletes who put their heads down and played to win. It took a long time for them to be able to smile at each other or feel comfortable if they were alone together. But it did happen. They didn't retain an enmity forever. They were just never going to be close friends.

I first had the idea for a book with Thurman just days after the MVP award was announced, but not until I left the Yankees in January did I decide how much sense it made, particularly with my no longer being the in-house publicist for the team.

Thurman's familiarity with my writing extended back to late 1976, when two cartons of galley proofs and original manuscript for my first book arrived at Yankee Stadium for proofreading. With good luck, I was leaving for the parking lot just as he was and he carried one of the cartons to my car for me. So he knew that my writing required heavy lifting.

The crazed events of 1977—when the Thurman-Billy-George-Reggie Show was beginning to take shape—were not on my mind when I approached him about the book.

I knew a Yankee winning an MVP award would spark book interest and I also knew he'd be reluctant to do one. Even if he did one, he really didn't talk to any of the sportswriters who might collaborate with him. His silence toward the media was now a full part of his persona.

I phoned him at his home in Norwood, New Jersey, and suggested a book.

"I'm only twenty-nine," he said. "No one does an autobiography at twenty-nine."

I explained to him that twenty-nine wasn't especially young in the celebrity world, and winning an MVP award with the Yankees almost guaranteed that *someone* would be pitching a book idea to a publisher.

"And if you don't do it yourself, you'll hate whatever is done without you—you won't make any money, you'll think it's all wrong, and it will just aggravate you."

"I'm not that interested in the money," he said. "And I'd want it to be a paperback so kids could buy it."

I talked him through the publishing cycle. If you start with a hardcover, you get library sales. Kids could read it for free. If it has some success, then there could be a paperback edition.

He still hesitated. This was really not something high on his "to do" list. But then he saw my argument that it was like an insurance policy against someone doing an unauthorized bio.

"Those are good arguments," he said, laughing. "Let's do it."

And so during one phone conversation we agreed on the project. I then mailed off proposals to several publishers. I got a phone call from one, Coward, McCann and Geoghegan, the day they received it. It was a decent offer and my inclination was to wait to see what else came back. So I bought some time, but after a few days they called again and said, "Look, we want to do this, it's a fair offer, and you shouldn't wait any longer; you should jump at this. We'll have to pull it back next week and move on."

I conferred with Thurman. We agreed on the process with which we'd do it, our own revenue split (on a handshake), and made the deal. (I have been offered a lot of money for the signed book contract, but I still have it.)

I loved having this deal in place. I was feeling withdrawal symptoms after nine seasons with the team, and this got me into a project with the team captain.

We would work throughout the 1977 season at his home in Norwood when the Yankees were at home. I was living in Tarrytown, New York, at the time and it would be an easy drive over there.

The process would involve my taping him, transcribing the tapes, creating the book, and his reading and reacting to it. During the tapings we would sit opposite each other on a sofa and a chair, or he would sit at his big mahogany desk with the nameplate T. MUNSON at the front. He'd be interrupted by calls about his real estate holdings. "Six percent on that sewer project?" he would say. "Let's sell!"

Sometimes one of his children would come in, which automatically meant stopping the tape while he dangled them on his knee and asked what they were up to.

By the time we finished, the 1977 season had finished as well, with a happy conclusion—the team's first world championship since 1962. So the book was generally upbeat.

But there wasn't much humor in it; Thurman's stories didn't translate into really funny tales. "Can you make it funnier?" he asked at one point. "Sure," I said, "give me more funny stories." But he didn't have many, and he didn't want to share much about his childhood. So what we had was a pretty traditional baseball bio.

Their home on Fifteenth Street in Norwood was magnificent, and I remember its greatest feature being not one but two spiral staircases to the second floor.

Still, I could see a loneliness there in Diana. When the team was on the road, she especially missed her family in Canton. Work was progressing on a great new home for them near Fifty-fifth Street NE and Market, and ultimately they decided that for everyone's greater happiness, home would always be Canton.

In wrapping up work on the book, by now in the spring of 1978, Thurman happened to mention to me how he had discovered flying as a great means of spending more time at home in Canton with his family, and of purchasing a twin-engine, six-seater Beechcraft Duke. It was how I first learned he had been flying his own plane. Almost as an afterthought for the book, we inserted it into a single paragraph.

The Reggie-Thurman issue still hung in the air in the Yankee clubhouse as the 1977 season progressed. It was not an easy one to put to rest. Two high-profile guys, two former MVPs, and it was all creating a terrible distraction to the business at hand.

Of course, Billy and Reggie weren't getting along either. Billy resented having to take "Steinbrenner's boy" onto his roster, and for most of the season refused to bat him cleanup. Things all came to a head in Boston in June, when he pulled Reggie out of right field in the middle of an inning for loafing on a base hit. On national TV, the two of them went at each other in the dugout, nearly coming to blows.

There were talks of a suspension for Jackson, and certainly a lot of talk about firing Martin for "losing it" as he did in public. The team lost five straight before escaping Detroit with a 12–11 win on June 22, finding themselves in second place, four and a half games behind Boston.

At this point, as the story continued to have traction, Steinbrenner went to Munson and said, essentially: "You better start getting along with Reggie, or Martin's going to be in trouble!"

That put Thurman in what he saw as an impossible position.

"I was suddenly put in the middle and made responsible for Billy's job!" he said. "I wish I hadn't gone along with Steinbrenner, but I got Fran Healy to bring Jackson to me for a talk to try and patch things up."

The three of them went to dinner in Detroit. It was tense. Munson challenged Jackson to name one thing he had that Thurman would want. According to Thurman, Reggie didn't answer.

"After that talk," he said for the autobiography project, "we were able to at least say hello to each other. We even had some conversations. But I think he felt very uncomfortable and self-conscious about our relationship. I think when I confronted him with the reality of life—that baseball may be a great ego trip, but there's a lot more to this world than baseball—he found himself unable to deal with it. For the sake of the team, we did no more interviews on each other. But we didn't become the best of friends, either."

During the dinner, Munson, direct as always, said to Jackson, "Did you get a Rolls Royce when you signed?"

Jackson said he did.

Healy said to himself, *Oh boy, here's a problem.*

And the next time Healy saw Steinbrenner, he said to him, "Mr. Steinbrenner, guess what—you owe Thurman a Rolls-Royce."

He never got one.

Meanwhile, the Red Sox were coming to town.

This is when the great Yankee-Boston rivalry was really kicking in, and 55,000 fans turned out for the first game of the series, giving Martin a tremendous ovation as he took the lineups to home plate. Billy could really work a crowd, could really get them behind him.

A game-tying, two-run homer by Roy White, perhaps the team's most important hit of the year, helped to send the Yanks to a 6–5 win, with Reggie getting the game-winning single in the eleventh. This was where the season began to take fire.

The Yanks swept that series to move just two games back, continued to enjoy a strong July, and stayed in first or second with the Red Sox for much of the summer. Baltimore got into it as well, and it was a terrific pennant race.

It was a summer of discontent for Billy Martin, of course, with the threat of being fired constantly upon him. He would have been gone had not third base coach Dick Howser said no to an offer to replace him.

In Baltimore on July 11, Munson turned to a rare use of the newspapers to advance a cause, telling Murray Chass and *Newsday*'s Steve Jacobson, "George is calling the shots from upstairs and dictating the lineup to Billy." He said to attribute it to "a prominent Yankee."

"George tells him who to play," he said. "He doesn't want competition, he wants a slaughter. To win, you need nine good players, plus some capable utility players and a pitching staff. George wants twenty-five superstars. George doesn't care about anybody's feelings. To him, we're not professionals, we're all employees. He treats everybody like that. Everybody on the club has experienced it. He's done something to everybody. He's destroyed Billy. He's made him nothing. Not a single guy on the club is happy except Willie [Randolph]."

Things were getting so heated that Steinbrenner made a rare

road trip to meet up with the team in Milwaukee on July 12. This was almost a month after the Fenway Park meltdown, but the Boss was still after Billy for embarrassing the Yankees.

The pressure on Billy was weighing down the whole club, which at the time was still just one and a half games out of first.

In Milwaukee, after a night game, Piniella and Munson went to Sally's, a popular ballplayer gathering spot, to have some drinks and talk about the team's situation. To them, it felt unlikely that they could win another pennant with this cloud hanging over them. They decided to go to the Pfister Hotel and confront Steinbrenner in his room—telling him to either fire Martin or get off his back.

Steinbrenner opened the door in his pajamas. For two hours, the three men sat and talked. As bizarre as the incident appeared, it was a sign of leadership that these two respected players—one the team captain, the other a future manager of great success—would decide to take this fight on.

Martin's suite was on the same floor. Arriving back at the hotel well past the start of the secret meeting, he heard voices and knocked. Piniella and Munson, trapped like lovers when the husband returns from a business trip a day early, dove into the shower and pulled the curtain closed. They didn't want Martin to see that they had gone over his head to solve the team's problems.

Martin knew he had heard voices and helped himself to a tour. He found them.

It was a ridiculous moment at two o'clock in the morning. And it didn't really clear the air, or if it did, it cleared it for a few days, at best.

Meanwhile, the story with quotes from the "prominent Yankee" ran in all the New York papers. Seemingly wishing to make the story go away, as though insignificant, Steinbrenner decided that the prominent Yankee was Carlos May, who played sixty-five games that year for the team, mostly as a designated hitter. (I liked Carlos because a year earlier, Steinbrenner had actually sought out my opinion on whether to get him, and I said he was a good gap hitter.)

If the use of May's name was a ruse to get the real player to reveal himself, it worked. Munson went to Steinbrenner and told him that it was he who was the "prominent Yankee" quoted in the story. But he didn't apologize for it. He just wanted him to know it wasn't May.

At the Sheraton Royal Hotel in Kansas City the next day, Steinbrenner called a team meeting—most unusual for an owner—and delivered a pep talk to pump up the team for the second half of the season. It wasn't a lovefest. He cajoled the players to live up to their high salaries, and then jumped on anonymous players who leaked things to the press.

"The one funny note in it," recalled Fran Healy, "was that Ted Turner had recently worn a uniform and taken over as manager of the Braves for a day. Steinbrenner threatened that he would do the same thing if necessary. The thought of that was pretty funny."

The reference to players who leak to the press really angered Thurman, who had let his teammates know that it was he, and that he had told Steinbrenner it was he. But the Boss's comments made Munson look like a liar—that he had said he had taken responsibility but in fact hadn't.

"So as the All-Star Game arrived," he said for our book, "I was in a bad frame of mind. Jackson's magazine story bugged me, I felt deceived over my contract, and I felt I'd been made to look like a fool in Kansas City."

The All-Star Game was played in Yankee Stadium. Fisk outpolled Munson again to be the starting catcher, another embarrassment for Thurman for the game in his own home ballpark. He was getting grumpier by the day.

And then there came "the beard episode."

Steinbrenner's no-beard policy was to be enforced, of course, by Martin. Munson happened to be a guy who liked growing a beard and often did so in the off-season. Now, on top of all that was going on around them, Munson decided not to shave for eleven days, starting in late July.

"Let this walrus off at Sea World," said Piniella to the team's bus driver. It was funny, but everyone knew it was actually growing into a political issue. Would Martin order it shaved? Would Steinbrenner order Martin to order Munson? Or would he just explode on Billy for having lost control of the team?

The drama, as well as the beard, was growing. Never mind how uncomfortable it must have been to wear a catcher's mask with the beard. Now it was the George-Billy-Thurman Show.

When Murray Chass called Steinbrenner to ask him point-blank about Munson's beard, Steinbrenner said, "Beard? What beard? I didn't even know about it. What do you mean, Thurman's beard? Does he have a beard?"

With the press now fueling the "crisis," Thurman quietly shaved it off before an exhibition game in Syracuse on August 8. The Yankees were there to play their Triple-A farm team, and Don Ross, a well-liked restaurateur and friend to many players who had played for the Chiefs, went to Munson's room at the Sheraton armed with a pizza, a razor, and cream, and stood by for the "historic" shave.

Apparently Martin had quietly spoken with Munson the day before. Diana had cried on the phone over stories of Thurman creating tension between Martin and Steinbrenner.

It became a nonissue in the bathroom of Munson's hotel room around 1:15 in the afternoon. Another crisis passed. But the very act of his shaving was a huge story in New York and even made the national wires. The Yankees were now giving papers all over the country game stories and off-the-field stories, and journalists were jumping over one another to be the first with the latest.

"I was more determined than ever to get out of New York," he said for the book. "The problems at the ballpark made me feel

closer to Diane and the children, and seek more gratification from
my business interests. It all added up to my wanting to go home,
where I could play ball in peace and attend to the things in life that
matter to me."

Distractions aside, there was a pennant race to be fought. On August 23 in Chicago, Mike Torrez beat Wilbur Wood and the Yanks
went into first place to stay. They wound up with one hundred wins,
three more than in 1976, and won by two and a half games. It took
a lot out of everybody.

Coming off his MVP season, Munson had another big year at the
plate, hitting .308 with 18 homers and 100 RBIs. He was seventh in
the MVP voting.

Again facing the Royals, Billy Martin defied conventional wisdom
by benching Jackson in the fifth and deciding game; one last effort
to show the Boss who was boss, even if it meant he was managing his
last game.

In the eighth inning, Jackson pinch-hit a run-scoring single, the
Yanks went on to take the lead, and Sparky Lyle, who would win the
Cy Young Award, nailed it down to give the Yanks another pennant.
In the clubhouse, Martin poured champagne over Steinbrenner's
head and said, "That's for trying to fire me."

Thurman hit .286 in the Championship Series with a home run,
and then .320 in the World Series against the Dodgers with a home
run in the fifth game. As Munson rounded the bases after the
homer, Dodger pitcher Don Sutton shouted, "Is that as hard as you
can hit it?" Thurman laughed.

Between games two and three of the Series, Munson broke his silence with the press and let out a lot of frustration. "I've been in the
middle of controversy all year that I didn't cause," he told the assembled press corps. "There was the magazine article where Reggie
put me down. Then I'm told by Steinbrenner if I don't get along
with Reggie they're going to fire the manager . . . You'll never read

an article that I haven't stuck up for Billy. I've got five more games at the most to put up with this crap. All year I've been trying to live down the image I was jealous of somebody making more money. Somebody asked me, 'Did you bury your pride?' No, I postponed it.

"We have a chance to win a Series ring, and a guy is second-guessing the manager. If I was hitting .111 I wouldn't be second-guessing the goddamned manager. And I'm going to stop talking because the more I talk the madder I get."

The .111 remark was directed at Jackson, who was fuming over Billy sitting him down against Kansas City. And with sarcasm, Thurman inadvertently coined a name that would live on for decades, would appear on Reggie's Hall of Fame plaque, and would be copyrighted by Jackson for marketing purposes. Said Munson: "Billy probably just doesn't realize Reggie is Mr. October."

A nickname born out of sarcasm. It's even part of Reggie's e-mail address today.

That is the Series that is best remembered for Jackson's remarkable game six, in which he hit home runs on three consecutive pitches, putting his name in the record books with five homers in a World Series and three in one game. He thrived in the big spotlight, and he proved that he was indeed the missing link, the cure for what had been the Yanks' failings the year before.

After the third home run, Thurman had a huge smile on his face, visible to all watching TV or seeing still photos. The smile said it all: *Big guy, you may have been a pain in the ass to have around, but you gave us what we needed, and I tip my hat to you. You are a money ballplayer.*

This was it, this was the dream fulfilled. Tuesday night, October 18, 1977, Yankee Stadium. The Yankees beat their historic rivals and won their twenty-first World Series. In his eighth full season in the major leagues, Thurman Munson was the captain of a world championship club. He had played every day of every year as though that was the goal, and now it was realized. He was exhausted, exhilarated, and energized all at once.

The usually camera-shy Munson did go on TV with Bill White during the clubhouse celebration on ABC. White, uncomfortable but
being pressed by ABC to ask tough questions, tried to get Thurman
to talk about whether he wanted to play in New York the following
year, but Munson would have none of it. He didn't dislike being a
Yankee, but his flirtation with playing for the Indians or retiring
would have to be dealt with on another day, in another place.

12

After the 1977 season, Thurman had surgery on his right shoulder to alleviate friction in the acromioclavicular joint. He had it done in Los Angeles, and George Steinbrenner flew out to visit him and lend support at the hospital. The surgery was deemed to be successful, and it left him feeling good about his throwing again. He would be at his physical best since 1973.

Then he did his first television commercial.

Yes, the grouchy, reclusive, scruffy ragamuffin that was Munson, actually did a TV commercial. Not that many active baseball players did commercials—Rose, Bench, Seaver, Jackson; that was about it.

The product was Williams's Lectric Shave preshave lotion, of all things, and the thirty-second spot was a surprise to everyone who had listened to him for years about not getting respect, not getting opportunities like this. He had fun doing it and showed some personality and sparkle with his delivery. And it did recall his adventure with his beard.

In a mock office of George Steinbrenner, not unlike the set we came to see in the later Seinfeld programs, Munson, in uniform, tells his boss, "I wanna use Lectric Shave and I'll be the best-looking catcher in the game . . ." Then, exiting, he looks over his shoulder and with a nice smile says, "Well, one of the best."

"That commercial captured him," said Scott Davis, an old family friend from Canton. "He had a good sense of humor and he didn't take himself too seriously."

He groused and pouted, sometimes admitting that retirement was an option, sometimes saying Cleveland was the only solution, and sometimes acknowledging that New York was the only place to play.

As much as he might have complained about playing in New York, there was no way the Yankees were about to trade him to Cleveland—or anywhere. He was the heart and soul of a world championship team—irreplaceable, really.

So he went to spring training in 1978 and shut off the media. He was in the third year of a four-year contract he had signed in 1976, and it continued to gnaw at him, knowing, as he felt certain, that Jackson was making more than he was. Finally, peace on this issue would come to him during spring training, when without announcement he signed a new four-year contract, good through 1981, that would peak at just under $387,000 a year, guaranteed. He was satisfied, but still bitter over his pay from the preceding years.

He turned his attention to the Beechcraft Duke parked next door at Fort Lauderdale's Executive Airport. There, he took flying lessons and got away from the ballpark and the writers. Sometimes Piniella flew with him.

Piniella told Maury Allen, "He enjoyed the freedom. On a few occasions [that spring] I went up with him. A pilot-instructor was at his side. Thurman was at the controls. I would listen to the instructors talk and they all seemed impressed at how well he was doing, how fast he was learning, and how rapidly he was progressing."

The first plane he bought was a Beechcraft Duke twin-piston engine, around the time he was licensed, June 11, 1978, after ninety-one hours of flight time, twenty-five of them solo. Four days later he received the FAA multi-engine rating, and by December 22 he had an instrument rating after just under three hundred total flying hours. The instrument rating allowed him to use larger airports, which relied on ground control, and to fly in inclement weather using only his instruments as guidance. It was a big step.

"He was proud of the possession," Piniella says. "He didn't have much as a kid. He kept his cars spotless. Baseball was a means to make his family and his life comfortable and enjoy the material things he had worked hard for. He knew his career wasn't going to last that much longer."

The camp was in its usual disarray anyway. In the never-ending pursuit of glamour players, the Yankees had gone out and signed Goose Gossage, the great relief star, despite the fact that they had one in Sparky Lyle, the reigning Cy Young Award winner.

"He went from Cy Young to *sayonara*," quipped Nettles.

There is a tendency, thirty years later, to run the 1977 and 1978 seasons together as though they were one. Both had clubhouse tensions, both were world championship seasons, both involved beating Kansas City in the ALCS and then the Dodgers in the World Series. Nineteen seventy-eight was known as the season of *The Bronx Zoo*, after Sparky Lyle and Peter Golenbock combined for a best-selling book of that name. Nineteen seventy-seven was featured in *The Bronx Is Burning*, an eight-hour miniseries on ESPN (shown in 2007), which was first a book by Jonathan Mahler called *Ladies and Gentlemen, the Bronx Is Burning*, published in 2005.

The biggest differences were that Billy Martin managed the entire 1977 season, while '78 was split between Martin and Bob Lemon. Nineteen seventy-seven saw a late-summer course correction that sent the Yankees into the postseason; 1978 needed one of the great comebacks of all time to overcome the deficit they had created. Ron

Guidry's 1978 season was one of the greatest of any starting pitcher in baseball history; Jackson's 1977 World Series was one of the greatest of any hitter in baseball history. The 1977 season had Lyle as the closer; '78 had Gossage. Brian Doyle played second base in place of the injured Willie Randolph in the '78 postseason.

Gossage's replacement of Lyle as the "closer" meant Munson had to accept his friend's demotion and welcome a new friend. The two got along just fine. As Gossage told Bob Cairns for the book *Pen Men,*

> Munson was a hell of a guy, his own man, but you know, that's the way the whole team was. There were a lot of those guys. Everybody was a man's man, did what they wanted to do and said what they wanted to say. If they felt like saying "Fuck you!" they'd tell you, "Fuck you!" Munson was probably even more outspoken than everybody else except Reggie. Munson was smart. Sometimes when I was pitching he'd just throw his hand out and wave for the ball, show me and the hitter exactly where he wanted it, "Come on, bring it up, bring it right here, fastball!" And I'd say, "Damn, Munce, at least do that down so they can't see it!" And he'd say "Why? You're not gonna trick anybody!" It wasn't an argument; it was just a fun thing between us. And I'd say, "At least give me a fuckin' sign or something." But he'd just wave it so the whole world could see, here comes the fastball.
>
> For two months [in 1978] I stunk. I'd come onto the mound and Munson would say, "Hey fuckhead, how are you gonna lose this one?" And I'd say, "I don't know, can I get back to you? I have a feelin' we're gonna find out! You just catch!" It was unbelievable. One time I'm having trouble and I'm getting the sign from Munson. He calls time out and walks out there and says, "Hey shithead, check Rivers out!" I turned around and look out at center field and here's Rivers in a three-point stance, facing the wall getting ready to run

down the next pitch. All I could see was his ass, sticking up
in the air. I said, "That son of a bitch!" But we had the greatest senses of humor on that team. Shit happened like that
all the time.

Munson was more actively in the midst of swirling clubhouse controversies in 1977 than he was in '78, when he seemed to keep his
head low and stay out of the news as best he could. Inwardly, he was
still pouting over what he felt had been a betrayal over Steinbrenner's not raising his salary to match Jackson's.

He skipped the mandatory Yankees "Welcome Home Luncheon"
in April (along with Nettles, Lyle, and Rivers) and was fined five
hundred dollars. Little was asked of him as team captain; his skip-
ping the event no doubt infuriated Steinbrenner.

For Thurman, small nagging injuries began to take their toll. His
arm (technically his hand and shoulder) had improved to the best
it had felt since before the 1974 backswing injury. He was back there
when Guidry fanned eighteen in June for a Yankee record, the day
the fans began to rise on two strikes to help encourage a strikeout.
It still happens to this day.

But his knees and legs were starting to betray him. The idea of
his being behind the plate for 125 games or more seemed to stretch
reality.

In the 1978 season, he would play thirteen games in right field,
and actually hit .351 in the games he started there, as opposed to
.289 when he caught. He got by in right field, but in one game he
made a costly error when he dropped a fly ball. It wasn't the best situation, but the Yankees wanted him hitting third in the lineup, and
they recognized that he might be a defensive liability from time to
time. Mike Heath and Cliff Johnson caught when he wasn't available.

The growing pain in his knees made him less potent at bat, where
he hit only 6 homers for the season, just two of them at home. His

.297 average and just 71 RBIs ended the streak of three consecutive .300-average, 100-RBI seasons.

Without Munson central to the mix, the season's controversies fell on Martin and Jackson and the continuing power struggle between Martin and Steinbrenner over how to use Reggie in the lineup.

On July 17, Martin ordered Jackson to bunt. No one could believe it. Baseball just wasn't played that way any longer. The team had thirty-seven sacrifices all season.

The bunt sign was removed, but Jackson continued to attempt to lay one down, eventually striking out on a foul as he sought to show up his manager. The incident passed but the Yankees lost in eleven innings, partly on the fly ball dropped by Thurman in right field.

Martin went crazy in his office after the game and called Al Rosen, the team president, to demand that Jackson be suspended for the season. Rosen suspended his superstar for five games for defying the manager's order once the bunt sign was removed. The team was now fourteen games behind Boston and sinking quickly.

This was the beginning of the end for Martin. He was drinking heavily and had a self-destructive gene within him anyway. He was about to throw away the best job he ever had.

The suspension over and Jackson back with the team, comments were being made by both Martin and Jackson to select media. Finally came the fatal line. Referring to Jackson and Steinbrenner, Martin said, "The two of them deserve each other. One's a born liar, and the other's convicted," the latter comment referring to Steinbrenner's conviction for illegal campaign contributions.

It essentially resulted in Billy's first firing as manager, although conversations with his agent turned it into a tear-filled resignation. I had nothing but compassion for my young successor as PR director, Mickey Morabito, who was trying to maintain some Yankee dignity through all of this, and trying to keep up with the news as it happened.

In came Bob Lemon to succeed Martin. Lem had been fired as manager of the White Sox on June 30.

Everyone in baseball loved the affable Lemon, who had been the Yankees pitching coach in 1976, the year he was elected to the Hall of Fame. He was such a good baseball man, and so admired, it was actually hard to figure why he had to wait until 1970, with Kansas City, to get his first managing job—and then, after three seasons, to wait another six years for another chance. Probably it was because pitchers don't get sufficient respect as managing prospects, and because he was such a mild-mannered, easygoing guy. Once asked if he ever took a loss home with him, he said, "No, I usually leave it at a bar on the way."

In any case, after the turmoil of the season's first four months, it was a good tonic to bring in someone as much fun as Lem. That, combined with a New York newspaper strike that removed irritant journalists from the clubhouse, brought a level of calm to the ball club.

Another moment of drama occurred before July ended. On Old-Timers' Day, July 29, just days after Martin's "resignation," at the same event at which he had been hired in 1975, fans were shocked to see Billy introduced on the field as "the manager for 1980 and hopefully for many years to come." There were a lot of stone-cold faces in the Yankee dugout. Not everyone was pleased with the news. Lemon was to become general manager.

Steinbrenner had spoken with Martin, had felt the emotional pull that Billy had on people, felt sorry for him, and couldn't resist the temptation to bring him back. It was a bold and dramatic move, but the team was now taking on an attitude of "1980 is a long way off; a lot can happen, stay tuned."

Meanwhile, they began to play like the defending world champions that they were. Fourteen games out on July 19 would be the biggest deficit. Then they began to creep forward. They won ten of twelve in early August, then ten of eleven in late August and early September. They arrived in Boston on September 7 having won five of six and having cut the deficit to four games. Picking up ten games in seven weeks was a great feat, but now they had to face the Red Sox four times in Fenway Park.

When the Yanks played in Boston, Thurman liked to go to Wonderland Greyhound Track in Revere with his teammates. Roy White, Ken Holtzman, Gullett, Rivers, and Piniella were familiar travel companions on the trip. The track probably had more of Rivers's money than his many wives did, not to mention his bank account. Thurman came to know one of the dog trainers, twenty-year-old Phil Castinetti, a big Yankee fan with a major Boston accent.

"Because of my knowledge of the dogs, I was able to give the guys tips," says Phil. "There was nothing improper about it, and it wasn't like I was always right. But when I was right they loved it. Thurm was always generous in giving me some cash from his winnings and buying me dinner. I ate with him on maybe six occasions and he knew me by name and thought of me as a friend. He just treated me great. He signed a lot of stuff for me too, but I only saved the first track program he signed, the night I first met him. I gave away a lot of stuff.

"You'd see all sides of him there. He could be great, as he was to me. Or there was the time a guy threw a program in front of his face for an autograph just as he was preparing to cut into his chopped sirloin. The guy said, 'Munson, sign this.' He gave him a 'Get the fuck out of here,' that was for sure.

"During that big '78 'massacre' series, he asked me if I knew who was pitching the next day and I said, 'Yeah, Bobby Sprowl; Bill Lee is in Zimmer's doghouse.' And he said, 'Who the fuck is Bobby Sprowl!!!' and he laughed and laughed."

Castinetti owns Sportsworld in Saugus, Massachusetts, today. He sells autographed goods but keeps his special Yankee collection at home, for himself.

"A single signed baseball from Munson is worth about $17,000 today," he says, shaking his head. "You know how many I had and gave away? What they would be worth! He just didn't sign very many."

The games came to be known as the Boston Massacre. The Yanks swept, winning 15–3, 13–2, 7–0, and 7–4. They would have been happy with a split; this was nirvana. Munson went 8 for 16 in the series, but it was a total team effort, a historic annihilation, and a series that lives forever in the history of the Yankee-Boston rivalry, just as the 2004 ALCS will forever be "the answer" for the long-suffering Red Sox Nation.

During the 1978 series, Thurman was hit in the head with a pitch from Dick Drago and had to be replaced.

"When he came to, he started looking around for his catching gear," recalls Willie Randolph. "He thought we were in the field."

A few days later in Detroit, he was experiencing terrible headaches, and was sent for a brain scan to a local hospital.

"My first reaction was that I didn't want to die," he said. "I never experienced anything like that. This wasn't a headache, it was tremendous pain."

But he would be okay.

People who think of 1978 forget that the Red Sox did not roll over and die after those games. The Yankees couldn't shake them, even after winning two of three back in New York a week later. The Yanks played inspired baseball, Guidry was on fire, and everything was clicking. The team won seven of their last eight games. But Boston wouldn't die; wouldn't go away.

On Sunday, October 1, the final day of the regular season, a Yankee victory would have clinched the division. The team was playing the Indians at home. In the first inning, Thurman singled and Piniella doubled him to third. When Jackson grounded out, Munson scored, a gritty, "money" run. Had it been a 1–0 game, his bulldog trip around the bases on bad knees would have been a Yankee play for the ages—a bit like Joe Girardi's big triple in the deciding game of the 1996 World Series.

But it wasn't to be, as Catfish, the starter, didn't have it that day and the Yankees lost 9–2. To Hunter, a great kidder who could give as well as he could take, it recalled an earlier exchange with Piniella on a team bus (naturally) in Boston, when the driver got lost and wound up giving the players a historic tour of the city.

"This is a Revolutionary War cemetery," he said at one point.

"That's where Catfish's arm is buried," announced Piniella.

Boston won on that fateful Sunday, and the two teams, perhaps destined for this all year long, wound up tied for first. A playoff game needed to be held the following day in Boston to decide who would play the Royals for the pennant.

It was not hard to find 32,925 Red Sox fans to fill Fenway Park on Monday afternoon on short notice for one of those "games for the ages." The Yanks got to town on Sunday night, with Munson, Piniella, Lyle, Nettles, and Gossage heading for Daisy Buchanan's saloon near the Sheraton. They were confident and relaxed. Lemon had created a tone of peace over this franchise. They had come this far, and they intended to finish the Sox—again—in a few hours.

It would be Guidry, 24–3, against their old teammate Mike Torrez. Everything was perfect about baseball on this day. The weather—cool, crisp, October baseball—the ballpark, the rivalry, and the fact that two elite teams were about to go at each other with this great historic rivalry at its zenith.

Munson batted second and went 1 for 5 with three strikeouts. But he and Guidry were in a good rhythm, and even though the Sox jumped to an early lead, the confidence didn't wane. And Thurman's one hit would be a big one.

In the historic seventh inning, with the Yanks down 2–0, Chambliss and White both singled. With two out, Bucky Dent came to bat

and we can still hear Bill White saying, "Deep to left . . . Yastrzem-
skiiii's . . . not going to get it . . . It's a home run!" and the Yankees
took a 3–2 lead. Kind of a highlight moment in Bucky's career.

What followed was important as well. Rivers walked, and Bob Stanley replaced Torrez. Rivers stole second, and then Munson laced a
double to drive in Rivers and make it a 4–2 game. A big RBI, lost in
the memories of the Dent homer, in perhaps the most famous game
he ever appeared in.

Jackson homered in the eighth to make it 5–2, and that would
prove to be the winning run, as the Red Sox, noble to the end,
scored twice in the eighth, and the Yanks needed Gossage to save it
in the ninth for the 5–4 victory. Yastrzemski, with two on, could have
won it with a double, or maybe even a long single off the wall. Memories of the Impossible Dream of 1967?

Gossage got Yaz to foul out to Nettles and the Yankees won.

The Red Sox went home; the Yankees went on to face the Royals
for the pennant.

The Royals, well, the poor Royals found it their destiny to face the
Yankees again, and although this was a top-rate club with a fine manager in Whitey Herzog and first-rate players throughout the lineup
and on the pitching staff, the Yanks just had their number in the
1970s.

The Yanks won this one in four games, but for Munson, everything about his gifts as a major league baseball player came together
in game three in Yankee Stadium. Not only did he call another fine
game for Hunter and Gossage, but when he came to bat against re-
liever Doug Bird, the series was tied at a game apiece and the Royals were winning 5–4 in the last of the eighth, prepared to take a
two-to-one lead in games. George Brett was prepared to take his
place in playoff history with a three–home run game.

Munson, who had hit just two home runs in Yankee Stadium all season, tore into a fastball and sent it soaring deep, deep, way deep to the Babe Ruth monument in left-center field's Monument Park area, measured to be 475 feet. Very few balls had been hit there. Tape-measure home runs were not part of Munson's game. The unexpected nature of this titanic clout, and the fact that it set up a 6–5 playoff victory and a two-games-to-one *Yankee* lead, made it the most important home run of his career.

Where did that power come from!? On replays of the shot, the swing looks like a normal Munson swing. The power was always there; he was a very strong man. He simply didn't swing with an arc that lifted it as that one was lifted. He had a very disciplined swing and didn't give in to temptation, not even in Fenway. But here, for a moment at least, he let it all out.

Everyone must have one "longest ever" in them, leaving you wondering why it is never duplicated. Why did Mickey Mantle never again hit one 565 feet as he did that afternoon in Washington, D.C., when he was twenty-one years old?

Everything had come together just right—a moment of baseball perfection. As a hitter, that was Thurman's moment.

And the next day, the Yankees won the American League pennant.

"That home run was the greatest individual baseball feat I ever saw," says Henry Hecht, who covered the Yankees for the *New York Post* during the "Bronx Zoo" years, and was often in the middle of controversy himself. "Thurman was physically incapable of hitting a ball like that anymore because he was a broken-down catcher by then. I'm still in awe of what he did—because he couldn't do it."

The World Series rematch with the Dodgers found Thurman batting in five runs in game five, just one short of Bobby Richardson's World Series record, to help put the Yankees up three games to two. That was longer than Munson wanted the Series to last. As Guidry recalls, "There were a bunch of us in the clubhouse on the day I was scheduled to pitch. Thurman came in steaming. He had just read some more Dodger quotes saying this was going to be their year, and he said, 'If this was any other team but Los Angeles, I might just say forget it. But the way these guys have been carrying on, mouthing off, I would like nothing better than to kick their asses four straight.' "

Prior to game six, Hunter learned that his father had lung cancer. He was scheduled to pitch the game, and he did, but he also planned to skip game seven and get home to his dad. So there was a big desire to win it all that night in Los Angeles.

He wasn't sharp. He was doubtless distracted. A finesse pitcher like Hunter needed to have his concentration at full strength.

In the third inning, Munson went to the mound and said, "Well, Catfish, you better make sure you hit my glove exactly where I put it because you ain't got diddly-squat tonight."

The two of them could banter like that. Munson often talked to his pitchers like that. Jim Kaat remembers Munson coming to the mound and saying, "Are you fucking *trying* to lose this game?"

Hunter responded to Thurman, "Hey, Captain Bad Body, just get back on behind the plate and catch it after I throw it. I'm in a hurry to get home."

He threw a double-play ball to kill the Dodger rally.

The Yankees won the game 7–2. The last batter, Ron Cey, hit a high foul pop behind the plate. Munson turned and tossed his mask to his right, settled under the ball, and snared it for the world championship out. He turned toward Goose, took a quick glance at his mask with a momentary thought of retrieving it, but forgot about it and ran for the mound in triumph.

Lemon's steady hand and noninterfering approach were just the tonic the Yankees needed. It was their twenty-second world championship—and the last they would win until 1996, a gap of eighteen seasons.

An emotionally spent Thurman Munson went home to the tranquillity of Canton.

13

Over the winter of 1978–79, Thurman, now a mature, 31-year-old veteran ballplayer and businessman, busied himself in Canton with his off-field interests, particularly aviation, as well as with attention to his family, always the priority. A couple of times, he visited his mother at the senior citizens home. He had joined the Congress Lake Club and played golf there and at Prestwick and Tam O'Shanter in Canton when the weather permitted. His roots in the community were deep. Even as a Yankee star, he'd go back to Lehman and talk to the teams.

"He was always the same guy, he just had more money," laughs his boyhood battery mate Jerome Pruett. "The same lovable sarcastic Thurman."

He'd play racquetball with Jerry Anderson, grab lunch with Tote Dominick at Lucia's, survey his property holdings, fly his plane, and hang out a lot with Diana and the kids. They were full days.

In November he was a secret guest speaker for the Plain Local Midget Football League banquet, agreeing to appear only if the press wasn't informed.

In February there was a "Munson Roast" in Canton that raised $51,000 for three local charities, which was certainly the only reason he agreed to be honored. Several teammates came, including Roy White, whom he could always count on to show up for him. Reggie Jackson came too, to the surprise of many.

"He didn't even hesitate," said Thurman. "He told me he'd be happy to come in, at no expense. That doesn't sound like a guy who hates me, does it?"

He remained loyal to Canton and loyal to its public schools. Bob Henderson, his senior year basketball coach at Lehman, called the Yankees to see if Thurman might come back to visit classes during Right to Read Week. "I never expected he would do this at this stage of his career, but he spent a whole day with us, visiting various schools, talking about the importance of reading and getting an education. It was a wonderful day."

Contractually, he was modestly content. His baseball salary, through the deal signed for four years—1978 through 1981—moved progressively from $317,500 to $417,500, and it grudgingly accepted his flying. Dick Moss, the former number two man to Marvin Miller at the Players Association, had negotiated the deal with the Yankees, managing to remove the standard clause in the contract that absolved the club of compliance with the agreement if the player dies while piloting a plane. Thurman, who had never used an agent, had reached out to Moss, a top-tier guy, when he knew he wanted to deal with the no-fly provision of the contact. But much bitterness had preceded the signing, and Thurman was never happy about the deal. "It was satisfactory the way it should have been before I was disgraced for two years," he said. "In the respect that it satisfies me finally yes, but it doesn't help my attitude. Are material things supposed to help a guy who's had these things eating at him for two years?"

"Munson would have flown anyway," says Moss. "He had two important things in his life at that time: playing baseball and flying his airplane. It was an easy deal to do, but there was the problem of that flying clause. It took George a couple of weeks to come around, but the provision was stricken."

Spring training of 1979 had a great air of sadness over it. Bob Lemon, shortly after his great triumph in the World Series, had suffered the loss of his twenty-six-year-old son Jerry in a car crash in Arizona. Lem tried to give it his all but he was filled with grief. What should have been a glorious spring was one of melancholy.

"He was never the same after that," said Joe Garagiola Sr., who had taken Lem's phone call in Arizona and rushed to the hospital until Lemon could get there.

Thurman blew off Jim Bouton, who had sought an interview during spring training, evoking old memories of *Ball Four* and reminding people that Munson was old-school and not ready to forgive Bouton for breaking the clubhouse code of silence almost a decade earlier. Days later, Thurman did a rare interview with John Dockery of WNEW TV from New York. He always preferred TV or radio to print, feeling his words could not be edited.

> **MUNSON:** Well, we're having fun, there's not as much excitement around here this year, problems with the manager and problems with everyone else, you know, we're just trying to have some fun and get our work done. He's running a very light camp right now and hey, we really know the guys who are going to be here and we're getting in shape our own way.
>
> **DOCKERY:** Does it take "nasty energy" for the club to win?
>
> **MUNSON:** Nobody needs that stuff mentally, last year, a lot of that stuff, everyone says, well, maybe it helped us. Well, after it was over and we started playing ball around

July it didn't help us to win all the games we did, so I don't believe anybody feeds on that kind of stuff, they might feed on, ya know, different aspects of the game, of course, failure and pride will do a lot of things for people, but I don't think anybody feeds on that kind of crap.

DOCKERY: Is there talk of this being a dynasty?

MUNSON: Well, I think with the addition of [Tommy] John and of course [Luis] Tiant, even though they're older players, with quite a few of the younger people we have and the younger pitchers coming up, I think for the next four or five years we've got a super chance to win.

DOCKERY: What is your role as captain as you see it?

MUNSON: I just come out to the ballpark and play every day. If somebody needs help with something, we've got seven or eight guys on the club who try to help everybody they can, you really just let things take their course, that's all.

DOCKERY: Sports is a big business now, what do you see as the media's role?

MUNSON: Well, the media *is* sports, really—no one knows what we do unless they come to the ballpark, unless they read about it. The only bad part of the media, it's like TV shows, too many things are elaborated on, you know, just for interest, which is great, but a lot of times a true story doesn't get told, and it's really one reason why a lot of times I don't mind talking in front of cameras to the people, but you talk to newspapers and not the right thing is written.

DOCKERY: Has the media been fair to you?

MUNSON: Well I have to say this, New York itself in general, the fans, the press, and everybody my whole career have been great to me. I made a statement last year

that I want to go home to play baseball because I love my
family, I love my children and my wife, I do love to be
home but it's not because of New York, because they've
been great to me.

DOCKERY: Are you reluctant to talk, do you have
negative feelings towards me?

MUNSON: I don't feel any negative feels towards
anybody. I have too many nice things in life to have
negative feelings. I think one thing we all have to do is just
do what we want to do and, you know, and for me, it isn't
really going out and having a lot of small talk sometimes
and I'm not saying what we're doing now is small talk, but
most things or a lot of things that people ask in the press,
they're all controversial and small talk!

DOCKERY: If you were doing this interview, what is the
most relevant thing I could ask you?

MUNSON: Well, kind of what you did, what the Yankees
are going to do, talk about the team in general, like
yesterday, the first question I get is what about Jim Bouton.
The next question I get is do I think it will be better this
year now that Billy Martin's not back. Those kind of things,
you can't win, guys come up to me and ask me about my
arm, well, I've got a seven-or-eight-inch gash in my arm,
they took part of my clavicle out, well, they ask the trainer
something, they're not going to coincide so I'm in trouble
right away.

DOCKERY: Do you want to tell the other side of the
Bouton incident?

MUNSON: The other side that I can tell you about Jim
Bouton is Elston Howard's my coach, Ralph Houk was my
manager for five years and Mickey Mantle's a good friend
of mine. He wrote a book that ripped those people pretty

well. I'm just not the type of person that can lose Ellie's respect or Ralph's or anyone else's. So I told him very nice three times that I couldn't do an autograph, or interview with him, and I meant it. I will never do a session with Jim Bouton because of my respect for those three people.

DOCKERY: The book was an invasion of your privacy?

MUNSON: It wasn't an invasion of privacy to me, it had nothing to do with me. The invasion of privacy was what he said about Elston Howard, Ralph Houk, and Mantle.

DOCKERY: But it was a violation of the locker room?

MUNSON: I think what's in the locker room should stay there, and besides *Ball Four* wasn't written the right way anyway, it was the way it was so he could sell books, so he goes and says, "How long do I have to pay for something like that?"—as long as he's associated with this game, or as long as I'm in it or a few other people are in it, he has to pay for it, that's all.

DOCKER: Talk to you in October?

MUNSON: I hope we get a chance to talk in October, it'll mean we'll be in the Series. I think the Yankees will be in the Series this year. Boston has another fine team, but we've got a bunch of good people on this club and as long as we keep the trouble away like I think we're going to, as long as things don't get stirred up too bad, we could eliminate everybody.

The Yankees had a new assistant trainer in camp that year. Barry Weinberg had come up from the team's Columbus farm club to begin a major league career that would see him serve Tony LaRussa as head trainer in both Oakland and St. Louis.

The rookie trainer introduced himself to Thurman. "I'm Barry Weinberg," he said.

"Goldberg?" said Munson.

"Weinberg."

"Okay, Goldberg, nice to meet you." And he would continue to call him Goldberg.

One day Munson went into the training room for a rubdown. Gene Monahan was working on someone else, so Weinberg said he'd do it.

"Oh no, Goldberg," said Thurman. "I'm a German and I can't be rubbed down by a Jew." And he left.

That night, Weinberg and a friend were seated at a table in a restaurant, when a waitress brought over a drink, saying, "It's compliments of the gentleman at the bar."

Weinberg looked up and Munson was sitting there with a big grin, giving him the finger.

"I wound up idolizing him," said Weinberg. "He was one of the greatest guys I ever knew. That April, we played in the cold in Chicago and I only had a short-sleeve shirt with me. He came over and handed me a flannel parka. Only that night did I see that inside in Pete Sheehy's printing it said MUNSON-15. It was his own parka. I still have it."

In the spring of 1979, Thurman bought a Beechcraft King Air Model E-90, a twin-engine turboprop, and flew it to spring training. It was an upgrade on his Beechcraft Duke.

"One afternoon we flew out together to the Bahamas," said Piniella to Maury Allen in his autobiography.

> He was in complete control and secure in his skills. We flew together several more times and I was fascinated with the fun he was having and started to think about getting a plane myself. We talked about my taking flying lessons, but I never got around to it. Still, I understood.

Early in '79 we played a game in Baltimore and after the game, Reggie and I flew back to New York with him. Thurman and Reggie were getting along okay by now. We hit bad weather over Pennsylvania, thunderstorms, but he just got a new flight plan from the control tower and went around the storm. [He showed] total confidence, total control. Very professional.

A few weeks later I flew with him from Teterboro [N.J.] to Canton to have dinner after a Sunday game. He buzzed his house to let his family know he was almost home. He got a kick out of that.

One night we were sitting in a hotel bar after a game, Bobby Murcer, Thurman and me. He was talking about flying and he said, "I'm buying a jet for a million and a half, a Cessna Citation, a real beauty."

Bobby made a face and said, "What do you need such a big plane for?"

"It'll be great. I'll get home much faster. I'm getting it in a couple of weeks."

Bobby and I, neither of us liked this at all. It was a whole different kind of plane. Plus it was very expensive to fly, with the fuel, repairs, insurance. "Now I'll have to play three or four more years to pay it off," he said.

Indeed, his friends and fellow aviators were astounded by the rapidity of his graduation to bigger planes. He had started with the Cessna 150 in spring training of 1978. By June of that year he was in a Beechcraft Duke twin-piston. By February 1979 it was on to a Beechcraft Duke Air Model E-90, a twin-engine turboprop. And now he had taken delivery of the jet on July 6, just five months later.

On the field, things weren't going well for the Yankees, and some felt there was a pall over Bob Lemon, still mourning his son, that took some fire out of the team. (Not that Lem was particularly fiery, but it was a whispered theory.)

Some felt the year was doomed from the start, when Goose Gossage tore a ligament in his right thumb during a scuffle with Cliff Johnson in the clubhouse on April 19. With that, they lost their closer until July 12.

Winning a fourth straight pennant would indeed prove to be a challenge. The Yankees played .500 baseball, more or less, through Memorial Day, but Baltimore was hot and between June 1 and June 30, the Yanks fell from three games out to twelve. Steinbrenner fired poor Lemon on June 18 and replaced him with Billy Martin, yet again. Did they have another comeback in them like 1978?

Nobody was feeling it.

Seattle, Thursday, July 12

The Yankees played a weekend series in Oakland July 6–8, during which a Cessna pilot delivered Thurman's new Citation to him. He was thrilled! With the Cessna pilot in control and Thurman in the copilot seat, he took it up that very weekend, joined by Bucky Dent and his old Cape Cod teammate John Frobose, who was now living in San Jose.

Thurman was loving his new jet, and was not shy about talking it up and inviting teammates to fly with him. Some just said, "Are you crazy?" and some said, "Yeah, I'll do it sometime." Like any cross section of society, ballplayers had varying senses of adventure when it came to flying in a small plane.

On Thursday night, July 12, after playing a game in Seattle, Graig Nettles and Reggie Jackson agreed to accompany Thurman in his Cessna on a trip to Anaheim, where the team would begin a three-game series the next evening. A flight instructor joined Munson in the cockpit.

Nettles told author Peter Golenbock:

Reggie and I were in the back, and his instructor was in the pilot's seat next to Thurman . . . We had finished a night game in Seattle, and we were flying south, and all of a sudden I heard a big boom in the back of the plane. It sounded like someone had thrown something against the plane. Reggie was napping and he jerked awake and looked around. "What was that?" he said, as oxygen masks were dropping down. The pilot said, "You're going to have to use the oxygen." My mask worked, but Reggie's didn't. I told Reggie, "Thurman told me to make sure you sat in that seat." Reggie laughed 'cause they were supposed to be feuding at that time, but they really weren't. It turned out there was nothing wrong with the oxygen supply, and we didn't need the masks after all.

Except for that one incident, the flight was spectacular. We flew over Washington, Oregon, and California, and it was a bright night and you could see the snow-capped mountains. I told Thurman how much fun I had and he told me that when he got back to New York he would be going to Teterboro to practice and that I could fly with him and bring my son.

Thurman took flying very seriously. After ballgames we would often sit around and have a few beers, but if he knew he was going to be flying, he would only have Coke or Pepsi. He wouldn't even have one beer.

Two days later in Anaheim, Jackson made out a hundred-dollar check to Munson and wrote "Plane fare, Seattle to Cal" in the memo. Thurman never cashed it.

Anaheim, Saturday, July 14

The Saturday night game in Anaheim ended late. Phil Pepe was on the trip covering the team for the *Daily News*. "I was in the hotel gift shop and I was about to go to my room for the night, when I noticed Munson in there picking out some snacks, a bag of Doritos, a bag of potato chips, etc. 'What are you doing?' I asked him.

" 'I didn't have dinner and I'm hungry,' he said.

" 'Don't eat that junk,' I said. 'There's an all-night burger joint up the street, why don't you go up there and get something nutritious?'

" 'I don't like eating alone,' he said.

" 'I'll sit with you.'

" 'You will?' he said. So we went and spent about two and a half hours, talking about life in general, no baseball, until about two a.m. At one point, Munson began to talk about flying, telling me how much he enjoyed the peace and serenity of being up in the air, alone with his thoughts. As if to convince me, he said, 'I'll take you up with me one day.'

" 'No way,' I said. 'I'm not going up there with you.'

" 'There's nothing to worry about,' he said. 'It's perfectly safe. Look, I don't care if you live or die, but I care if I live or die!' "

Anaheim, Sunday, July 15

After the Anaheim series concluded on Sunday, Thurman had the All-Star break off. (Darrell Porter, Brian Downing, and Jeff Newman were the A.L. catchers.) Billy Martin wanted to go fishing in Kansas City with his friend Howard Wong. He asked Thurman if he would fly him there on his way home to Canton. Munson was more than happy to accommodate him.

Diana was with Thurman, and this was her first experience in the jet. Thurman took his place in the copilot seat, with a Cessna instructor in the pilot's seat, as Thurman was not yet licensed to fly without one. Billy and Diana were in the back midsection seated across from each other.

As Martin told Golenbock (who also cowrote his autobiography):

> We were in the jet which Thurman had just bought, and he landed in Albuquerque to gas up, and coming out of Albuquerque we hit an ice storm. I was looking out the windows, facing the engines, and I saw a flash of flame hit one engine. I didn't want to say anything because Thurman's wife, Diane, was sitting right across from me and I didn't want to scare her, but when we landed in Kansas City, I took Thurman aside. I said, "You better check your engines. Did you see flames coming out of the right one?" He said, "Maybe that was when I switched on the deicer." I said, "No way. I've never seen flames come out of an engine like that. You better check it out." My car came and Howard and I got in, and two days later . . . Thurman came over and said, "You know we had to take another plane out of Kansas City after we dropped you off. We had to stay overnight and take a commercial jet out." I said, "You're kidding me." He said, "The rotors of the right engine were all mashed in, bent. They must have put them in wrong when they built the plane."
>
> That scared me. Here was a million-and-a-quarter-dollar plane, and the engines weren't working right. They had to put a brand-new engine on the plane.
>
> I told Thurman I didn't like him flying. I said, "Why are you flying this thing? Does George know you're flying?" He said, "Yeah, he gave me permission." I said, "You gotta be kidding me." . . . I didn't like it because here this guy could fly all over the country whenever he wanted, and I was yelling at other players that they had to be on the bus on time. He was

being treated differently than the other guys, and it wasn't right.

Indeed, Cessna had sent one of their pilots to fly the plane from Kansas City to Dallas, where repairs were made on the Citation at Cooper Industries. It had been flown back to Canton on July 31, while Munson was in Chicago, by Cessna pilot Morgan Lilly.

Wichita, Tuesday, July 17

During the All-Star break, Thurman slipped off to Wichita, Kansas, to fly a number of solo hours with an instructor, enabling him to move closer to his license. On Tuesday, July 17, the day of the All-Star Game, he received a Citation-type rating after doing four hours of training in a flight simulator in Wichita, allowing him to ultimately serve as his own pilot-in-command.

"The problem with this period of instructor training," says his friend Jerry Anderson, "was that you mostly sit back and cruise, most certainly on autopilot, and you certainly don't learn how to take off and land or recognize emergencies, while at cruise."

Edward McAvoy, an investigator for the National Transportation Safety Board, would later say, "Such rapid progress is unusual for a part-time flier." He was critical of the whole FAA system under which the licensing and rating of pilots were done by examiners who first teach them to fly, and then license them, while working for the companies selling the planes. It amounted to a conflict of interest, thought McAvoy.

And there was nothing unusual about the procedure. It was standard among airplane manufacturers.

"I agreed with McAvoy," says Anderson. "Cessna promised Thurman he could learn to fly with their instructors during the season so they could sell him the plane."

The Citation name is still used by Cessna for its business jets. Thurman had purchased a Citation I/SP, which was introduced in 1977 and enabled single-pilot operation and the use of short run-ways. It was thirty-two feet long and sat six, with a wingspan of forty-four feet, and was capable of flying at 300 knots (about 332 miles per hour), which was about twice as fast as the King Air C90 twin propeller. The first Citations had appeared in 1969. The company produced 312 Citation I/SPs between 1977 and 1985, when the Ci-tation II line was introduced.

"When I flew [it]," wrote pilot Richard L. Collins, speaking of the new Citation line, "the word from Cessna salesmen was to use it like any airplane. Just do what you do, only do it faster . . ."

"Looking back," says Anderson, "the King Air C90 was the per-fect plane for Thurman—fast enough for New York–to–Canton trips, but not so complex or expensive to operate that he struggled. I flew many times with him in the King Air; it was a very comfort-able aircraft for his piloting skill level and five-hundred-mile trips. Of course, he wanted 'faster and higher,' as all us pilots do at times."

Canton, Sunday, July 22

While the Yankees were at home playing the Mariners, back home in Canton Bill Shearer was having a Sunday breakfast with Jack Dole at a farm just outside of town. Shearer had played third base in American Legion ball when Thurman had been a shortstop. "We were the most scouted Legion team in the country," he says. "Four of our guys signed pro contracts. Gene Woodling used to watch us when he was scouting."

Dole's job was manager of the Akron-Canton Airport.

At one point, when the conversation turned to baseball, Dole looked at Shearer and said, "You know Thurman Munson pretty well, right?"

Told that he did, and that in fact Thurman often called him when he was in town, Dole looked him in the eye and said, "Please talk to him . . . this jet . . . he's not getting it done."

Shearer thought about his own conversations with Munson on the subject. They had been talking on Thurman's driveway after he'd come home from the 1978 World Series. Munson already owned one of the fastest propeller planes available. Why did he need the jet?

"Bill, I can get home between twenty-five and thirty minutes quicker than with the propeller plane," said Thurman.

"It was true," says Don Armen, who hangared Thurman's plane in Canton. "He bought the jet to save time. He could fly in all kinds of weather, high enough to get up over storms. And this way, he could start branching out, flying to the West Coast and taking his family and flying from almost anywhere after a game. It was for convenience."

On Monday, July 23, Munson fell under the .300 mark for the season and into what would be a 2-for-24 slump. He was so banged up it was amazing that he was in the lineup at all. This season was getting away from the Yankees, and they knew it. They said the right things, but it was looking like a lost year.

New York, Tuesday, July 24

Thurman always walked to the batter's box with what can best be called a herky-jerky walk. There was nothing gladiatorlike about his presence on a baseball field. He wasn't blessed with the body of Dave Winfield, nor the presence of Brett Favre. His teammates sometimes called him "Tugboat," which perhaps captured his manner best of all. He was their leader, their captain, but he didn't lead the pack with the grace of a luxury liner. He did it like a tugboat leading his charges, perhaps breaking through ice to do so.

He also waddled a little bit, like a bobblehead doll, set in motion with batteries. And yet there was a steely-eyed determination about him as he jerked his head back and forth as though never quite able to relieve some bothersome kink in his neck.

And oh, could he be annoying adjusting his batting glove. Over and over, unhitching the Velcro, then refastening it, stepping out after each pitch, adjusting, flexing, resetting his helmet, digging in, positioning himself. No pitch was too insignificant to avoid the rituals. It could be a Wednesday afternoon in June against the Brewers, Yanks up by seven, eighth inning, and yet each pitch was to be studied, considered, analyzed, and pondered. "How did he pitch me last time when we were 0–2?" he'd wonder. And then, as he was adjusting his batting glove, he'd remember. Breaking pitch, low and away. And his concentration would return and his focus would be steely, and he'd take his practice swing—one, two, three—and stare at the pitcher.

Mike Barlow was on the mound at this moment. Barlow, a six-foot-six right-hander out of Syracuse University, was thirty-one years of age, in his fifth season. Munson hadn't seen him much—he pitched for the Angels and matchups between this pitcher and this hitter had been few. Syracuse and Kent State hadn't played each other in college.

This was the first game of a three-game series with the Angels, and if you wonder if it was a different era for baseball, consider this. Of four home weekday games that week, this was the only one on TV. There was no cable. It was on Channel 11, and it started at eight o'clock, as night games did back then when the games could still end around a reasonable 10:30.

This being the fourth inning, it would have been just past nine p.m. The Yanks had a little three-game winning streak going. Martin, having replaced Lemon as manager on June 18, was starting to feel a bit of momentum, although the team was in fourth place, eleven and a half games out of first, and dealing with a seeming epidemic of injuries to key players.

Munson, catching and hitting second in the lineup, had struck

Clockwise from top: Darla, Duane, Thurman, and Janice. *His siblings had all left home as soon as they could.* COURTESY OF DARLA MUNSON DAY

Thurman with his older brother, Duane. *"I left home and missed his high school years. That hurt me a lot, and maybe it hurt him too."* COURTESY OF DARLA MUNSON DAY

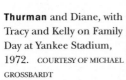

A photo in his Binghamton uniform, first day at Yankee Stadium, 1968. *You can always tell a rookie photo from a veteran photo by the poise, or lack of poise, on display. Thurman had some poise.* COURTESY OF MICHAEL GROSSBARDT

Thurman and Diane, with Tracy and Kelly on Family Day at Yankee Stadium, 1972. COURTESY OF MICHAEL GROSSBARDT

Munson awaits his turn at the batting cage on his first day in the big leagues. *"I had to go digging to find a pair of pants to fit him,"* said Yankee clubhouse attendant Pete Sheehy. *"His rear end was too big. I always kidded him about that."*
COURTESY OF MICHAEL GROSSBARDT

In his locker with senior Yankee beat writer Jim Ogle of the *Newark Star-Ledger*. *"I think he was edged away from us by Nettles, and maybe some others,"* says reporter Murray Chass. *"They didn't like to see him too close to the writers."* COURTESY OF MICHAEL GROSSBARDT

Thurman hustles to third on a hit by Bobby Murcer. *"He was the second fastest runner on our team, despite that body he was trapped inside of,"* says Kent State teammate Steve Stone. *"He could really run."* COURTESY OF MICHAEL GROSSBARDT

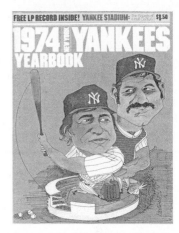

Old Timers' Day, 1976. Yankee catching heritage of (l–r) Bill Dickey, Yogi Berra, Elston Howard, and Munson. *"What time do you need me?"* he asked. *"Oh, he could be difficult."* COURTESY OF MICHAEL GROSSBARDT

Cover of the 1974 *Yankees Yearbook,* with the reigning "M & M" Boys, Murcer and Munson.

Boston's Carlton Fisk headed for a collision with Munson at Yankee Stadium. *It wasn't until the mid-'70s that both teams peaked, and Munson-Fisk seemed to be the symbols of both.* COURTESY OF MICHAEL GROSSBARDT

Munson with Reggie Jackson. *It was all Yankee fans could talk about, with few siding with Jackson. Munson was "their guy."* COURTESY OF MICHAEL GROSSBARDT

Thurman, full mustache, full polyester look, spring training. *"To get [a] picture, I had to take a punch [in the ribs],"* says Yankee photographer Michael Grossbardt. *"I suppose on some level it was a sign of affection."*

The author with Munson at the time of the autobiography project. *"I'm only twenty-nine! No one does an autobiography at twenty-nine."*

With his father-in-law, "Tote" Dominick. *"We're really shook up. It's unbelievable. Such a loss. A 32-year-old son-in-law."*

The cover of the 1977 Yankees media guide captures Munson's reaction as Chris Chambliss homers to win the '76 pennant. *The losing years were over. The Yankees were American League champions and going to their thirtieth World Series.*

With Joe DiMaggio and Commissioner Bowie Kuhn, first-pitch ceremony, 1977 World Series. This would be the Yankees' first world championship since 1962.
COURTESY OF MICHAEL GROSSBARDT

The scoreboard at Shea Stadium on the afternoon Thurman died, where the Phillies and Mets were engaged in a day game. *"I've never heard a ballpark that was any quieter than that,"* says Tim McCarver, Phillies catcher at the time.
COURTESY OF THE AUTHOR

Rescue workers at the scene of the accident on Greenberg Road, just north of Akron-Canton Airport. *Steinbrenner wanted to call his players before they heard the news on the radio.* THE CANTON REPOSITORY. USED WITH PERMISSION.

The moment of silence at Yankee Stadium, August 3, 1979, with home plate left empty for the missing captain. *For many, it was the single visual moment that evoked memories of the riderless horse in the funeral procession of President Kennedy sixteen years earlier.* AP IMAGES

Aisles are arranged for public viewing of Thurman casket, August 5, 1979, at the Canton Civic Center. *In Cooperstown flags were at half-staff on what should have been a more joyous New York event—the induction of Willie Mays into the Hall of Fame.* THE CANTON REPOSITORY. USED WITH PERMISSION.

Munson's casket leaves the Canton Civic Center as an honor guard stands watch before the journey to the cemetery. Diana, her daughters, and her father are off to the left. *Canton had not seen an event like this since President William McKinley's memorial service in September of 1901.* THE CANTON REPOSITORY. USED WITH PERMISSION.

Diana Munson's mother, Pauline, attends to restless four-year-old Michael, wearing his dad's number 15, outside the Civic Center. *"He's a handful, that little guy!"* AP PHOTO/BRIAN HORTON

Ruth Munson, Thurman's mother, leaves the funeral home, unrecognized by media or the Yankees. CBS NEWS ARCHIVES

Darrell Munson, back in Tucson, Arizona, about a month after his son's funeral. *"You always thought you were too big for this world. Well, you weren't!"*

NO GAME TODAY - AUG. 3, 1979   BY BILL GALLO

NAW, YUCHIE—
I JUST DON'T
FEEL LIKE
PLAYIN'
BALL TODAY...

Bill Gallo's poignant drawing in the *New York Daily News* following the accident. *"I wanted it to look like he's gone, but still looking at the symbol of baseball, which is kids."* BY PERMISSION FROM BILL GALLO AND THE *NEW YORK DAILY NEWS*

Thurman's gravesite at Sunset Hills Burial Park. *"Only Thurman would get buried next to a Burger King and a pizza parlor,"* said teammate Graig Nettles. COURTESY OF THE AUTHOR

Diana Munson surrounded by her three children, two sons-in-law, and five grandchildren in 2004. Michael Munson (top, center) has since married and added another grandchild to the family. JOHN F. GRIESHOP/ *SPORTS ILLUSTRATED*

out against Don Aase in the first inning. Now Barlow was pitching and the Yanks were up 4–3—thinking, a little bit at least, about winning a fourth in a row.

Willie Randolph was on third, Bucky Dent on second, with two out.

Thurman had settled into his batting stance, when Barlow delivered one right at his body that sent Thurman sprawling onto his ass, his bat flying out of his hands. It missed hitting him and went to the backstop, and Randolph scored the fifth run.

Thurman got up, adjusted his batting glove, touched his helmet, stared at Barlow, waved his bat, and took ball four. He hadn't seen a decent pitch to bring in Bucky, but that was fine, he was on base, and maybe Chris Chambliss could pick him up.

But as he headed for first, he knew he didn't feel right. The fall had played havoc with his already wobbly knees. It was as though he could hear the joint crack on every step as he trotted to first. And it hurt. He was used to playing hurt, and generally played through it. But if he couldn't run, he would hurt the team, and that was not something he was about to do.

Chambliss lined out and the inning was over.

As Munson headed for the first base dugout he exchanged glances with Martin and shook his head. He knew he was done for the evening, and trainer Gene Monahan went over to ask him about the knee. Martin shouted over to Jerry Narron to put on the catching gear and get out there for the fifth.

Thurman headed down the four steps at the rear of the dugout and then up the walkway toward the clubhouse. He was going to put some ice on his knee and watch the rest of the game on the clubhouse television set. What he didn't know was that he had just played his last game at Yankee Stadium.

During that home stand, Steinbrenner had called Martin into his office before a ball game. As Martin related to Golenbock:

He was madder'n hell at Thurman's flying. I said: "George, you're the one who gave him permission to do it." He said, "Billy, I'd appreciate it if you'd talk to him about it."

I went down and talked to him, and he told me that he and Diane were planning to take an apartment in New Jersey so he wouldn't have to fly anymore. I said, "I think that's a good idea. You'll be with your wife, and you won't have to fly anymore, and it won't take so much out of you." He agreed with me on that.

I went back up and told George about our conversation, and that's when George got mad about Thurman's hitting. He showed me his stats, that his average was down, his RBIs down. I said, "Don't you understand, his legs are killing him. He can't push off his legs to hit. The guy shouldn't even be playing right now." He was playing in great pain, playing in hell. That's the kind of guy Thurman was. I said, "He shouldn't be playing but we don't have anyone else." George said, "Why don't you bat him eighth, that'll show him." "Bat him eighth? I wouldn't bat Thurman Munson eighth," I told George. "I won't."

New York, Wednesday, July 25

Thurman didn't play the home game on Wednesday night the twenty-fifth, and Frank Messer told us on radio that he was still feeling the effects of the injury that caused him to leave the game the night before.

This sounded odd to me, since he had left after being decked by a pitch—not being hit, not suffering a collision. He was a catcher and took so much pain and punishment back there that for him to miss a game without a more meaningful cause was strange.

So on Thursday, the final day of the home stand, I drove to the stadium to visit with him. Off to see my coauthor.

I drove my 1976 Toyota Corolla from my home in White Plains to the stadium, a twenty-minute trip. The car had been the Yankees' bullpen car; it was a kick to own it, but then I found out I couldn't take it on certain Westchester highways because, with its pinstripes and Yankee logo, it was considered a "commercial vehicle." So I had to repaint it. But I knew it was the car of Munson's MVP season and of Sparky Lyle's triumphant entrances. Lyle's spike marks were on the passenger door.

I went into the clubhouse, didn't spot Thurman, but saw Catfish. It had been a tough year personally for this very special ballplayer. I had been the team's PR director when he signed, and we had gotten close during the weeks of intense publicity that accompanied his signing and Yankee debut. He had been the one who doused me with champagne after we won the '76 pennant. He had recently lost his dad and his "surrogate baseball dad," scout Clyde Klutz, the man who had twice signed him—once for Kansas City and once again for the Yankees.

I told Hunter I was really sorry about his losses, and that I missed Clyde too.

"Thanks," he said. "It makes you grow up. 'Specially when it happens twice."

When I asked him how he felt, he quickly said, "I feel a hundred years old. I can't pitch for shit. I'm not helping the team. I'm done."

Hunter was always a stand-up guy, the kind who would look a manager on a visit to the mound straight in the eye and tell him whether he had any pitches left. He wasn't the sort to be insecure about his standing with the club. You could take him at his word. Always.

I asked him if he knew where Munson was.

"Maybe in the sauna. He's an old man too. Squatted down too many times."

We laughed over that one.

I found it an interesting thought. How many times had he "squatted," I wondered. There was no way I could calculate that in my head. But I was wearing a Casio digital watch with a calculator on it and I decided to figure it out.

I came up with about 20,250 pitches a year, more with spring training and warm-ups, multiplied by ten seasons, and it was over 200,000 squats back there. No wonder his knees were breaking down.

Hunter was amused by these stats but intrigued as well.

"Don't raise your kids to be catchers," he responded.

With that I saw the naked Munson circle toward his locker. He was smiling; he seemed to have been coming down off a good punch line from someone. He was toweling himself off from the rear, singing, "America loves burgers, and we're America's Burger King . . ." I excused myself and walked over to him.

"Whaddya say, partner!" he said, extending a hand and motioning for me to slide over the stool from the next locker.

I told him I'd just calculated his lifetime squats on my Casio.

He laughed. "You think it's 200,000?" he said.

"Well, that's at 150 a game, 135 games a year plus warm-ups."

"Well, no wonder I'm so messed up then! I didn't need to hear that!"

I told him that I came down because I didn't like to see him out of the lineup. Plus, it took a lot to sit him down, and I thought it might be more than it appeared.

He acknowledged that he was indeed hurting "like hell," and couldn't catch even in an emergency as it now stood. He was hoping that maybe a few days off would help, but he seemed resigned to going through more tests to see what was up.

I told him it just wasn't the same team without him catching, and he said, "Get used to it." The chances were good he wouldn't catch again for the rest of the season.

"It kills me not to be out there. I can't sit still in the dugout. I try to go to the bullpen for a few innings just to break things up."

We shifted gears and talked about my wife's pregnancy, with our first child due in about six weeks. I asked him how everything was in Canton.

"Yeah, I need to get back there soon, I've got this little strip mall property I'm looking at buying, and I miss the family. When am I going to get you up there with me in the jet?"

I laughed. "You have a jet? I didn't know that. Are you kidding me? I hate the turbulence in a 747! I couldn't be in a small plane, I'd be a nervous wreck."

"Oh, you don't know what you're talking about," he said. "It's a beautiful experience! Ask Reggie, he was up with me. Nettles too. And Billy."

"That's okay, they might have thought it was great, but it's not for me."

With that, I stood and shook his hand and said I'd see him soon.

"Any book sale numbers?" he asked.

"That's pretty much done, Thurman. Any sales at this point don't really amount to much. It did okay, it wasn't a big hit, but we didn't get very controversial, and that was the result. It's a book you're proud of, right?"

"Yeah, it was good. I know we could have taken more shots. But it was good we didn't, I don't want to be like those guys. Especially after I boycotted Bouton. I wish it was funnier though. There were funny stories I could have put in there."

That was our last conversation. He headed for the trainer's room; I headed for the press room. The conversation was not as free and easy as when I was the team's PR director, or when we had done the book together, but when you're not an everyday insider, relationships change. And I knew he had a lot on his mind.

New York, Thursday, July 26

Ron Guidry shut out the California Angels 2–0 in the afternoon game of July 26 before a Yankee Stadium crowd of more than

43,000, many of them kids enjoying summer-camp outings. The practice of wearing "Yankee blue" T-shirts with favorite players' names on the back hadn't yet begun. That was a marketing plan waiting to happen. If it did exist, there would have been plenty of MUNSON 15 shirts in the stands. JACKSON 44 might have sold the most, but there would have been plenty of Munsons. The fans just connected with him. He was a "grinder," in the words of NBC announcer Joe Garagiola. He was the one who went out there and grinded it out, pumping his fist, pointing here and there, keeping everyone in the game, quarterbacking the day's flow of events.

Guidry put down the Angels with his shutout, and it was always nice to win on a travel day. It had been a duel of complete games, almost impossible to imagine today, with Jim Barr taking the loss despite an eight-hitter. Mickey Rivers, the clock ticking on his Yankee career, played the last two innings after Murcer led off and left the game with a sore right shin and a strained tendon behind his left knee. The M&M Boys—Murcer and Munson—were walking wounded, as were Chambliss, Rivers, Randolph, and Jim Spencer.

"It was Munson, however," wrote Murray Chass in the *Times,* "who posed the most bothersome problem for the Yankees. The catcher has a chronically sore right knee and he aggravated it when he fell Tuesday night. He has missed the last two games and no one knows when he will be able to catch again."

Martin said, "From what the doctor told me, he won't be able to catch for a while. If I can afford to, I'd like to rest him for about a week, but I don't know if I can do that."

It was Billy's way of using the press to say, *The front office isn't giving me the players I need to win.*

Jerry Narron caught and batted seventh, going 1 for 2 with a run scored. Martin needed another catcher, the likely fellow being Brad Gulden, a left-handed hitter at Columbus, but the front office was not anxious to bring him up and Martin was seething over it. Slow personnel call-ups handicapped his ability to fully manipulate his roster during a game; being unable to pinch-hit for Narron might cost him one of the twenty-seven outs he had to work with, and perhaps cost him the game. He was always on a short leash, and so he was displeased with being shorthanded.

Further, the Yankees hired Jeff Torborg that day to join their coaching staff. He had recently been dropped as manager of the Indians, and he was going to be assigned to the bullpen to help out with the faltering pitching. The last thing Billy liked was to have coaches around who were not of his choosing, let alone former managers.

The team would dress and fly to Milwaukee, arriving around nine, time enough to go out for some beers with the guys.

Into the clubhouse came Bill Kane, the Yankees' traveling secretary. He had some bad news. Their plane was delayed, so there was no need to board the bus for LaGuardia at that time. Better to hang out in the clubhouse, kill time there, and head for the airport when all was ready.

Munson looked at Nettles and smiled the all-knowing, "nothing is running smoothly anymore this year" look. With all the stars in the room, this was still a team that was not only not going to Milwaukee on time, but also not really going anywhere in the American League East. Yes, they had just won five of six and were 5–2 since the All-Star break, but they had managed to lose ground to the Orioles during that time and were just not playing like the Yankees of 1976–77–78.

"Sauna?" suggested Nettles.

"Yeah, let's do it," said Munson. It meant getting undressed again, but it seemed like a decent idea under the circumstances.

The sauna in the Yankee clubhouse was off-limits to the press, which also made it attractive. The added time in the clubhouse, if the players chose to just sit by their lockers, would only be an invitation to the pesky newspaper guys, the day game giving them a rare opportunity to finish their stories in plenty of time, and then fish around for some Yankee gossip. Nope, didn't need that.

Already in the sauna were Dom Scala, the Yankees' bullpen catcher, and Fred Stanley, who had been the team's regular short-stop in 1976, but who had become a bench player with the coming of Dent. A good guy was Stanley, known as Chicken, mostly for his scrawny build and, well, "chicken legs."

In the sauna was a copy of the team's 1979 media guide, warped by humidity, lying on a bench with a photo of Goose Gossage jumping into the arms of Munson after the last out of the 1978 American League Championship Series. "The Great Comeback" it said on the cover. "World Champions 1978."

The funny thing about a world championship is that you win it on the last day of the season, and you raise the pennant on opening day of the following season, but by then—it's a new season, time to start all over again. The opportunity to strut through an airport in the company of your fellow world champions, feeling awfully good about yourself, doesn't last very long. If you win the Series at home, there isn't even the satisfaction of that last flight home together as a conquering team. You win, you celebrate, and by the time you are together again, there are roster changes, and the guys you went to war with are different. It's already time to prove yourselves all over again.

Munson glanced at the media guide and flipped it over to look at the upcoming schedule. Two night games in Milwaukee on Friday and Saturday, a Sunday day game, then down the road to Chicago for night games Monday, Tuesday, and Wednesday. As a catcher, he would look at the schedule, almost routinely, and translate each game into who was pitching. Ed Figueroa, hurting, wouldn't be able to take his turn in the rotation. That meant perhaps giving the veteran Jim Kaat a start, along with Tiant and Hunter in Milwaukee, with Tommy John and Guidry pitching the first two in Chicago. Losing Figgy was tough; he was a solid, dependable starter. Munson liked working with him.

"It's tough about Figgy," Thurman said to his three sauna partners. "It's a big hole to fill, maybe fifteen starts down the stretch. Hopefully he's not done for the season."

He realized he was thinking like a catcher as he pondered the rotation, but in reality, he had bigger things on his mind. It was the matter of his own future as a catcher. And he was having to face up to it.

The matter was the arthritic state of his beaten-down knees. It was even affecting his concentration behind the plate.

Figueroa would one day write his own book, *Yankee Stranger,* and in it he spoke of Thurman's troubles in 1979:

> Munson told me how much his knees and shoulder were paining him and confessed that he felt very depressed because of all the pain in his body. He said to me, "Figgy, I am crazy for killing myself. I feel like dying. I would like to die right here now."
>
> When I arrived in New York in 1976, Thurman helped make me a big league pitcher, showing me how to pitch to the batters and in what situation to throw a pitch. I always respected Munson as a person because he himself gave respect to all his teammates.
>
> I had been aware of how troubled he was. Even back in May, he was not himself behind the plate. He was not mixing up the pitches he was calling, but I did not want to throw off every sign.

Milwaukee, Friday, July 27

A late arrival in Milwaukee, not a favorite city for traveling ballplayers anyway, made for few happy players on the Yankees. The Pfister

Hotel, on Wisconsin and Jefferson, was stately and classic, but had a depressingly gloomy lobby and very old-fashioned rooms. The hotel had opened in 1893, and early on was considered too elegant for actors or ballplayers, who were usually relegated to lesser accommodations. But eventually it opened its doors to baseball teams. Those who visited to play the Milwaukee Braves, and later the Brewers, knew it well.

It was perhaps best known to baseball for the Yankees' lobby brawl in the closing days of the 1974 season.

The team checked in more politely this time. Only seven players—Tidrow, Chambliss, Nettles, Piniella, Murcer, White, and Munson—remained from that team.

Although the bus to County Stadium on this Friday, July 27, would depart the Pfister at five p.m., many players took taxis and headed to the park early. In towns that offered little of a downtown to walk through, it was common to get to the park early, hang with the guys, play cards, run on the warning track, take extra batting practice, or do whatever got you out of the hotel and the boredom of daytime TV.

This was going to be a big weekend for the Brewers, a team of coming stars who would go to the World Series in three years. Nearly 150,000 fans were expected for the three-game series with the Yankees. Despite their slumping campaign, the Yankees were always a big draw on the road. Many had bought tickets well in advance of this slump, and a summer weekend with the Bronx Bombers was a big event in town.

Munson got to the ballpark around 3:30. The clubhouse, old-fashioned, humid, and cramped, did not lend itself to sitting around. Besides, these guys were athletes, ballplayers; guys who liked being outdoors and feeling the competitive juices rise within them as the early activity on the field took form.

Groundskeepers went through their paces and early-arriving vendors sat and watched the lazy activities on the field as brats began to cook and kegs of beer began to move to the vending stands.

Thurman put on his underwear, his jock, and got his sanitary socks and navy blue stirrups on just right. He'd been going through this ritual since he was a kid. It was the routine, the daily chore that went with reporting to work. On the back of his sweatshirt, in capital block letters, was MUNSON with "15" below it, carefully printed in black felt marker by Pete Sheehy, the clubhouse attendant since 1927.

He pulled on his gray baseball pants and threw a windbreaker over his head, postponing his actual uniform top until after batting practice. Lacing his spiked shoes and heading through the tunnel, he emerged onto the turf and began to run toward left field. He wanted to get a general feel for how his legs were going to operate on this day.

To his pleasant surprise, it wasn't so bad.

He ran to the left field foul pole and stopped short. No real pain. He headed for center field, stopped, and turned. There was a sensation in his knees that wasn't right, but he thought he could play with it.

And so despite telling everyone he might be done catching for the year, he decided he might in fact be able to play this very night.

"Yogi, old man, I'm gonna catch tonight," he told his coach. Berra, a lifer at ballparks, was always there early too.

"If you think you can, then tell Billy early before he makes out the lineup," said the Yankee legend. "He should be here anytime."

Anytime, of course, really meant "anytime" when it came to Martin. It could even mean thirty minutes before the game. But Billy arrived with Elston Howard around five, and Thurman went into his office.

"Skip, I can catch tonight. Write me in there," said Munson.

Billy was surprised. Based on everything he'd heard and things Munson had said, it seemed that option was no longer in play.

"Really, I tested it, I did some running, some turning; I can do it. At least let me go and see how it plays out."

So Billy wrote out the lineup card and had "Munson, c," batting third. Figueroa, also among the walking wounded, would start and test his arm, and see what he had left.

"We're gonna be like two guys from the old soldiers' home out there," Thurman said to Figueroa. "I hope they have two stretchers ready in this place."

Before the game Thurman headed for the training room, where he saw Gene Monahan and said, "I'm gonna give it a shot tonight, Geno; give me a good rubdown."

"You got it, Thurman," said the Yankees' trainer. "I hope this is the start of a good turnaround for us! We need you back there!"

The game was to be an eventful one.

Cecil Cooper, the tall, thin Brewers slugger who had come up through the Red Sox system, homered in the first. When he came up in the last of the third, Figueroa threw one tight to him, but didn't hit him.

In the top of the fourth, with Reggie Jackson leading off, Mike Caldwell twice dusted the Yankee cleanup hitter and sent him sprawling.

"Uh-oh," said Phil Rizzuto on the radio.

Hitting a high foul pop-up toward his old Oakland teammate Sal Bando at third, Jackson flipped his bat in Caldwell's direction while headed for first. It was a provocative act; bats don't get flipped toward the pitcher's mound. And confrontation was already in the wind.

Jackson rounded first as the high pop settled into Bando's glove. Caldwell, incensed by the bat throwing, walked over, picked up the bat, and slammed it into the ground, breaking it. That was all Reggie needed on his way past Caldwell and back toward the dugout. He threw off his batting helmet, charged Caldwell, and grabbed him by the throat. They both hit the ground as teammates raced out, dugouts and bullpens emptying. Munson, wearing his shin guards and chest protector, joined in the scrum, which was quickly halted by the umpires. John Shulock, the home plate umpire, tossed Jackson from the game. Martin angrily fought with Shulock and the other umpires, insisting that Caldwell be ejected as well. He was in Shulock's face, finger pointing, but to no avail. As Martin left the field, the normally placid Brewers fans threw garbage at him and cursed at him.

This could have gotten uglier because Billy looked to the stands and thought for a moment about exchanging words with fans close to the dugout who were cursing him. Yankee players, who had returned to the dugout, now popped out again and looked over the roof to see what was going on. Milwaukee security officers hustled atop the dugout to keep the peace.

Martin informed Shulock that he was playing the game under protest, claiming that Caldwell should have automatically been ejected for throwing at Jackson. The public address announcer was instructed to inform the fans, which only elicited more howls. It is hard to get a Milwaukee audience riled up, but Martin had done it. Now this was a game in very hostile territory.

"Shulock let the game get out of hand," Martin told reporters afterward. "He should have thrown Caldwell out. When he ejected Jackson and not Caldwell, that's when I made the protest."

"The pitch slipped," said Caldwell after the game. "It looked like a good knockdown pitch. He sure thought it was."

Reggie said, "I asked him if he had thrown at me on purpose, and he denied that he had. He just said that the pitch had gotten away from him, that it slipped off his fingers. I thought it was a knockdown, and I felt I had to do what I did to preserve some respect. But I had no idea of trying to hurt anyone. Thank God no one got hurt. If someone gets hurt, whoever it is, I'm going to be the loser publicly because I'm Reggie Jackson."

"When the press came in later, I left," he added the next day. "Because anything I say gets blown out of proportion, it was better to take a little time to think about it. Last night would have been a big story if I had said anything, but I didn't want that. I think I made my point."

Some catchers return to home plate after such an episode and make light of it; maybe even make a joke of it with the umpire. To spend the rest of the game looking for close calls from the man a foot behind you could make for a very high-tension evening, to be sure. But Munson wasn't like that. He began jabbering at Shulock, defending Martin, even saying, "This is one protest the league is going to accept, and you're gonna look bad."

But of course, that wasn't going to be the case; the league allows a protest maybe once every thirty years. No matter how obvious an infraction may be, the logistics of doing so were more than it could ever be worth, and only on the rarest of occasions would a protest ever result in a game being replayed.

Munson knew that; he knew the politics of the game. But he also wasn't about to give ground to Shulock.

In the seventh, with Ron Davis on the mound, Cooper homered again to give the Brewers a 5–3 lead, but then Willie Randolph hit a two-run homer in the eighth, driving in Rivers ahead of him, to tie it up at 5–5. Willie hit only five home runs all season; this was a big one. Munson liked Randolph a lot and certainly knew this was a key blow, a "money homer." As the next hitter, he greeted him at home plate with a big smile and a firm handshake. Then he grounded out to first.

It had been a tough day at bat for Thurm. He hadn't gotten the ball out of the infield. A grounder to second in the first; a 6–4–3 double play in the third, another groundout to short in the sixth, and now this groundout to first in the eighth. Not a Munson kind of ball game.

Thurman donned his shin guards and his chest protector and flipped his mask over his face as he headed behind the plate for the ninth. Gossage had come into the game an inning earlier. This had been an unusual game for Thurman, not only at bat, but even behind the plate. No strikeouts, no putouts. Figueroa, Davis, and Gossage hadn't managed to strike out a single Brewers hitter.

Paul Molitor led off by grounding out to Jim Spencer at first, Spencer making the play unassisted. Don Money (born the same day as Thurman, thirty-two years before) flied out to Rivers in center, Mickey making that patented snap catch of his, flipping his elbows as he threw the ball back to the infield. Two down.

Cooper came up. He of the two home runs, one off Figgy, one off Davis. Thurman settled behind the plate and called for an inside fastball. It went over the black for strike one.

The next pitch was also inside, but missed the plate, and it was 1 and 1.

The third pitch was fouled off.

Munson crouched down and gave a signal for another inside fastball. This was, by that earlier rough math, maybe the 200,000th squat behind the batter over his ten seasons in the majors. And he felt every one of them as he grinded this one out.

Gossage pitched and Cooper connected.

"Ah, shit," said Gossage as the ball took off.

"Shit!" said Munson out loud, wishing he could have that one back.

"I was just trying to meet the ball and drive it somewhere," Cooper would say after the game. "I didn't think it would go out."

It did. It was a 6–5 Brewer win, a three-homer game for Cooper. Munson walked toward the dugout, pained, tired, and beaten.

While the fans outside cheered Cooper, who came back out for a curtain call, Munson flipped his mask into his locker, lifted his chest protector over his head, and sat down to unbuckle his shin guards. The tools of ignorance, they had once been called in baseball, a nickname long forgotten by this generation of players.

The mask was in its first year. His previous mask had been tossed aside and lost after he caught the final out of the 1978 World Series.

Now his equipment lay in his locker, the clubhouse silent after the sudden defeat.

He would not wear the catching gear again.

Milwaukee, Saturday, July 28

The Yankees played a Saturday night game at Milwaukee on July 28—a "date night" idea, which few teams embraced. Saturdays were for day games, even when it seemed that it was a nice thing to do, to give couples an option of a night at the ballpark.

Billy gave Thurman the night off, but during batting practice Munson borrowed a first baseman's glove and did some time at first base. Four years earlier Munson had played two complete games at the position, one in Anaheim and another at Shea Stadium, handling twenty chances without an error. He was an athlete, a former shortstop, and he took to it well, playing the position as though it represented a day off, to relax a bit. Of course Munson was too competitive to really relax, and he was aware that his concentration was not the same as when he was behind the plate.

His presence at first during BP led to speculation that he would indeed be back there one of these days, to give his knees a rest while keeping his bat in the lineup. But the bat—oh boy—he'd only gone 11 for his last 52, a .212 showing, and ten of the eleven hits were singles.

He watched the Saturday night game partly from the bullpen, enjoying the playful horsing around that goes with the early innings in the pen, and then moved to the dugout later in the game in case he was needed to pinch-hit. He wasn't, and the Yanks lost 9–2 before 52,000 people, as they fell thirteen games behind the Orioles.

Milwaukee, Sunday, July 29

On Sunday, Thurman played first base.

He went 1 for 4 with a triple in the ninth, Jackson driving him home, but the Yankees lost again, this time 5–3, to fall fourteen back. It had been a wonderful weekend for the Brewers, sweeping the Yankees before three packed houses, and as though to put an exclamation mark on it all, Jim Gantner and Lou Piniella got into a fight in the sixth inning over a tag play at third, with Gantner ejected to the supportive cheers of the Millered-up fans. Third base coach Mike Ferraro had tried to step between the two after the hard slide, but wound up being taken down with Piniella by the charged-up Gantner. When Piniella went to left field, he was pelted with baseballs and play had to be stopped while the PA announcer asked for calm.

"It was a good play for [Piniella]," said Gantner. "I would have done the same thing."

Piniella, always calm in the clubhouse after the most fiery displays on the field, said, "I made a bad play going to third; I was just trying to make up for it."

Lou had to deal with the teasing of his own teammates all weekend as well. There in center field for the Brewers was "Jim Fucking Wohlford," the journeyman outfielder who had long been the butt of Yankee humor at Piniella's expense. The onetime "successor" to Lou in the Kansas City outfield had already been sent away by the Royals.

At first base, Munson had eight putouts, no assists, and no errors, keeping alive his career 1.000 fielding percentage at first. His game there was otherwise uneventful; he seemed comfortable and didn't screw anything up.

But it had been a miserable weekend. Now it was on to Chicago. But first there would be a side trip.

After the game, Thurman and his father-in-law, Tote, flew home

to Canton to celebrate Michael's fourth birthday. If there was a perfect example of why the plane meant so much to Thurman, this was
it. The ability to fly home to be with the family on a special occasion, and then still be able to be easily in Chicago the next night,
made it all feel worthwhile.

14

Bobby Murcer had been traded back to the Yankees on June 26 in exchange for a minor leaguer and cash. He was in his third season with the Cubs following two with the Giants, and it had never felt right—not to Bobby, and not to Yankee fans.

So his return to the Yankees was a joyous moment, even if it signaled the end of his days as a regular, star player.

He was, from this point forward, though only thirty-three, an elder statesman on the team, the senior player in terms of having gone back with the organization the farthest, never mind the forced separation.

That Munson and Murcer should have a warm friendship was not surprising. They had a lot in common. They were both the local star athlete who married the prettiest girl in town. They had both been schoolboy shortstop. They were both anointed as "the promise of tomorrow" after joining the Yankees. They were admired by fans. They should have been teammates forever.

Back on October 21, 1974, I was sitting in Gabe Paul's office in the Parks Administration Building across the street from Shea. He had called me into his corner office, once occupied by Robert Moses during the days of the 1964–65 World's Fair. With no advance warning to me, he called Pearl Davis, his secretary, and said, "Pearl, get me Bobby Murcer in Oklahoma."

I sat on the couch facing Gabe's desk and heard only his side of the conversation.

"Bobby? Good morning, Gabe Paul.

"What's that? Well, remember what they say, Bobby: Only whores make money in bed."

Gabe loved to use that line; he also loved calling people in the earlier time zones when he knew they would be sleeping.

"Well, I have some good news for you this morning, Bobby," he said. "At least I think you'll come to realize it's good news . . . We've traded you to the San Francisco Giants."

As I said, I couldn't hear Bobby's reaction, but it was easy to tell he was shocked. He had not that long before been told by Steinbrenner that he was the franchise player, the guy who could count on being there for life.

Gabe had been making calls like this since the 1940s. He covered the speaker part of the phone and whispered to me, "What's his wife's name?"

I answered, and he continued, "Bobby, I think you and Kay will love San Francisco. It's a great city. Lots of great restaurants."

I sensed there was silence and astonishment on Bobby's end. Then he asked a question.

"What's that?" said Gabe. "Oh, yes, Bobby Bonds."

It was a last question; he wanted to know whom he had been traded for.

After Gabe hung up, I sighed to him, "He's a good guy, I'll miss him."

And that of course was just another straight line for Gabe, who said, "Marty, I'll take you to church any Sunday you want and introduce you to twenty-five of the nicest guys you'll ever want to meet. But they're not going to win us any pennants."

Murcer and Munson had become friends from the day Munson joined the team. Now, with Murcer's return at the end of June 1979, the M&M Boys were back. To me as a PR guy, it was a wonderful story. While not Mantle and Maris, they were top-shelf players. On the 1974 *Yankee Yearbook,* I had an artist sketch the two of them, larger than life, forearms bulging, ready to take on the world.

Bobby and Thurman were friends the way ballplayers were friends—teammates first, friends second. They genuinely liked each other and there was no jealousy there. They ate together, shared taxis together, played catch together, played cards together. Did they pick up the phone during the winter to keep in touch? Not really. That wasn't the way it was with players. You called if you had something important to discuss, like "Can you play in my celebrity golf tournament?" but you didn't call to see how the kids' flu was coming or to wish a happy birthday.

The wives did that sometimes. Diana and Kay would call each other, and then they might put the husbands on if they were standing nearby. It was just more of a wives' thing to do.

Thurman was disappointed when Bobby was traded, but part of him knew that Bonds was a helluva player and that Steinbrenner was indeed serious about going all out to win. He didn't criticize the trade, but he did call Bobby to say how badly he felt for him. But Munson wasn't the type of guy who would miss his pal in the sense of having your best friend in fifth grade move to another state. They'd follow each other in the box scores and know how each was faring, and that counted as still being close.

And so Murcer was thrilled to be back with the Yankees but sad to have missed out on the pennants of 1976–77–78 and the glory that went with them. He was now one of the all-time favorite Yankees who had never played in the postseason. And here it was, 1979, and the team was struggling. Yes, it seemed like old times.

Murcer still had his apartment in Chicago, a small townhouse condo near Arlington Race Track, and after the Yankees left Milwaukee on Sunday, July 29, that would be his destination. He invited Munson and Lou Piniella to stay with him and Kay, rather than at the Continental Plaza on Michigan Avenue with the team. It would be three old pals together again, the Murcers playing host. It was a great break to the routine of hotels.

With the Murcer children away, Thurman took Tori's room and Lou took Todd's. On the first morning, Kay arose early to make a wonderful breakfast, with ham, eggs, biscuits, gravy—the works. And the houseguests seemed to enjoy it all.

"Thurman must have been too embarrassed to say anything other than thanks," Diana told Kay later on. "He never ate a traditional breakfast—not ever. Breakfast for him would be something like Oreos and milk."

Kay would always think of this teddy bear of a man in this way: caring of someone else's feelings, pushing down Oreos and milk for breakfast if left to his own devices.

Murcer, no stranger by now to baseball's fates and fortunes, knew that his happy return to the Yankees might in fact be short-lived. It was clear almost from the start that he wasn't brought in to be a big contributor in the middle of the lineup as he had been in the old days. He was in fact put on a roster in upheaval, Steinbrenner being convinced that the team was going to underachieve for the season, and thus that heads needed to roll.

"Yankee Purge Begins" headlined the *New York Post* the day after Mick the Quick Rivers, ol' Gozzlehead, was shipped off to Texas. He was informed of the deal by Cedric Tallis, the Yankees' general manager, around 3:30 in the afternoon, left immediately for Texas, and got there in time to pinch-hit that night in a loss to Detroit. This was most unusual for Rivers, who could take as long as five days to get from Miami to Fort Lauderdale for spring training.

He went off for three players and one to be named later. That was believed by all to be Mike Heath, a Steinbrenner favorite, who had been traded by the Yankees to Texas over the winter with Sparky Lyle (the Yankees getting Dave Righetti), and then dealt by Texas to Oakland for two players. It was "understood" that he would be going back to Texas at the end of the season, but now it was also "understood" that he would in fact be going back to the Yankees.

This seemed necessitated by the fact that as a right-handed hitting catcher, Heath could be the player to move behind the plate in place of Munson, whose days as a catcher may have run their course.

"Munson's days as the team's regular catcher are over," wrote Larry Brooks in the *Post*.

"People in the stands didn't know how that man was playing in pain," said Guidry. "He was taped ankle to neck, like a walking cast. He was always in pain—knees, thighs . . ."

So much more was in play. Would Munson move to first? What of Chris Chambliss and Jim Spencer, lately the first base platoon, both seasoned and proven major leaguers?

Well, guess what. As had become a pattern with Yankee deals, which had been regularly failing inspection by baseball commissioner Bowie Kuhn, this one wasn't going to be a smooth one either. Kuhn didn't like the structure of Rivers for four minor leaguers and wanted someone else in the deal. It looked like it might be Rivers's old pal Oscar Gamble, a Billy Martin favorite.

Young Bobby Brown was being called up from Columbus to replace Rivers in center. If Gamble were sent to the Yankees, it would crowd the outfield, with Jackson to remain in right, and with Piniella in the mix. Gamble would surely threaten to take Murcer's precarious spot on the roster, just a month after he arrived.

So there they were, Munson, Murcer, and Piniella, all tucked into Bobby's apartment, left to figure out the roster, or to watch TV and drink beer and call it a night.

As was often the case with Piniella, the subject turned to hitting, and he had an opinion on almost everyone in the White Sox lineup, which, even after midnight, he decided was a good thing to discuss.

Piniella was always like that. A few years earlier, I had the room next to his at the Fort Lauderdale Inn during spring training. One night—after midnight—he and Catfish Hunter returned from a night out, and both had obviously had a few beers. The walls in the hotel were thin, and their arrival woke me up. It was clear that they were resuming their conversation from the drive home—an analysis of every hitter in the league. Piniella, although a right fielder, thought he knew more about it than Hunter, a future Hall of Fame pitcher. And so team by team, batter by batter, the two began arguing about whether you throw a breaking pitch or a fastball away with the count 0–2 to Wayne Nordhagen, and I knew it was going to be a long night. Lou could outtalk Hunter, but Hunter was the wise one, and as I settled in for the night's analysis, I somehow favored Cat's opinions more. But Lou had an opinion on everyone, even from out in right field. I guess this served him well when he became a highly successful manager.

So Murcer and Piniella argued the hitters and Munson, the catcher who should have been right in the thick of it, said, "I'm going to sleep."

As for whether Murcer would remain a Yankee with the latest roster reconfiguration, well, as Rivers once famously put it, "Ain't no use worrying about things you got control over 'cause you got control over 'em. Ain't no use in worrying about things you don't have control over 'cause you don't have control over 'em."

In this case, control fell to Bowie Kuhn. Going back to his veto of the Yankees' signing of Andy Messersmith as a free agent during spring training of 1976, the Yankees had often come under disagreeable scrutiny. But in this case, if they wound up with Gamble, it would be okay with Martin.

Piniella, Munson, and Murcer arrived at Comiskey Park around 2:30, right around the time that the team bus showed up. Miserable old Comiskey Park, where the Black Sox had thrown a World Series and where the White Sox had unintentionally dropped one in 1959, had a steamy old clubhouse down the right field side of the stadium. Piniella, who was one of the last Yankee players who smoked cigarettes, sometimes held back in the clubhouse for just that purpose. Murcer and Munson joined the other players who liked to get out to the field early.

The new face in the clubhouse that evening belonged to yet another outfielder, Juan Beniquez, who hadn't played since July 7, when he went on the disabled list. With Rivers gone, Beniquez was activated and placed in the second spot in the batting order. Munson would play first base and bat third, as the Yankees tried to snap their three-game losing streak.

Rich Wortham would oppose the Yanks' Tommy John that evening in a battle of left-handers. John had pitched for the White Sox from 1965 to 1971 and still had a good following in Chicago.

The Yankees did get a victory out of the evening, played under very humid conditions, but not without a cost. Beniquez, of all people, fell between second and third in the ninth inning and had to be carried off on a stretcher and sent back to New York. It was a pulled groin muscle, and he wouldn't be seen again until September. One game and out. And on the day Rivers was traded.

"I couldn't believe it," said Martin.

Murcer would now have to play center.

As for the game, the Yanks broke a 1–1 tie in the fifth when Willie

Randolph singled, went to second on a groundout by Beniquez, and scored on a single by Munson off Wortham.

It was career hit number 1,558 for Munson, and RBI number 701.

John, with his sinker working well, pitched into the seventh and gave up plenty of ground balls, with Munson recording thirteen of the team's twenty-seven putouts at first without a miscue. Ron Davis finished as the Yanks won 7–2 to stay fourteen games behind Baltimore.

Piniella, Munson, and Murcer returned to the Murcer apartment after the game, with the rest of the team going back to the Continental Plaza.

Chicago, Tuesday, July 31

On Tuesday, the second game of the series, the routine continued; Murcer drove his buddies to Comiskey; the team bus arrived around the same time. The injury report was going deeper in what was shaping up as a lost season. Figueroa, slated to pitch on Wednesday, told Martin he would warm up, but with bone chips in his right elbow already diagnosed, it was possible he might be done for the year. It would be another challenging week for Martin.

Wrote Figueroa, "In Chicago that night I told Munson that I was going to California the next day to see Dr. Frank Jobe, and as Munson had his plane in Chicago, I asked him jokingly if he could fly me to California. He answered that if it were not so far, he would take me.

"After, he told me, 'Figgy, we are two beauties. We can't do nothing to help the club win.' "

One wonders if his old line to Brian Doyle about complaining players—"So retire!"—ever entered his mind.

Having DH'd the night before, and with the team having won two in a row, Munson was as rested and as happy as it was possible for him to be, given his physical condition and the season looking like

a lost cause. Sensing this might be a rare opportunity to grab an interview with the team captain, broadcaster Frank Messer took a shot
at doing his pregame show with Thurman before the final game of
the series.

It was about 3:30 in the afternoon when Messer, tape recorder in
hand, ambled up to Munson and asked if he'd mind.

Everybody liked Frank Messer, a genuinely good guy, a guy who
liked to play cards with the players, a guy with a perpetual good attitude, day in, day out. He was also a terrific broadcaster, nestled between the playful Rizzuto and the skeptical Bill White, keeping the
flow of the game, dutifully reading the team promos, maintaining a
high level of professionalism. This was his twelfth season with the
team, and fans were comfortable and entertained by the Rizzuto-
Messer-White years. They complemented one another well and respected one another.

Messer was prepared for Munson to say no, which Thurman
would have done politely, since he was among those who liked Frank
a lot. And Messer knew Thurman didn't particularly like doing interviews, even though one normally assumed that a team captain
would do a lot of them. But he knew Thurman had things on his
mind and that he trusted broadcast media more than print, and that
Frank wouldn't do him wrong.

Munson ended up agreeing to the interview, so twenty-four hours
before he would unknowingly play his final major league baseball
game, he spoke with Messer. He tended to ramble on a bit in discussing
his future and his health, he spoke rapidly, and there was a discom-
forting air of uncertainty in his responses. Still, the pride of his accomplishments came through, and he did make it clear that he wanted
to remain a Yankee, if indeed he continued to play after 1979.

MESSER: Good evening, everybody, this is Frank
Messer on the New York Yankees pregame show sponsored

tonight by Abraham and Strauss. Game number two between the Yankees and the Chicago White Sox. My guest on the Yankee pregame show is Thurman Munson. We'll be back to talk baseball with Thurman in just one minute.

MESSER: Thurman Munson, the question being asked by Yankee fans everywhere these days is: What about the future of Thurman Munson; the report that the knees are bad; you're not able to catch anymore; just what is this story? Thurman?

MUNSON: Well, Frank, my knees are bad and I saw a doctor last week. They've both been X-rayed and he said that I am not gonna catch for a while, and how long that exactly is I don't know. I've got a lot of pain there and I probably won't be catching for quite a while. And if it'll clear up, I'll go back but if they don't and they're right, maybe I won't catch. [Short laugh] I don't know.

MESSER: Is it possible your career as a catcher could be over?

MUNSON: Well, anything is possible, Frank. I won't be that dramatic. I'm talking about what the Yankees are gonna have to do. I think my knees have some stress on them. It has some problems. And I think what the Yankees have to do to make up their minds. I want them for me to work me around for another two or three years. And I think that's one decision that they would have to make. As far as right now, Thurman Munson is not gonna catch for a while and . . . that's coming from me and not from the Yankees' office. And you know, they're bad and—and when they hurt like they do, I just can't do that much. I had the problem most of the year and I went ahead and played with it and I don't wanna hurt myself and the ball club, and I just decided not to play.

MESSER: What about Thurman Munson? Does he want to be around for another year or two or three more years?

MUNSON: If I go and play, so that I might retire from baseball but I wanted to go to Cleveland or somewhere else, that's not true anymore. And whether my last year is not this year, as long as my career lasts, I wanna play with the Yankees. And I wanna play as long as I am physically capable of going out there and having people remember me the way that I once was. And I don't mean maybe having good statistics that I used to have and this and that . . . remember me stretching the singles into doubles and taking extra bases, going first to home and all that kind of stuff, and if I can't do that then I'm not gonna play.

MESSER: Thurman Munson, the last few games, you've been playing at first base. Tonight, you're penciled in as the designated hitter, so Billy Martin obviously wants to keep your bat in the lineup.

MUNSON: Well, I told Billy before that when I'm catching six or seven days a week as I had been I can't hit. One thing about hitting or pitching, if your legs do go, you're in more trouble. I've got a lot of trouble, I've got a lot of problems, I couldn't make a decent turn at the plate. It cuts my power down and all of a sudden, you started cheatin' to do things, then you're not good together. So I told them if I did get out and play another position that I would be a much better player and a much better hitter like I was once. I think it proves that if I took four or five days off in a row, I wouldn't play first base in Milwaukee and I hit these three balls right to the fence, and one of which would have been a home run if it hadn't been for the wind blowing in and I hit a couple of balls really well so I'm convinced in my own mind, and, and I think the Yankees are too, that if I catch and I'm just gonna get back into the recession that I've had, because physically, I can't do it.

MESSER: My guest, Thurman Munson, will be back in one minute.

MESSER: Thurman, let's talk about another position for you. If there is to be another position, what would it be? Where would you like to play?

MUNSON: Well, I think if there's gonna be, I think the outfield would be worth playing. I haven't played infield since I was in college. And everybody says, he's a good athlete, he can learn to do things but it's a lot easier said than done. I think that if I could go to the outfield, at least learn to be an average outfielder and run, keep my legs in shape and do the things that I'd like to do without hurting. And there's a lot of pressure at infield; you better know your position pretty well and I'm sure you couldn't take an infielder and make a catcher out of him. Just like it's hard to take a catcher to make an infielder. And I think physically, I can do it, but mentally, I don't know. It's kinda tough, it's just something that—that happens after thirty years, you kinda wanna be left alone, you don't want somebody else's problems either.

MESSER: Now, all right Thurman, if you would go to the outfield, which outfield position do you think would best suit you?

MUNSON: Well, either left or right, to me it really doesn't matter. Left field's kinda tough at Yankee Stadium because of the fence. But the fence isn't as bad as it once was and anyway, it doesn't matter really to me. The only thing that I'm concerned about is to go out and get enough work to be able to play the outfield respectable and in order to do that, they have to let you play every day out there.

MESSER: Do you feel you have the arm it takes to play the outfield?

MUNSON: I don't know how much of an arm it takes, I don't know how many assists there are a year in the outfield. I sit back to catch. I don't know how many people get assists as an outfielder. How many would it take is a pretty reaction that what it takes for wanting to do things. If you wanna stop a guy from going first to third, you charge the ball, not worrying too much about making a mistake, and let's face it: you field the ball and you come throwing to the infield and people just gonna know, even last year I wanna play ball, I played eight to ten games. I can't remember anybody doing first to third on me. I take charge and I get the ball quick out as I did and you don't have to have a strong arm to intimidate people.

MESSER: Final thought from Thurman Munson after this.

MESSER: Well, Thurman, we talked about every aspect of it. The fact that if the knees may not let you catch anymore, that the future will decide that. What about hitting? You think you would still be in the major leagues for another two or three years as long as you want to play?

MUNSON: Well, it's not even a question, Frank. I'm just thinking that it really depends on the legs, it depends on turns, it depends on having enough power to push off to go into the ball, to do the things that you wanna do. You know, hitting so much now, people don't realize you have something physically wrong with you. All of a sudden, you start trying some other things, you start trying to get your hands out, and you get started having problems. I know that if my legs feel good, and probably because I've hopefully been a little smarter around, or a little better.

MESSER: Thurman, in retrospect, do you wish now you had not caught as many games a year as you had?

MUNSON: Well, Frank, I been asked that before and maybe I could have caught three or four more years if I'd caught a hundred games a year but I tell you, you know I'm a pretty proud guy, I'm pretty proud of the fact that as a catcher I always averaged 140 games a year for the ten years. I've been a damn good player doing so; not too many catchers have ever done it. I think I got more games. I got more hits in ten years than any catcher in the history of the game, and I can't say that I'd, there are not too many guys who'd had the chance to get the awards that I received and to win championships like we had. And I don't regret it at all because one thing anybody can say about me is that I like to win and I think that constitutes of playing every day.

MESSER: Thurman Munson, wherever you play, I hope it is every day. The outfield, first base, designated hitter, the Yankee lineup card just would not be the same without Thurman Munson's name in it.

MUNSON: Thanks, Frank. I hope so too.

MESSER: The pregame show has been sponsored by Abraham and Strauss, I'm Frank Messer and stay tuned for New York Yankee baseball.

Munson that night would DH against Randy Scarbery, the White Sox starter, who was 1–5 going in. Murcer would be in center, Jerry Narron behind the plate, and Jim Spencer at first. The Spencer move was a good one: he hit a three-run homer in the sixth off Scarbery to lead the Yanks to a 7–3 win, giving Guidry a win and Gossage a save. Neither had been pitching well of late; the win made Guidry only 9–7 a year after his 25–3 season, and Gossage's save was only his sixth after 27 the year before.

It wasn't a good game for the aching Munson. He went 0–5, with four groundouts and a fly to left.

It wasn't a good day for the White Sox player-manager Don Kessinger, either. Kessinger, the last player-manager the American League would see (Pete Rose would hold both jobs in the NL from 1984 to 1986), would be out of a job by week's end, with Tony LaRussa taking over on August 3 to begin an illustrious managerial career of his own.

Back at Murcer's apartment, Bobby, Lou, and Thurman were talking baseball, drinking scotch, talking flying.

Back in Canton, Diana watched *A Star Is Born* with Barbra Streisand and Kris Kristofferson on TV and cried at the end when Kristofferson's character, John Norman Howard, dies.

She called Thurman after the movie and told him she was scared of his flying. He reassured her that she was his best friend and he was privileged to share his life with her.

"I love you very much," Murcer and Piniella heard him say.

Piniella would tell Maury Allen for his book *Sweet Lou,* "He didn't need it, but you couldn't argue with him about anything.

"That night, it was baseball, friendship, and our happiness to have Bobby back. It was very sentimental; Bobby was almost in tears.

"Then Bobby started saying to Munson, 'What do you need that for?' Thurman brushed it off. 'I'm comfortable, I'm confident,' he said."

Chicago, Wednesday, August 1

August began with a night game in Chicago to wrap up the series, a game televised back in New York on WPIX.

Piniella recalls, "After breakfast, Bobby drove us out to the airport. [Thurman] talked about the plane the whole time. We drove to the hangar area. We got into the plane. It looked like a rocket, long and sleek. We sat for a few minutes, and finally Bobby and I looked at each other. We shook our heads. 'Let's do it some other time,' Bobby said. I unbuckled my seat belt, Thurman let the ladder down, and we got out.

" 'Ahh, hell,' he said. 'There's no need to worry.' "

In the afternoon, Commissioner Kuhn finally approved the deal that sent Oscar Gamble to the Yankees, but Gamble would not join the team until Friday in New York.

Don Hood, who was 3–0, pitched seven strong innings for the Yanks, with Jim Kaat hurling the final two in an easy 9–1 Yankee win. Hood had been told he was starting only eight minutes before game time, when Luis Tiant complained of a stiff arm. Tiant was moved up to start Friday night in New York. The Yanks benefited from three homers, Reggie Jackson's nineteenth, Lou Piniella's tenth (both in the first inning), and Jerry Narron's second. Narron caught and hit eighth. Thurman was at first base and hit third. It was the 1,423rd regular-season game of his career.

In the first inning, batting against left-hander Ken Kravec, Munson walked and scored on the Jackson homer. In the third, again facing Kravec, he struck out. In so doing, he strained his right knee, exchanged a nod with Billy Martin, and left the game, replaced by Spencer at first. He had made two putouts at first before departing.

When a Chicago reporter approached him afterward to ask about why he had left the game early, he cursed at him and sent him on his way. A normal day for Thurman and the press.

After the game, with most of the team preparing to fly back to Newark Airport, the Murcers drove Thurman to Palwaukee Airport north of Chicago, where his new Cessna was waiting. Piniella watched Munson throw a suit bag over his shoulder, tip the clubhouse man, and walk out the door. "Take it easy, Thurman," Piniella said. Munson didn't hear him.

Thurman invited the Murcers to look into the cockpit, and they wound up sitting inside for about twenty minutes, listening to Thurman describe the features of the plane. Thurm borrowed some money from Bobby for fuel.

"Thurman had been after Lou and me to fly from Chicago to Canton with him after the game," Murcer told Bill Madden for his book *Pride of October*. "I told him I couldn't do that. I'd heard from Reggie and Nettles—who had both flown with him—about his plane and I just didn't want to do it."

The Murcers got out of the plane and Thurman asked them to go to the end of the runway and watch him take off.

"So we positioned ourselves at the end of the runway in our car in this tiny airport, and then he took off and I'm watching this big old powerful jet go roaring over our heads and I thought to myself, 'I cannot believe Thurman is up there all by himself in that powerful machine, flying that crazy plane.'"

In a little more than an hour, he landed at Akron-Canton Airport in the middle of the night. He got home around three a.m., and then was up at seven to greet the kids. He hadn't had much sleep, but he was where he wanted to be.

15

Cessna Citation cockpit. PHOTO COURTESY CESSNA AIRCRAFT COMPANY

It was eight and a half miles from Thurman's home to Akron-Canton Airport. The drive took about fifteen minutes, with Everhard Road merging onto I-77, and then exit 113 taking you into the midsized airport at Lauby Road.

But first he stopped to see his father-in-law, Tote Dominick, at Prestwick Country Club. The club made for a really pleasant setting on a summer morning, except for running into a member of the media, Gene Dillon, a WHBC radio sportscaster, whom he told that his knees were "fine." Thurman could even blow off the hometown press when he wanted to.

Tote told Dillon how excited Thurman was about his new plane and what a great family man he was.

As difficult as Thurman's relationship had been with his own father, that was how easy it had been with Tote. Tote had, like Diana, known Thurman since he was a boy, but now they were adults, friends even. And of course he was in many ways the father that Thurman never had.

Thurman drove to the airport in his Mercedes 450, the one he had gotten from Nat Tarnopol in New York. He was no doubt feeling prosperous with all the trappings: cigar in his mouth, sitting in the 450 Benz, on his way to see his new jet, real estate holdings, second-highest-paid player on the New York Yankees, terrific family . . . life was good! John Denver (who would die piloting a small plane in 1997) was singing away on his tape player as he pulled into the airport shortly before three. It was a beautiful seventy-six-degree day. He was not planning to fly at all that day, and in fact had a four o'clock meeting with Diana downtown to hear about plans to name a road in his honor. So his stay at the airport would be brief. He just wanted to check out a few things. He didn't even lock his car. He just wanted to look at his possession one more time.

Naming a road in his honor was not the sort of thing that would have made Thurman rush to be on time. While generally reliable when it came to keeping a schedule—players, after all, are never late for a game—the whole idea of a road in his honor would have embarrassed Thurman.

Celebrity just didn't fit him well. His friendship with Jerry Anderson, whom he called "Munchkin," had nothing to do with celebrity. He was a guy his own age that he met at the YMCA and teamed up with to play handball. Just five feet seven and 155 pounds, Anderson was physically more diminutive than Munson, but he had a pilot's license and growing skills in real estate, two areas that Thurman found interesting. Anderson himself was no great baseball fan, and didn't seem to be swept away by Thurman's fame, as Nat Tarnopol and others had been.

There would be no free Mercedes from Anderson. Even free real estate advice used to elicit a joking comment from Jerry about money owed for his time.

Celebrity is about being in the right milieu anyway. A soap star is only a celebrity to those who watch the show. Otherwise, meeting someone who is on *Days of Our Lives* would hardly cause a non-watcher to break into a sweat. Baseball players feel the trappings of hero worship in their daily lives, but they also meet a lot of people who are unimpressed. Anderson liked Munson for reasons other than his Yankee career.

"What a competitor he was at handball," he remembers. "If the score was 20–20, you knew Thurman would not lose that twenty-first point. Impossible. He won every time.

"His interest in real estate was always very appealing to me. We spent hours talking about 'where the market was going' and which parcels would be in the path of progress. My visits to the Yankee locker room were full of conversations about real estate investing and how to earn a living once his playing days were gone. We seldom talked baseball. Our topics were always (1) real estate and how we would set up partnerships with his contacts, (2) airplanes, and (3) our next handball tournament. Some of the most pleasant days were spent flying over vacant land looking at growth patterns of roads and development. Most of that was done in his Duke or King Air around Canton and its suburbs. As a pilot it was easy for one of us to fly and the other to take notes and make sketches of what one day might be below us."

At the airport, Thurman bumped into Anderson, and into David

Hall, a flight instructor of Anderson's whom Thurman knew, but who was not otherwise a close friend. Hall, thirty-two, was Munson's age; Anderson, a year younger.

Anderson, Hall, and Munson walked around the jet, stroking it, patting it, enjoying it as grown men enjoy their new toys. There was the N15NY painted on the tail, a curious selection for a guy who was always talking about getting traded to Cleveland. They peered inside, and perhaps the glance at the control panel reminded Thurman that he had wanted to test a few things, perhaps a check to see if things on the panel were working properly. He had had that curiously difficult flight with Jackson and Nettles a few weeks earlier, and then the flash of flame on the flight with Diane and Billy Martin.

So rather spontaneously, Thurman just said, "Let's take it up." And Hall and Anderson nodded at each other with a "Sure, let's do it" look. It was unplanned, and seemingly forgotten was the four o'clock meeting.

Dave Hall took the copilot seat and Jerry Anderson sat behind him, facing the rear of the plane but keeping his lap belt loose enough so that he could easily turn around to observe. Hall had been Anderson's instructor, and the priority that gave him the front seat went unspoken. And Anderson had, to that point, never been up in a private jet, despite many hours of experience in single-engine aircraft.

Thurman also put on his lap belt, but not the shoulder harness, which was affixed to the wall. At that point, Thurman had logged 516 hours of flying time, thirty-three of them in the new Citation.

Thurman gave no emergency instructions to his passengers, even though this was their first time in the plane and Anderson's first time in any private jet. Although the men were friends, it is accepted practice to run through the safety procedures, even when the passengers are seasoned travelers. Without flight attendants aboard, it falls to the pilot to handle it.

Still, Hall and Anderson asked some questions as they looked around. They wanted to know what certain gauges meant on the control panel. They checked to see where and how the handle locked the entrance door, and to see where the emergency door was and that it worked.

The interior of the plane was beautiful. Thurman had selected "Yankee blue" as the interior color, and coupled with the designation of N15NY on the tail, it was hard to believe that he was serious about wanting to be traded to Cleveland anymore. If anything, the plane told the truth about that. The passengers spoke aloud of how taken they were by the beauty of the interior and the plush leather seats.

"Thurman was in a great mood that day," Anderson told ESPN nearly a quarter of a century later. "He was having a good day. He was in Canton. He didn't have to rush off to Yankee Stadium that night. He got to spend the night in town. He made a call to the tower and taxied out carefully. And on our way, I think he had his head on square that day."

There was enough fuel in the tanks, about nine hundred pounds, to travel perhaps eight hundred miles without refueling.

There was not a lot of activity going on in the control tower. N15NY was in fact the only plane in activity mode, as George Ackley, the air traffic controller in the tower, looked down.

"Know who's flying that N15NY?" asked another controller at his side.

Ackley didn't know.

"It's Thurman Munson," he said.

"Thurman has a Citation? When did he get that?"

"Just last month."

Ackley was unaware that Thurman was already on his third plane, and had no idea he had moved up to a jet.

"Let's do a few touch-and-goes," Thurman said to his passengers. Up to that moment, they had no idea what his flight intentions were.

Now it was clear that he was going to stay within range of the airport, just taking off and landing, then taking off again without stopping, a series of drills that could show off the plane's power and give everyone a feel for the aircraft, while Thurman checked whatever it was with the control panel that was giving him pause.

Cleared for takeoff, Thurman took the Citation down runway two-three at 3:41 p.m. and lifted the plane uneventfully into a left traffic pattern, the kind favored by pilots and airports because, with the pilot seated on the left, left turns provide greater visibility and feel more natural. A right turn requires a bit more strain to achieve desired visibility.

The Citation achieved an airspeed of about 200 knots and then slowed to below the "gear-down" limit of 174. The plane's altitude was about 1,300 feet as it headed out about a mile, made another left, and headed back for runway two-three.

"He was trying to give us a sense that day of the smoothness of the aircraft," said Anderson. "I recall him saying over and over again how smooth the aircraft is and how quiet it is, compared to the King Air."

The landing after the first loop was fine; Thurman handled it all like a pro, the landing gear was lowered, and the flaps were extended. As is done on touch-and-goes, the plane immediately raised its flaps and took off again from runway two-three.

With the landing gear and flaps retracted now, Thurman pulled the right throttle back to demonstrate the single-engine climb capability. The right throttle was then returned to normal thrust and a left traffic pattern was again flown. The altitude this time was between 2,800 and 3,000 feet.

On this pass Thurman advanced the throttles to demonstrate the acceleration of the jet. Both Hall and Anderson, in interviews with the National Transportation Safety Board (NTSB), recalled that Thurman had used the speed brakes to reduce the airspeed below maximum gear-lowering speed, 174 knots. But he lowered the land-

ing gear, extended the flaps, and retracted the speed brakes, bringing it in for a second normal landing on two-three.

For the third pass, Thurman invited Hall to take control. Seated
in the right seat, Hall put his hands on the control yoke and famil-
iarized himself with the responsiveness of the aircraft. At this point,
Thurman had Hall fly a zero-flap approach, later called "unbelievable" by an experienced pilot, given that this would be Hall's first
landing in the Citation and the hardest one you can make.

Hall would tell NTSB officials that Thurman did not recommend
a final-approach airspeed, but Hall thought that the speed flown was
"considerably faster than the reference speed on the airspeed indicator."

Thurman was handling the throttles and made a few power ad-
justments. Hall was handling only the control yoke and trim.

This was not an expert landing. The touchdown was long (about
midway down the runway), at which point Thurman immediately
prepared for a fourth takeoff.

Hall was a bit startled when the aircraft suddenly lifted and began
to float in the air about ten feet above the ground. He told the NTSB
investigators that he was surprised, until he realized that Thurman
had not lowered the flaps to the takeoff position, causing the aircraft to do what is called "ballooning."

There was no comment from the tower as they surely observed
this oddity. It was also considered unprofessional for Thurman to
fail to tell Hall that he had not lowered the flaps.

Still, neither of the passengers was alarmed by it; no one aboard
seemed to say, "Whoa, what are we doing here?" Professionalism
seemed to be in play. They were ready to go again.

This time, due to the arrival of other traffic in the air, the tower
told Munson to enter a right pattern on takeoff. This is the more difficult pattern for a pilot because his view of the direction he is headed
is not as clear. Still, it was not something that he hadn't done before.

The right downwind leg was entered at 3,500 feet and 200 knots indicated air speed (KIAS). Munson reduced the throttles to dissipate airspeed and altitude. Hall and Anderson would both recall that the throttles were reduced to a point where the landing gear warning horn sounded. The horn indicated they were going too fast for the landing gear to be extended.

Thurman shut off the horn.

"I knew that when we were at 3,500 feet, those throttles were pretty much all the way back," Hall told the NTSB.

Seconds before four p.m., the tower controller contacted Munson and told him to extend the downwind leg of his pattern for about one mile. One other plane was landing and another taking off ahead of him. Twenty-two seconds later, the tower told him he could begin his base turn "anytime now." He would come into runway one-nine over Greenburg Road on the north end of the airport.

Thurman piloted the aircraft into its base leg at once. Neither passenger recalled him using the speed brakes, and both said that he did not lower the landing gear or extend the flaps on downwind.

Flaps are used on wings to slow the aircraft sufficiently to allow it to land. When an aircraft slows too much, the wings don't develop enough lift to keep it in the air. With the extension of the flaps, or "flaps down," the surface area of the wing increases to create more lift. At the same time, the flaps create more drag, or friction, on the plane, so they are only used when it is necessary to reduce speed.

The flaps are panels built into the wings at the rear of the wing surface. They can be lowered in varying degrees to adjust for the amount of extra lift required. Anyone who has flown in an airplane has experienced the activation of flaps. In commercial jets, you can hear the noise of the electric motors that lower them and can feel the pitch of the plane change as they are extended. It feels as though brakes are being applied in midair.

Flaps are also used sometimes during takeoff, to allow the plane to become airborne faster. Once in the air, however, the flaps are retracted to allow for faster flight.

Thurman was about to approach the ground with too many things wrong with his basic mechanics. On strike three for the final out of an inning, he knew to roll the ball to the mound for the opposing pitcher to warm up with. It came naturally to him; he knew the game's subtleties. His piloting skills weren't as natural.

Mistakes were being made.

16

Jerry Anderson was happy to avoid the media for decades. With a common name, and with an eventual move to Florida, he just disappeared from sight. Yes, he had been linked to Munson through the tragedy, but no, it was not something he wanted to relive at all, despite his remarkable good fortune to have survived a plane crash. He's never been to the grave site and says he'll never go.

"Thurman was my friend," he said twenty-eight years after the accident during a long conversation with me. "We sort of lived vicariously through each other. He loved to talk to me about real estate and aviation, and while I would have loved to talk more about the Yankees with him, that was office talk as far as he was concerned, and when we were together, he preferred to leave stories about his 'day job' out of the conversation. And that was fine; we had plenty of other things to discuss."

Anderson has had a fine career in commercial real estate and still pilots a plane. He is the chief operating officer of Sperry Van Ness Commercial Real Estate Advisors, overseeing the firm's day-to-day operations, including marketing, technology, finance, operations, and human resources. He is coauthor of several audiotape programs on commercial real estate, and one of his books, *Success Strategies for Investment Real Estate*, is a classic in the field.

He is a frequent guest speaker around the world on real estate investment, and has appeared on NBC, CBS, ABC, and PBS over his career without anyone realizing his connection to the fateful flight.

"It's so ironic," he notes, "that I recovered reasonably well in terms of physical signs of the accident. Dave Hall became an air traffic controller. He works in a dark, closed environment. He had the more disfiguring scars on his arms, his face, his hands—the wrinkled skin. I became a public speaker and have few noticeable scars. A little on my right ear and right side of my face, but you have to look carefully. Some on my arms, but I can keep them covered. Ironic how that worked out."

Anderson spoke little of the fateful day to anyone until the twenty-fifth anniversary in 2004, when I had suggested to Willie Weinbaum, a producer at ESPN, that they might try to locate him. They were doing a feature on the anniversary, and Willie had asked me if I could suggest something that hadn't been done. I told him I didn't think I'd ever seen an interview with the two passengers.

Willie managed to track down Anderson, who had left Canton in 1982. Jerry agreed to talk for the first time. Three years later, he expanded on it with me.

"Thurman used to talk about the autobiography when it was in progress," he says. "He was pretty excited about doing it."

That was news to me, as I hadn't detected much enthusiasm from him at the time, other than heading off any would-be biographers from doing unauthorized books. But it was nice to hear.

"It's funny, the things you remember, the things you forget," he said to me. "For instance, I couldn't remember that David and I went to different hospitals after the accident.

"I don't think about it often, but I do if I'm landing on a runway marked one-nine. For a number of years after the accident I would fly into Canton and I always hated when I had to land on one-nine. But my flashbacks aren't of the accident but of the moments before.

"I also always try to avoid flying on August 2. I'm not a superstitious guy, but I guess on that one, I am. One year I couldn't avoid it, though; I had to be in Los Angeles for a speech and that was the way it worked out. Well, you won't believe this, but I'm on the plane, a commercial jet, and I'm sitting there and hear, 'Good morning, ladies and gentlemen. Welcome aboard. I'm Captain Munson, and I'll be your pilot today . . .' "

"No kidding."

Anderson first learned of Munson when Thurman was a high school star, one year ahead of Jerry. Jerry, a swimmer, would read the local sports section in the *Canton Repository,* and Munson's name was always there. Very much in the football stories, a lot in basketball—the "glamour sports," so to speak. And of course, he was in the baseball stories, but high school baseball didn't get that much coverage.

They first met while Anderson, a student at the University of Akron, was taking some classes at Kent State. They would see each other from time to time over the years back in Canton, but became really close after the 1975 baseball season when handball brought them together more frequently at the local YMCA.

"He was so competitive in handball, and he had such quick hands," said Anderson. "He'd never really played before, not seriously, and yet he was as good as anyone. It would piss me off, because I was a very good player. In the off-seasons after 1976, 1977, and 1978, he'd return to the Y, tired from the baseball season, and I'd beat him for a few weeks. But then as January and February came around, he was ready to beat me. And he did, almost all the time. We wound up playing doubles together and even won a tournament.

"He did love real estate. He would talk to me about it a lot. I became his confidant. Jess Tucker, a big Canton developer, used to suggest investments for Thurman, and he'd run them by me. Tucker had bought a massive piece of land in the seventies and got Thurman to invest in it. He was one of ten partners in what would become Belden Village, a major shopping center. I guided him through the process. It helped that Thurm knew Canton. He was a visionary, and just as he could see the coming innings of a baseball game in progress, he could see a good real estate opportunity. He knew what could work and what probably wouldn't. I think he probably owned real estate worth about $1.5 million eventually. And he had that good sense to know if something was going to be built on the wrong street.

"I believe he once told Diana, 'If anything ever happens to me, don't sell Belden Village!' "

Today, if you go to the west end of Munson Street where it meets Everhard, at the top of the hill, you can see the shopping center (which is now called Westfield Mall). Yes, there is a Munson Street, the subject he was supposed to have addressed that afternoon.

"He was really a man's man," says Anderson. "The self-confidence, the cigar, the swagger. But he had this odd sense of humor too; he could be very clever with this.

"One day I remember we were hanging around the airport when he still had his King Air, not too long before he bought the jet. It was about three p.m. and he had to go to Toronto for a night game. He said, 'Would you fly right seat with me? I'll be tired after the game and you can fly it back.'

"So I went! It was just an impulse, but it wasn't a long flight, and the beauty of engaging in aviation is the ability to do such a thing.

"So we land in Toronto and quickly went through customs, but then someone from the airport said, 'Oh, you guys must be ballplayers!'

"And Munson said, 'Yeah, and we're here to thump you guys.'

"They asked him for an autograph, which he was always happy to sign, despite a reputation otherwise, and then he turned and said to me, 'C'mon Willie, give 'em your autograph,' and he told them that I was Willie Randolph. I'm a five-foot-seven white guy and Willie was already an American League All-Star who had played in three World Series. But they were all like, 'Nice to meet you, Mr. Randolph.'

"So I signed and we had a good laugh over that, and he said, 'C'mon, let's get outta here before they discover us.' "

To Anderson's thinking, Thurman had no displeasure with the Yankees by 1979, and talked about playing for Cleveland strictly as a matter of convenience. Despite later statements from people who said he had given up on that notion by '79, he would tell Anderson, "This shit's wearing me out. I'd really like to play closer to home."

Munson and Anderson had no formal business relationship, other than two guys with common interests, until May 1977. And while Anderson collected no Yankee or Munson souvenirs, has no autographs, no caps, he did hold on to a ticket from a game on that May day when he sat in the Yankee Stadium clubhouse with Thurman during a rainout and first talked about a business arrangement together. It would be their first formal collaboration. Anderson would find real estate investment opportunities, and Munson would find investors among fellow ballplayers. That would be the basis of their business.

It took time for this to eventually materialize with formal documents. With no e-mails and no cell phones in those years, it could be months between their next meeting. They used to get together occasionally at "a little hole in the wall" in Canton for breakfast, and that was where they were the day before the All-Star Game in 1979, talking real estate and talking about a partnership.

Jerry began drawing up the papers, but there would be an obstacle. He had invested in a racquetball court with two other partners. Thurman didn't like that deal at all, although he was not involved.

"It's going to drain you," he said to Anderson. "It's a fad. It won't work. Get out of it."

Anderson was hesitant.

"Listen," Thurman said, talking tough and with a cigar in his hand. "I don't want to get into business with you if you're being drained on the other end by that stupid racquetball court. Here's the way it is: Take your choice. You can be partners with the captain of the New York Yankees, or with a couple of boneheads in a racquetball court!"

It was one of the few times—maybe the only time—that Munson had invoked his celebrity. But of course, by using the word "bonehead," he had made it funny.

Anderson, knowing Thurman had taken advantage of his moment, withdrew from the racquetball court partnership. He sold his one-third share to his two partners and closed the deal on July 20, putting the cash in the bank.

"Here's another thing," he noted. "Had I not listened to Munson, I would have been in deep trouble. As it was, I was sort of living deal to deal off real estate in those days. After the accident, I was unable to work for months. The cash in the bank from the racquetball sale saved me. Without that, I don't know what we would have done. I would probably have had to declare bankruptcy."

Anderson finalized the paperwork for his now formal partnership with Thurman. The papers were in the briefcase he brought on board with him when he climbed into Munson's jet on August 2. The documents burned in the fire.

Few people live to describe a crash, let alone people familiar with all that goes on mechanically with the plane. And because Jerry's description of the day to ESPN is far more emotional and insightful than any secondhand account could be, we have chosen to let his words take the story from here. Tom Rinaldi conducted the interview with producer Willie Weinbaum at his side. It took place in New

Smyra Beach, Florida, on June 1, 2004, a week before what would have been Thurman's fifty-seventh birthday, and two months before the twenty-fifth anniversary of the accident.

JERRY ANDERSON: Well, on August 2, I had been out doing some training earlier that day in my Beechcraft Bonanza with a fellow by the name of Dave Hall, who was my instructor. I was working on my instrument rating. And we came back to the ramp, taxied back in about three o'clock. And Dave said, "Oh boy, I think Thurman has his new airplane here." So we got out of our airplane, and sure enough, Cessna Citation, "November 15NY." We knew that was Mr. Munson's [*laughter*] new aircraft. So I jumped out of our plane, and I said, "Thurman, what are you doing here today?" And he said, "It's our day off." And I said, "Oh my gosh, that's right. It's your day off." He said, "I've been checking out a few things on the plane. Come take a look." So that was my first introduction. And I was in awe of it. It was beautiful.

TOM RINALDI: I was gonna ask. What was your reaction, and what was his, to showing you the plane, Jerry?

JA: You would have thought it was a newborn child. [*Laughter.*] I mean, we walked around that airplane. And he patted it, and he stroked it, and he showed it to me. He said, "I am so proud of this. This is something that's gonna enable us to really come back and forth. And I am gonna be able to see my family more." And he said, "Look at that. Look at that tail number." And that's when he pointed to "15NY."

TR: What was your reaction to the plane?

JA: I couldn't wait to go up in it. [*Laughter.*] You know? I

had just gotten out of my single-engine airplane, doing my
instrument training. And here was my friend who had a
brand-new jet. And I had never been in a jet. So I was very
excited to have an opportunity to fly. I couldn't wait to fly
out to Yankee Stadium and maybe take one of those trips.

TR: What happened next?

JA: Well, Thurman said, "Hey, you guys want to go for a
ride? We are gonna, we are gonna take it around the
pattern. And I need to check a few things out."

TR: He got in the plane, and what happened from
there, Jerry?

JA: Well, this is about three o'clock in the afternoon,
and we walked up, and started looking at the plane. I think
it was about 3:30 in the afternoon when we finally got in,
and started looking at all of the, at all of the . . . [coughs].

TR: So, he showed you the plane?

JA: Right. And we walked around the outside of the
plane. And in fact, Thurman was explaining what a
preflight was like on a Citation jet, versus maybe in the
airplane that I just come out of, the single-engine aircraft.
And they ask if we wanted to take a quick flight. And he
said he had to check out a couple of things on the
announceator panel, which is basically the panel of lights
that tells you whether or not things are working on the
aircraft. And he said, "Come on in. Let's take a look." So
Dave Hall and I looked at each other, and said, "Hey, let's,
let's go." And we hesitated to see who was gonna go in the
front right seat. And I said, "Oh, you win the toss. You go
ahead." I acquiesce to him because Dave was an instructor.
And I had not been in a jet. And he sat in the right seat,
and I sat in the jump seat. And we sat in the airplane for a
few minutes, and talked about the differences of the

turboprop aircraft versus the jet. Thurman was looking at
his checklist, reviewing a couple of things in the book.
David and I ask a couple of questions about the different
lights and the different panels. And what this item meant
on the panel versus that, that particular item. And we
looked over the emergency door. Saw how the emergency
door were, where to be if needed, how the emergency
door were to come out. And, of course, I think we all
thought the same thing, that, well, we are not gonna need
that emergency door today. Both David and I looked at the
entrance door. And we knew how that handle worked.
Pretty much just basic training, just to make sure that you
understand how the doors work. Sat there for a few
minutes on the ramp, looked over, said, "Thurman, this is
fantastic. It smells great. I mean, the leather is beautiful.
It's a beautiful airplane." And he said, "Well, let's go. Let's
take her around the pattern."

TR: How did he seem to you right then, Jerry? How
would you characterize his mood?

JA: Well, Thurman was in a great mood that day. He was
having a good day. He was in Canton. He didn't have to
rush off to Yankee Stadium that night. And not that he
didn't love baseball, but he didn't have to rush out that
night. He got to spend the night in town. I know he always
looked forward to that. Wasn't rushed. And looked at the
checklist. And made a call to the tower. Taxied out
carefully. And on our way. I think he had his head on
square that day.

TR: What happened from there?

JA: The—well, it's well documented. We stayed in the
pattern that day. Meaning, we just flew around the airport.
We didn't fly off-site. We taxied to runway two-three,

which is southwest to the inbound runway. And got our
clearance, and we took off from that runway. And I could
remember just being thrilled with the acceleration, you
know? Coming from my little, uh, 285-horsepower single-
engine plane that I had just flown an hour ago, this was
phenomenal. And we flew, what we call, around the
pattern. You know, basically means that we flew down the
runway, we took off, we made a left turn, we made another
left turn, and we paralleled back to runway, to come back
to runway two-three, for a landing. And, of course, during
that time frame the tower asked us what we wanted to do.
And Thurman responded, it was gonna be a touch-and-go.
Which basically means that the airplane would touch
down, and then we'd take back off again.

   TR: What was his goal? What was he trying to do with
you guys, for people that don't know, Jerry?

   JA: Well, he was just trying to give us a sense that day of
the smoothness of the aircraft. I recall him saying over and
over again how smooth the aircraft is, and how quiet it is,
compared to the King Air.

   TR: You make a couple of passes. And what happens
next?

   JA: We made a couple of passes around the pattern. We
made three passes on runway two-three that day. After the
third pass, we were asked by air traffic to control, to extend
our, our pattern a little bit, to extend our runway, to
extend our downwinds. Meaning that we were told to fly a
little further, before we turned again back toward the
runway. And this time though, instead of turning us to the
left, it took him back to runway two-three, the air traffic
control asked us to turn to the right, off to line up for a
different runway, a runway that was headed due south,

runway one-nine. And, at that time now, things were
happening pretty fast, because we had accelerated. And
because we had extended our takeoff, we were a little
higher than maybe we should have been. We were a couple
of hundred feet higher, as I recall. No big deal. Thurman
banked the aircraft around to the right. And we
descended. Lost some of that altitude. Got back down
closer to pattern altitude. And now, we were gonna land,
land on a runway that was off to our right side, versus
before where we were always landing on a runway that was
off to the pilot's left side. So now we are coming back
around for one-nine.

TR: What happened as the plane started to descend,
Jerry, toward one-nine?

JA: As we got ready to make our, what's called 180-
degree turn from, or a ninety-degree turn. As we got ready
to make our ninety-degree turn, from what you would call
"base leg." Meaning, perpendicular to the runway to make
one more ninety-degree turn, to line up for the runway.
There were a couple of things that were happening
around the airport. And I have, of course, since learned
much more than I knew at the time. And as a pilot, I am a
much more experienced pilot than I was twenty-five years
ago. But what happened at that particular point, when we
started to turn back toward one-nine, is we had a series of
diversions take place. And two of the diversions that took
place were: we heard traffic being talked to by air traffic
control, by the tower. One plane landing on runway two-
three, another plane landing on one-nine. So, as pilots, we
recognized, we have other airplanes out there. And we
need to find them. So we had both Dave Hall and myself,
and immediately looking for, *Where is the other aircraft? Let's*

make sure we know where those other aircraft are. So we had a diversion. I suspect, I don't know for a fact, but I suspect Thurman too was looking for those aircraft, as good pilots do. *Where is the other aircraft?* You don't just depend on the tower.

As we turned then toward final, on one-nine, one of the things that we noticed is that—and David and I both noticed the same thing—is that we were a little bit lower than what we had been on previous landings. No big deal. On final approach, you always have to adjust upward or downward. What was different though about this approach is that, unlike the other approaches, this one was different. We had turned to the right. We had a lot of other traffic we were looking for. We had been a little bit too high in the pattern. There were a lot of things going on that were different than the other ones. So, from the standpoint of a pilot, I can recall thinking, *We are not as stabilized, on our approach this time, as we had been in the past.* And it was not of concern. We were just, were not as stabilized as we had been.

So those diversions that maybe took us off of a coordinated final approach to the runway, were now out of the way. And we were now descending toward one-nine, relatively rapidly. And I felt us sinking. And I noticed that as we were sinking, of course, Thurman is reaching for the throttles. And he pushed those throttles forward. But it was a very unusual feeling that we had, because although we were, had just started to accelerate, we were sinking as well. As a pilot, I knew that that sinking feeling was not something that was [*laughter*] advantageous to us. And I was waiting for those engines to kick in. But the engines didn't seem to kick in nearly as quickly as they should have. I subsequently learned, of course, that jet engines have to spool up. But they just didn't seem to be kicking in the way that I felt they should.

TR: How long was that moment, Jerry? The recognition of the sinking, and the waiting for the rise?

JA: The recognition of the sinking, and the waiting for the acceleration were literally seconds. I mean that. We are not talking about minutes here. We are talking about five, six, seven seconds, maximum. But it was also time, the point at which, I realized that this descent was probably not going to be arrested, and that we would probably crash short of the runway.

TR: I don't know how difficult it is to answer this, Jerry, because I—I didn't live through it. But what are those six seconds of recognition like?

JA: Well, I think for anybody that's ever been through any type of a crash, whether it's an airplane, an automobile, or even a bicycle. There is a moment in time that freezes for you, and you recognize that you are about to make impact. You don't know what the outcome is going to be, so your initial thought is, *Oh my gosh,* you know? *Am I gonna be able to walk away from this?* I had been scooted off to the side, looking into the cockpit. When I realized that we were gonna make impact with the ground, I, my seat, my seat belt was on, but loose. I quickly turned around, to try and shield myself from the impact. And that is probably one of the things that, that saved me, because although we had some, or a lot of hard impact, as we hit the ground, and then as we went some, through some trees, I felt the fuselage just taking the pounding, [*claps*] boom [*claps*] boom [*claps*] boom [*claps*] boom. And then, as we finally hit [*claps*] what appeared to be, my initial impression was, we must have hit a ditch, and sort of popped up. [*Claps.*] And I realized, as we came to a stop, *mm-hmm* [*claps*], that I was still intact. I mean, unbelievable as it might seem, I thought, *My God, I have survived this.* And I looked up to the cockpit, and David was moving, and, and Thurman's head was twisted a little bit. And I thought, *This is, uh, unbelievable. We are going to walk away from this airplane. And we have just crashed an airplane, and we have all survived.*

TR: And what happened?

JA: Well, things didn't quite go like my mind had initially thought. The right side of the aircraft was engulfed in flames. I knew that we had popped up, because I felt it, that we popped up onto a ridge. I didn't realize that we had popped up onto a road. And of course the flames were being created by the fuel. I knew that, as a pilot. But I was feeling pretty good about it, because the right side of the aircraft was not the side of the aircraft we needed to go out. The door was on the left side. And the left side was relatively clear. I didn't see any smoke or flames there.

So my job, being closest to the door—I already knew how to open the door—was to turn that handle, and get it open. What I quickly realized is I could not get it open. The door had jammed. At that point, I didn't know why it had jammed. And David came back, and he gave it a try, and he couldn't get it open either. And I took a good solid kick at it. And now as I think about it, it was probably ridiculous, but I think I should have been able to kick open that door. But, nonetheless, that main entrance door was jammed. And it was then that we turned our attention back to getting out of the aircraft, because at that point the aircraft has started to fill with smoke.

And the two things that I remember—and I will hang
on this for a long time—is that Thurman mumbled to us.
He said, "Are you guys okay?" At this point, he says, "Are
you guys okay?" And we said, "Yeah." I don't remember
whether David said it, or I said it. But one of us said, "How
about you?" And he said, "I don't know. I can't move. I
can't move." And he said that somewhat with a gasping
breath.

And it was at that point that, almost instinctively, David
and I split up the responsibilities. I was closest to the door.
Obviously, I needed to get us out of there. He was closest
to Thurman, he was gonna lift Thurman up. We felt that
we could probably collectively get him out of there. I know
that, because the communication that we had—and this is
all in seconds—was, "Let's go. Let's get us all out of here."
I cracked the emergency door. And when I cracked the
emergency door, flames shot in and above our heads into
the cockpit. And again, this cockpit is, you know, only
about four feet wide, so it's not as if there are two or three
of us standing there together.

Um. Thurman was somewhat slumped over. And he did
have some blood coming from his nose and forehead. But
I, at that point, felt, *We are gonna get him outta there. We are
just gonna haul him out. I mean, it's no big deal. There are two of
us, there is one of him. And we are gonna drag him right through
there.* But what I quickly realized was, when the flames
came into the cockpit, and started to catch fire in the air,
and the black smoke was so overtaking, we couldn't really
breathe. And at that point, we didn't have a choice.
Unspoken word. I pulled the emergency door into the
cockpit. And I departed the aircraft. And pretty much
dove into the puddle of fuel that was on fire on the right
side.

I know that, as I was departing the aircraft, David gave one last tug on Thurman, and he couldn't, he couldn't move him. And neither one of us could move him. And David followed me, right outside that door. And I rolled around on the ground for a moment, and then was unconscious. I don't really remember anything after that, until waking up in the hospital. The hard part of that of course is that there was a point in time that I knew that I was gonna leave that airplane, and that my friend was not. And that was a terrible feeling.

TR: And when did you realize that, Jerry?

JA: I think I realized that when David and I both tried, at the same time, to get Thurman to move. We couldn't move him. The whole seat was moving. And I have now come to learn, of course, that his seat—because of what we hit on the, underneath the fuselage—that whole seat track had come loose. And I had no idea of course at the time, that that's what had happened. But that's why we were not able to lift him and move him. So we just couldn't get him to where we needed to get him outside that emergency door. And he was unconscious at the time. He was not helpful at all to us, in terms of movement.

TR: And how long a period of time elapsed, between hitting the ground, and getting the door open?

JA: You know, it's funny you ask that question. What was the period of time, from the time that we hit the ground, till that door came open? It, it seemed like a long time. But the truth is, I now know—and I realize, realize then—that we were on fire immediately. I mean, all that fuel. And I don't know how much fuel we had that day. But probably close to, well, full tanks, and, and, uh, the full, fuel in both tanks. It was now burning. And we were sitting in it. So it was just moments, from the time that that whole right side of the aircraft caught on fire. The time that it took both myself and David to try that, that entrance door, to realize that it was jammed, that we could not get it open. The quick realization that there was only one other way out, and if that door was jammed, we were all going to perish in this. You know, would probably, were just minutes. Minutes.

TR: That journey, from recognition, that the door would not open, to the option to get the emergency door open. And you mentioned something, Jerry. You mentioned the division of labor, and an unspoken word. How does, how did that happen, Jerry?

JA: Well, I think, anybody that's involved in a tragedy, or anybody that's involved in conflict, and is certainly, every person that's ever been in the military would know that you react. And when I say "the division of labor," and "the unspoken word," I mean that from the standpoint of, where each of us, where each of us were sitting. David was in the copilot seat. He was on the right side of the aircraft. And I was closest to the door. He couldn't get around me, to try the door. I had to step aside. When I stepped aside for him to try the door, and that entrance door didn't work, it was natural for him to go back to our other pilot, Thurman, who was there. And it was just unspoken. I had to get the door open. I was closest to it. And the door was beside me. *Get the door open, Jerry.* This is the unspoken word. *Get the door open. We'll all get out of here.*

TR: At what point, if any? And maybe the better way to ask you, Jerry, is: How much contemplation were you able to, to exercising, in your first recognition, that something has gone wrong with the landing?

JA: When I first realized that something had gone astray, was really that sinking feeling, and the feeling of acceleration, at the same time. Those senses, that sensation of sinking and acceleration at the same time, it was not something that I was accustomed to as a pilot. Pilots don't like things they never experienced before. [*Laughter.*] So when we made contact with the ground. You know, you have to remember, Tom. The throttles were full forward.

TR: Well, would you, would you? But the point I want to get you to, which is, Thurman's reaction. His reaction. I realize where you were sitting, Jerry. And yet you admit, you were craning over, to look into the cockpit. But how did Thurman react to that sinking sensation?

JA: Well, Thurman reacted, I think, well. And he did what needed to be done. He immediately went to those throttles. I saw the little frown on his face. My interpretation of that frown was, *This isn't quite right. I don't like it. We are gonna go around.* Throttles all the way forward. *We are gonna go around one more time, and try this again.* Again, a natural reaction for a pilot. After he pushed the throttles forward, and then we felt that acceleration, and yet still felt the sinking, is when I realized that the impact with the ground was gonna be made.

TR: And what, if anything, happened in the cockpit, when, in your mind, a crash was inevitable?

JA: Well, once we realized that a crash was inevitable, I am sure the other two pilots, Thurman and David, probably realized at the same time I did, you had a second to prepare yourself. A second to prepare yourself for impact. Irony is a strange thing, Tom. And we went through a clump of trees, four or five inches in diameter

as I later learned. And those trees slowed us down.
Remember, the throttles were pulled forward. Those trees
slowed us down. And we skidded along those trees,
eventually to the point where we crashed back to the
ground, and we hit a stump. Now, while we were crashing
through those trees, those were the bumps that I heard.
I now know that. Those were all those bumps. [*Claps.*]
That was [*claps*] as we bumped along. [*Claps.*] That slowed
the airplane down enough, for us to, two of the three of
us, to survive. Um. Thurman was doing everything
possible, as a pilot, to put that aircraft on the ground
safely. He did what he was trained to do. He had full
throttles. He was trying to accelerate and get the airplane
climbing again. That day, it was not to be, though. It was
simply not to be.

TR: When you look back at the day and what happened,
Jerry, what is the significance, in ultimately what
happened, of the stump?

JA: Well, the stump. The stump is—it's now gone.
About a four-by-five-foot area. A large tree that had been
cut down. That stump hit our aircraft. No. Our aircraft hit
that stump, right on the pilot side. I know now, that's why
the door wouldn't open. I know now, that's why Thurman's
seat had come loose. Because that stump, when the aircraft
went over the stump, completely ripped off the bottom of
the aircraft, on the left-hand side. At that side. You know,
Tom, the irony of the stump is, we hit the stump with the
left side of the aircraft. And that's what tore the seat loose
from Thurman. That's the reason Thurman couldn't
move, is because of that stump. The reason we couldn't get
the door open on the left side was because of that stump.
And ironically enough, the left side of the aircraft was the

clear side, when we, initially when we finally stopped moving. But that was the side we couldn't get out. And had that stump hit on the right side of the aircraft, I suspect David would have probably had the same outcome as Thurman. And I suspect Thurman and I would have gone out the entrance door. Fate is something one can't explain.

TR: But Jerry, as you ponder fate, how do you make sense of it, or reconcile it?

JA: You know, that's very difficult. And you don't, you don't know for sure what the future holds. But we were in the air that day, thirty minutes. Thirty minutes. It changed Thurman's family. He didn't see his three children grow. And his wife became a widow. And a lot of Yankee fans lost their captain. And, yeah, baseball lost a good player. But a lot of us lost a lot that day. And I lost a friend. I remember finally reading all the news articles and thinking that the whole country was somewhat mourning the loss of this ballplayer. And I had, up until that point, even though I had laid in the hospital for a couple of weeks of burns that I was recovering. I hadn't thought about Thurman as the New York Yankees' captain. I found him as my friend. And I didn't realize how many people were being affected. I certainly knew that Diana and the children would be affected. I knew that my life would be different. Sometimes twists and turns that take place. I knew my life was gonna be different now, because I wasn't on the same track, businesswise, as I was before, with Thurman. But now that I look back on it, twenty-five years later, so many people have had their lives affected by that.

TR: But just you, Jerry. And go back to something that you, you summed up in a sentence. What did you lose that day?

JA: Well, what I lost that day was a friend. And I lost somebody that stimulated me. And I lost someone that I lived vicariously through. And Thurman and I used to joke with each other that I live vicariously through him in baseball, and he lived vicariously through me in commercial real estate. And we said many times, "What would really shake 'em up, Jerry, if you showed up at Yankee Stadium, and I showed up out selling real estate." And I said, "Well, I have. I think, Thurman, you would be a lot better in real estate than I would be playing baseball." [*Laughter.*] So I did lose that. But I think what I also lost was a future that was going to be interesting. And Thurman was a very interesting guy. And Thurman was a guy who was so much more than a baseball player. And I lost the opportunity to really see him grow.

TR: How did you cope, in the immediate aftermath of the accident, Jerry?

JA: Well, any time you are involved in an accident, and you survive, versus others, guilt is natural. And Dave Hall and I haven't communicated in years. Not that we don't want to. It's that the only memories we have are painful ones. And you go through the feeling initially that you should have been able to get him out of there. Then reality sets in. You talk to the county coroner, and the county coroner gives you the report. And you talk to folks that witnessed the aircraft afterward, and you realize that you were very fortunate to get out, let alone get someone else out. And you read all the official reports, and you realize that there wasn't a whole lot that you could have done that day, to change the events.

TR: So why did you [feel guilt]?

JA: The—the guilt comes and goes. And the natural feeling is to be feeling guilty that you were not able to, as a

pilot, maybe change that last approach. As a pilot, not to
be able to recognize something. Gosh. Are the flaps down?
Is there a gear down? Are we established? So you have the
guilt, as a pilot, for not recognizing what needed to be
done on the flight. But you also then, of course, have the
guilt as a survivor. And the guilt is not something that is . . .
overwhelming. I thank the Lord every day that I am
around an airplane, that I survived. I still fly, Tom. I, I am a
pilot today. I own an airplane. I have much more respect
for aviation. And so yes, there is guilt. But I can't ever feel
guilty, I suppose, for not trying. And we did try. And we
stayed in that airplane, both David and I stayed in that
airplane, until we possibly realized, until we finally
realized, that if we stayed any longer, we both would
perish.

　　TR: Yet you still maintain . . . guilt over not getting him
out. Why?

　　JA: Well, it's a natural reaction, to be able to. It's a
natural reaction, to want to be able to do more than what
you did. As a reporter, you know, you have the opportunity
sometimes to look at a film and say, "Gosh, I wish. If I had
that to do over, I'd do it a different way." But aviation
accidents, you don't get to do over. There are no do-overs.
There are no mulligans. And we, in an aviation accident,
when you crash—aviation is much less forgiving than some
other situations.

　　TR: What did you learn when the coroner's report came
back, Jerry?

　　JA: One of the things that I learned when the coroner's
report came out, that probably has helped me over the
years, is that, um, at the time David and I left the aircraft,
that there might not have been a whole lot we could do to

save Thurman at that point. That he had spinal damage. That his neck had been broken. And that when we left that aircraft, we had probably done everything that we could have. And when I met with Diana, after the accident, it was so hard to look her in the eye, and say, "You know, Diana, we did what we could, to get Thurman out of there. And we just couldn't do it." And that was tough then. That was really tough. [*Cries, coughs.*] That was probably the hardest part of it all. Sorry about that.

TR: The report. You mentioned how often your mind goes back to the report, in a sense, as a comfort.

JA: Yeah. The National Transportation Safety Board report, which details the accident almost in the third person, which then gives me the ability to read it in the third person, offers me a lot of comfort sometimes, in recognition of what we did, was the right thing. And as difficult as it is to accept the loss of Thurman at a very early age, two of the three people in that accident that day survived. And that's a blessing, because three people could have perished. Certainly one perishing was bad enough. But it could have been a lot worse. And when you read that NTSB report, what you realize is that Thurman was a well-trained, competent pilot, who made a mistake, a couple of pilot errors that day. And pilots are human. And when pilots make errors, aviation is not very forgiving. So we have to be very careful, in that regard.

TR: You mentioned, just before we broke, Jerry, that Thurman made a mistake or two. What mistakes did he make?

JA: Well, in the last, the last time around, as we now all realize from all the reports, we probably should have put the flaps down. And as we got into our sinking and acceleration, the gear had not yet been put down. So probably the two mistakes that were made on the last time around, is that we didn't have our approach flaps in position, and that the gear was put down late. The gear was put down. It was just put down a little bit later than normal.

TR: What's the biggest misconception, all these years later, about what happened?

JA: The misconception, in my opinion, is, is that you hear a lot of people talking about Thurman as a pilot. I have heard other baseball players—I have had contact with pro ballplayers over the years. And I hear them giving their opinion of Thurman as a pilot. And I think to myself, "Well, they are not a pilot. What qualifies them to judge Thurman's skills? And have judged his skills twenty-five years ago?" So the misconception, I think, that a lot of people have is that Thurman was not a good pilot, that he was "rushed through his training much faster than he should have been." There is no question that his training was accelerated. No question about it. He did it in a very short period of time, what takes many pilots years to do. In a year and a half, he went from flying a single-engine aircraft to a jet. However, he did it within the regulations.

TR: And when we were talking earlier, Jerry, you mentioned something with a lot of flair. That's Thurman's approach to life. And you, you made a bit of a baseball analogy. He lived. "He did most things as if it were a full count and two out," etc. If you wouldn't mind, reprise that, and elaborate on what you meant, and why you believe in that.

JA: Thurman was a very intense, focused individual. And he lived life with the throttle to the fire wall. With the

pedal to the metal. And he was a "get it done, come
through"–type guy. You know, 3–2 count, bases loaded,
bottom of the ninth, you wanted him at the plate.
Handball is a game that's played, first one to 21 wins. I can
remember matches [tied at] 20–20 with him. And if we
would have 20 points, I knew we'd get 21. He could always
punch the ball over the goal line. That's how he was. The
intensity that he had, the focus that he had. He just
couldn't be stopped. When he learned to fly, he was also
that intense. He would study the manuals of the airplanes
that he was learning to fly. He would know the page. Not
just the information, he would know the page number
where the information resided.

TR: How has that intensity, and that legacy, Jerry,
shaped who you are now?

JA: Well, twenty-five years is a long time. And of course,
Thurman didn't live his complete life. So, you know, we
only have him, and his memory, for a short period of time.
But sometimes when I feel myself getting a little bit lax, or
when I don't think I might be able to come through in a
situation, I think about Thurman. Because Thurman
would just say, "Just get it done. Focus. Concentrate."
Punch the ball over the goal line. Get the base hit. Score
the twenty-first point. Land this airplane.

TR: Why do we remember him, twenty-five years later?

JA: It absolutely amazes me that Thurman's memory is
as alive and well as it is. Tom, I travel the country, and
people say, "Well, you are from Canton, Ohio." I say, "Yeah,
I am from Canton, Ohio." They say, "Football Hall of
Fame. And Thurman Munson." And then we start talking
about Thurman. "Did you know Thurman?" "Yes, I did."
"And you did? Thurman? And you worked with Thurman,

on some of his real estate? Well, what did you think?" They always want to know. They know him. Then they will say, "Oh, I remember that August as if it was yesterday." Most of the time, very seldom do I ever tell people that I was a survivor of that crash. But they remember. And that was the only connection, is from Canton, Ohio. Amazing to me. I think they remember. I think they remember Thurman, because he was, of what he represented. He was an ordinary guy. Sort of a country bumpkin, in a way. And he went to New York City. He made the big time. He was the captain of the New York Yankees. And yet he lived in northeastern Ohio. Canton, Ohio, a small little community, a quiet community, a Midwest community, a very conservative community. And it was almost as if he had these two lives. He was dedicated to his family, which I think made him stand out. And I think that's much of the reason that he is remembered.

TR: You said you still fly.

JA: I do still fly.

TR: And what is it like, to fly back into that Canton airport?

JA: What is it like, to land on runway one-nine? The first time that I flew, after the accident, I was perspiring so profusely, that I thought I had wet myself. I was that nervous. The adrenaline was so high. And my tongue was so dry. When the tower cleared me to land on one-nine. And Tom, I can remember, not too many years after the accident, hoping, praying, that I would land on runway two-three, or five, any runway but one-nine, please. Because every time I fly on the final approach to one-nine, I would have to look down at that terrible place where we had crashed. Of course, now it's all grown over, and all the trees are gone, and the stump is removed. But all those memories get resurfaced, as I flew over the approach for one-nine.

TR: I had a few different points, when we spoke, Jerry. You have said twenty-five years is a long time. But at several other points, during our talk, you have worn a lot of emotion on your face, twenty-five years later. Why?

JA: Well, twenty-five years is a long time. But when I think about the accident now, it's almost as if I see it as a movie. Because I have learned so much. I have learned as a pilot. I have learned as a practitioner. I have learned as a father. I have realized all those things that Thurman missed. I mean, remember, Tom, we were in our early thirties. I mean, we were kids. And now, I have lived most of my life, and I have had my career. The reasons these conversations spark the emotion that it does, is that it's very deep. And it was a time that was very exciting. I had given up another business to be able to go and get involved with Thurman in a partnership. I didn't want to give up that other business. He said, "Give up that other business, or we are not going to do our partnership, with putting ballplayers together, to invest in real estate." That was a turning point for me, in my career. And it's the turning point that never took place. And we turned the corner, but never traveled the road.

WILLIE WEINBAUM: A couple of things. Just real quickly. You mentioned that people say to you, "The Football Hall of Fame, and Thurman Munson," when you mention Canton. One of the things that, in all honesty, most people do not remember is that Thurman Munson was not alone. If you can, what are your thoughts on what most people do remember about that day, and the fact that you and David Hall are sort of footnotes to that history?

JA: Well, Dave Hall and I are footnotes to the history. And we are not public figures. Thurman was a public figure. He was a professional baseball player. His memories live on on TV. And you can watch him. You can, you could watch the 1978 World Series tape. And you see him in action. And David and I were just two friends with him that day, along for a ride. And we should be footnotes. We are survivors, but we were not the public figure. A lot of things have changed. And a lot of things have changed in baseball, and aviation, for the better, after that crash. I think many baseball contracts now exclude the ballplayers from being able to fly. I think that the FAA has tightened up some of the requirements for training. I think some aircraft companies have put less of a full-court press on public figures to buy aircraft. And Payne Stewart was killed in an airplane crash.

TR: Yeah.

JA: How many people know who else was in the airplane? Payne Stewart was the public figure.

17

Within minutes, fire and emergency rescue vehicles arrived and doused the flames in thirty to forty seconds. Emergency vehicles were parked end to end along Greenburg Road, where the plane had come to rest. It was, of course, too late to save Thurman.

The initial rescue team got there in minutes. Ed Hutchinson of airport security and Harry Yoder, an FAA technician who was with the airport fire unit, got close enough that they needed to be treated for smoke inhalation. Rescue units arrived from Greentown, Green Township, Uniontown, and Jackson Township. The City of Green was the closest fire department. Jeff Mashburn of the Summit County sheriff's office said he couldn't get closer than thirty feet because of the blaze.

Mashburn saw Anderson and Hall running from the flames. Detective William Evans reached the site and found Hall under a nearby tree, gasping for breath. He had burns on his hands and was taken to Akron Children's Hospital by ambulance. In television coverage of the accident, Anderson can be seen on the ground, being treated by paramedics. Another ambulance took him to Timken Mercy Medical Center suffering from burns of his face, neck, and forearms.

Mashburn knew that there was another person in the wreckage, but the flames made it impossible for him to get to him.

The coroner's report stated that Munson expired at 4:06 p.m., after four minutes of consciousness during which he would have realized the helplessness of his situation. A. H. Kyriakides, the Summit County coroner, found that the official cause of death was asphyxiation resulting from inhalation of superheated air and toxic substances.

The police, now aware that it was Thurman Munson in the plane, called Tote with the news. Thurman and Tote had eaten lunch together hours before.

The three Munson children were playing in their backyard when Don Armen, head of the flying school at Akron-Canton Airport, arrived, along with two instructors. Thurman had kept his planes in Armen's hangars. Before leaving the airport, Armen had called Jody Anderson, Jerry's wife, to tell her, "There's been an accident."

Diana was alone in the house, having just returned from grocery shopping with the family station wagon. They had been preparing for Thurman to barbecue chicken. Instead, upon hearing the awful news, she rushed Armen, pounded on his chest, and screamed, "Tell me this isn't true!!!"

But then she summoned the strength to call in the children and gather them together in a side room, away from Armen and his companions.

"Daddy has gone off to be with God," she told them.

The girls broke into tears as Diana pulled them all closer.

Michael said, "If my daddy's with God, why is everybody crying?"

Armen didn't stay long. But within five minutes a reporter called to get a confirmation or a reaction from Diana.

"If we hadn't gotten there when we did, that's how she would have learned of the accident," says Armen.

Armen attributed the accident simply to fatigue. "He hadn't had enough sleep. He was a good pilot; he was capable of flying that jet. He was just going on too few hours of sleep after coming home from Chicago early in the morning and getting up to be with his kids."

Diana immediately began calling family and friends and Armen left after about thirty minutes.

Her friend Joanne would take the children to a fast-food restaurant to get them away from the house for a while. Later, Thurman's friend Jess Tucker would drive with Diane to the airport to pick up the Mercedes—without visiting the crash sight. There was a half-smoked cigar in the ashtray.

"There was no way Thurman would've left it unlocked if he'd intended to go flying that day," she later reflected.

Tote joined the police in going to the Munson home. Later he stood in the driveway in tears. "We're shook," he said. "We're really shook up. It's unbelievable. Such a loss. A thirty-two-year-old son-in-law."

The police set up guard duty at the Munson home and continued it there for days, helping to maintain the family's privacy at such a time.

George Steinbrenner was at his big round desk at Yankee Stadium late in the afternoon, meeting with two of his financial people. At the reception desk for the Yankee offices, not far removed, Doris Walden answered a call with her usual "Good afternoon, world champion Yankees." The voice on the other end said, "George Steinbrenner, please."

She put the call through to Gerry Murphy, the former batboy and traveling secretary who was now serving as Steinbrenner's executive assistant. The caller identified herself but withheld the full story, saying that she was calling from the Summit County sheriff's office in Canton, Ohio, and she needed to put the sheriff through to George Steinbrenner.

Steinbrenner had left strict orders not to be disturbed during his meeting, but Murphy sensed the urgency and went in just the same. He had put two and two together when "Canton" was mentioned, and he assumed something had gone wrong for Munson.

"Goddamn it, I told you not to disturb me," said Steinbrenner, predictably.

"I really feel it's urgent that you take this, Mr. Steinbrenner," said Murphy.

George picked up the phone. Murphy watched as his face fell, and he repeated, "Oh no . . . oh no . . . oh no . . . oh no . . ."

Steinbrenner would recall that the caller was the airport manager, but perhaps that was a later call.

He told *The Sporting News,* "I get a call from Canton, the [Akron-] Canton Airport. The manager was an old friend of mine named Jack Doyle. And he said, 'George, this is Jack.' I said, 'How are you? What the hell is going on? Where are you?' He said, 'I'm in Canton.' He sounded terrible. He says, 'I guess you can imagine why I'm calling.' And then it dawned on me—Thurman. And [Doyle] said he died in a plane crash . . . at the airport. [Munson] had two instructors. They were in the plane. He was practicing landing and takeoffs, which is difficult in a jet because in a prop plane when you give it power, right away you get the power. In a jet, that isn't the case. There is that little hesitation. When he saw that he was in trouble on his landing, he tried to get the power going again and it didn't take. It wasn't like the prop plane. And he was killed. That was one of the worst moments."

Steinbrenner allowed himself the human emotions of grief and shock and anger, and no doubt some thoughts about allowing Munson to fly in the first place. ("Can you imagine Dock Ellis saying that I'm responsible for Thurman Munson's death because I let him fly that plane?" he later exclaimed. "I didn't want him to fly that plane.") Then he swung into action. And on that hot August afternoon, George Steinbrenner shined. He was truly "the Boss," taking command. He was forty-nine years old, at the height of his power as a CEO, in his ultimate moment of guiding his club through its most awful tragedy.

He had Murphy round up his office team—Cedric Tallis the general manager, Bill Kane the traveling secretary, Mickey Morabito the PR man, Larry Wahl his assistant, Bobby Hofman, Jack Butterfield, and Bill Bergesh from player development, and others. (Butterfield, who was vice president for player development and scouting, would die in an auto accident on November 16, 1979, an event that further shook the mourning Yankee front office.)

In a clear and commanding voice, Steinbrenner informed his staff about the circumstances in Canton and the call he had received.

"He was composed, and at the top of his game," said Wahl. "There was no grief in the room at that time because we were suddenly all in emergency mode."

Within seconds he could shift from "helping the family" to "planning to go there" to "what are we going to do about another catcher?"

"He covered all the bases," said Wahl. "It was amazing to watch. It was like he had this emergency rulebook in his head. He even talked about black stripes on the uniform sleeves in the first minutes. He talked about retiring his number, retiring his locker, having Cardinal Cooke at the stadium the next night, and what the scoreboard should show during the moment of silence. He was amazing to watch."

Steinbrenner dispatched Wahl to go immediately to Canton to

do "whatever needed to be done." Murphy, who had flown with Munson about half a dozen times and considered him a friend, asked if he could go as well, and he did. So the two left the meeting at once to go home and pack bags, and then to meet at LaGuardia for a flight to Canton. Murphy, the former traveling secretary and in fact a pilot himself, was a good man for this assignment.

"We landed later that night," Wahl recalls, "but it was so late that we just found a motel and didn't go to the house until Friday morning. I didn't know Diana that well, so it was difficult for me to invade the home at such a time. But she welcomed us graciously and appreciated our being there. Later, I became a publicist for ABC Sports and would have dinner with her every year when we did the Hall of Fame football game. She's a great lady.

"Our mission was to take care of the family and to work with the city and the county, handling whatever needs anyone had as best we could. Looking back, it was very smart of George to send us there. Diana had Yankee representation at her side the whole weekend. And it was important to her.

"We didn't have a car, so the sheriff's office arranged for us to have a car and driver all weekend. The sheriff was great and took charge of everything. He was the key, he provided security at the home and kept people out."

It was quickly decided that a public viewing would be held on Sunday and a funeral on Monday at the Rossi Funeral Home, a plan that would have to change as the magnitude of the event became more clear.

"Back at the house," says Murphy, "Diana would be periodically overcome, and would say things like, 'What is to become of us?' She had the three small children and I could understand her real-world anxieties. Would they lose the house? Thurman's salary? She went from grief to her motherly duties, back and forth. It was good that she had her parents there. She was always gracious to us throughout the difficult weekend."

Tote showed Murphy and Wahl Thurman's office, with a model of the Citation on the desk. "There it is," he said. "There's the killer."

Minutes after Steinbrenner received the devastating news, he wanted to call his players before they heard the news on the radio. He split the task with Tallis; he would call the veteran stars of the team, and Tallis the others. The key was to be brief and move on so that they could reach everyone. Of course, as they worked their way through the roster, the news was starting to break on the radio, and the players were calling one another.

Cedric Tallis, a baseball "lifer," knew Thurman mostly as a ballplayer he had coveted while running the Kansas City Royals, and now grieved as the Yankees' general manager. "He always ran the ball out, always slid, never avoided contact despite the troubles with his knees," he would say. "In baseball, this is the measure of the man, the guts behind the glory. And even as an opponent who saw him a dozen times a year, you saw that quality in him."

One of the first calls was to Catfish Hunter in Norwood, where Munson had once been a neighbor. Hunter was not used to getting calls from Steinbrenner.

"Did you hear about Thurman?" he asked. Told that he hadn't, Steinbrenner said, "He's dead. He got killed in the worst way, crashed his plane and burned up."

Hunter told Armen Keteyian in his autobiography:

> Oh, no, not right after Daddy and Clyde. It was like George had said an oak tree standing tall in my front yard for the last 30 years had suddenly just fallen over. Oak trees don't just fall. Thurman Munson just doesn't die. Not now, not this way.
>
> I walked across the street to tell Nettles. He thought it was some kind of gag. "Right," said Graig, "what's the joke?"
>
> "No joke," I said, "Thurman's dead." Then the phone rang. Mr. Steinbrenner was on the line.

Dealing with three deaths in a span of three months was beyond belief. You try not to let it affect you, you know you've got a job to do, a game to play, but Lord, it's a lot to ask of a man.

In Nettles's book *Balls,* with Peter Golenbock, he says, "It took a few minutes to sink in. I just couldn't believe it. It was the first real tragedy of my life. I broke down and cried like a baby."

The calls went on. Steinbrenner called Guidry. "I knew there was something wrong," Ron remembers, "because he just doesn't call." Disbelieving, Gator sat silently in his rocking chair long into the evening with his wife Bonnie and her parents.

It was not unusual for Steinbrenner to call Piniella. They would speak frequently, even to discuss the roster. The two Tampa residents respected each other. Piniella would tell Maury Allen:

Shortly before 5, the phone rang. Anita answered. "Lou," she said, "it's for you. George." I didn't think much about the call. By now he was in the habit of calling me occasionally to talk about a player on another club, getting my opinions.

His voice was choked. He could barely talk. He was nervous and emotional. "There's been a crash in Canton. Thurman's plane, very bad . . . Thurman's passed away." Then he hung up. I ran out into the kitchen where Anita was beginning to prepare dinner for the kids. "Thurman's dead," I blurted out. "Killed in a crash."

"Oh my God," Anita shrieked, "Diane, what about Diane?"

We stood there in the kitchen, the two of us, holding each other tightly, our bodies shaking, gasping and sobbing and with tears running down our cheeks. Anita seemed like a rag doll in my arms, about to collapse and fall.

My first reaction was anger. I was mad at Thurman. "Why

in hell did he have to get into this thing? Why did he need that plane? Damn it, what did he need it for?"

Anita and I comforted each other. For the first hour or two, we were just angry. We had talked about this yesterday! I thought I was making progress getting him to give up the jet for financial reasons. It was so expensive. He hadn't sold his two small planes. I thought I was making sense.

Goose Gossage was another Yankee whom Steinbrenner called directly. He was getting ready to go to a concert when the phone rang in his bedroom with the news. "George who?" he said, not used to such a call.

"George Steinbrenner" was the response. "I have some terrible news. We lost Thurman today in a plane crash."

"I was in total shock," recalls Willie Randolph. "Stunned. You hear what people are saying to you, but you don't believe it. No, there's no way this happened. I was just with him the other night. We were sitting there joking, playing cards. It was a total shock. Disbelief. I broke down and cried."

There had always been a special bond between Thurman and Willie. In his rookie year, Thurman's MVP year, Willie had to battle a bit to get his swings in during batting practice. He thought he was being dissed. Thurman made sure he got to hit, and later gave him a T-shirt with ROOK printed on it. Willie has it to this day.

Chris Chambliss, one of the most sensitive men on the team, the son of a chaplain, said that he and his wife were in a car in New Jersey going for ice cream when they heard the news on the radio. "We just looked at each other and didn't say a word for I don't know how long. We were just stunned, quiet. We didn't say anything to each other for a long, long time. We were both so shocked."

Bucky Dent was having an early dinner at Windows on the World atop the World Trade Center on the off day. As he was leaving, someone said, "Aren't you Bucky Dent?" When Dent said he was, the stranger said, "Isn't it a shame what happened to Thurman?" Dent said, "What are you talking about?" And the stranger said, "He was killed in a plane crash!"

"It stunned me. I kind of fell back on the car. I said, 'No, that's not true.' He said it was and I asked him, 'Was there anybody with him?' And he said, 'Yeah, there were two other people in the plane.'

"My first reaction was I thought it was Bobby Murcer and his wife, because they walked out with Thurman in Chicago. I thought maybe Bobby and Kay were flying to Canton with him."

18

Mickey Morabito phoned Billy Martin, knowing what an emotional call this would be to a very emotional man. Mickey and Billy were close, and Mickey would eventually go with Billy to Oakland, where he remains traveling secretary to this day.

"I was twelve, and I was out fishing with Dad and Nick Nicolosi, who owned the hotel where a lot of Yankees stayed," says Billy Joe Martin. "Suddenly there were police on the shore with a bullhorn, paging Billy Martin.

" 'What did I do now, pard,' he said.

"We came ashore and they said that he had an emergency phone call. He jumped into the first car and I was in the second. It was Mickey with the horrible news.

"Just a few days before, I had been working out at second base and Thurman was watching me take ground balls. He said to Dad, 'I can't wait till I can see myself and my son like you are with Billy Joe.'

"He used to get me when I would be at second base; it was a

ballplayer's trick. He'd be shagging balls in the outfield, and then would throw them in on one bounce to hit me in the back of my knee. He was the best at it. I would drop like a tree falling.

"After the news, we went to our apartment, and Dad called Diana. He was just crushed. He said he wanted to go out, but I said, 'Dad, don't do it, somebody might say something about Thurman you don't like . . . ,' and he said, 'You're right.' So we stayed home and watched two John Wayne movies. He must have cried five or six times during the movies. I fixed him a Chivas and soda, but he didn't touch it."

Martin issued a statement through Morabito: "For the people who never knew him and didn't like him, I feel sorry for them. He was a great man. For his family and his friends and all the people who knew and loved him, my deepest sympathy. We not only lost a leader and a husband and a devoted family man, which is rare today. He was a dear friend. We would sit a lot and talk about our problems. I loved him."

Sparky Lyle, Thurman's fun-loving friend, was with the Texas Rangers, who were due into Cleveland for a weekend series. Sparky's two sons had been visiting him and his wife, Mary, during their summer vacation and they were taking them home. So they flew into Pittsburgh to drop them off and then flew to Cleveland. They were in a cab going to the hotel when the taxi driver turned around and said, "Wasn't that awful what happened today to Thurman Munson?" They had no idea what had happened, as they'd been on a plane all afternoon.

Rookie Jerry Narron was sharing a rented apartment with Ron Davis when Cedric Tallis called. Davis took the call. The next day, Narron would be the Yankees' "missing man" catcher in a never-to-be-forgotten ceremony at Yankee Stadium.

I was at my desk at the baseball commissioner's office. I had joined Bowie Kuhn's staff a year earlier. On the wall over my desk was a large oil painting of Munson at bat, painted by Arnold Cohen, my uncle, who had taken the image from the cover of Thurman's autobiography.

My phone rang, and it was George Steinbrenner. I knew he hadn't asked for me, and I don't know why it was put through to me, but he said, "This is George Steinbrenner, I have to speak to the commissioner at once."

"It's Marty Appel, Mr. Steinbrenner."

"Marty, there's been a terrible accident involving Thurman Munson, and he's been killed. Please put me right through to Bowie."

"Okay, hold on," I said.

I didn't want to take a chance on transferring the call. Imagine that call not getting picked up after being transferred. So I hurried out of my office and hustled down the hall, about sixty feet, to Kuhn's office. I stuck my head in the door and also realized I shouldn't be the one carrying this news.

"Commissioner, I have George Steinbrenner on my phone, and he needs to speak to you urgently—I'm going to transfer the call to your line, and I'm here to ask you to please pick it up yourself."

I raced back and transferred the call. This was well beyond the limit of George Steinbrenner's patience, but it worked and he delivered the news himself.

Meanwhile, as collaborator on Munson's autobiography, I began to get media calls myself, some looking for comment from the commissioner, some looking for comment from me.

No one had ever called me before for a statement about the passing of a celebrity, unless it was some old-time Yankee and I needed to speak on behalf of the organization.

I said something about the shock and the parallel to his predecessor as Yankee captain, Lou Gehrig, also dying young (Gehrig was thirty-seven). The quote wound up on the back page of the early editions of the *Daily News,* with quotes from Martin, Kuhn, Carl Yastrzemski, Pete Rose, Earl Weaver, and others. I didn't think I belonged in such prominent company when such a great tragedy had occurred. By the morning editions, people more highly placed than I had been heard from, and I was moved to an inner page. I felt relieved.

Bowie Kuhn called the death "an almost indescribable loss. He was a wonderful, enormously likeable guy and a truly great ballplayer. As tough a competitor as he was on the field, he was a warm friend of baseball people and a loving family man. Baseball sends its heartfelt sympathy to his wife and children."

In Cleveland, Gabe Paul did television interviews outside Municipal Stadium and talked about Thurman as a clutch ballplayer. "One year," he said, "I think it might have been 1977—I believe he hit .722 with men on second and third." It was a totally improvised statistic, at least three hundred points high and probably more.

Carlton Fisk said, "People always said Boston–New York was Fisk vs. Munson and there was a personal rivalry. If we were, as people said, the worst of the best of enemies, it was because we had the highest amount of respect for one another.

"We both thought for a while that we were the two best catchers in the league, and we tried to prove to one another that each of us was better than the other. I talked to him more than anyone else when we played them. We'd talk about catching, about how we hurt.

"People make baseball players out to be idols. They talk about how important it is to be the highest paid, to get the ink and print. And then this.

"I guess the point is driven home stronger to me because I respect the man so much. And because I'll really miss him."

Nat Tarnopol drove home from his record company office on Seventh Avenue, went into his study, and cried. "I never saw anything like that before," said his son Paul. "For a long, long time, he just wasn't himself."

Duane Munson heard the news in Laurel, Maryland, got in his car, and drove to Canton, where he would stay with Darla. The two of them went to the crash site the next morning and even took some photos. Duane was photographed viewing the wreckage. They, along with Thurman's parents, would be the forgotten family in the coming days. All attention would be on the widow and the children.

"I just wanted to stay in the background," said Duane. "I was asked to do some interviews, but declined. I couldn't believe Thurm had crashed. He had everything going for himself. I must admit I was a little bitter about all that. I wouldn't fly with him and I told him that he shouldn't be flying around too, but he wanted to do it, so he did."

"None of us got called, not one of us," says Darla Munson, speaking of her parents and her siblings. "I was walking down the street, and a neighbor called my husband over and whispered to him . . . I was wondering, what's going on, and my husband said, 'Your brother just died in a plane crash.'

"Janice was on her way home from work and heard it on radio. Mother heard about it in her nursing home. Someone said, 'Your son's dead.' Just like that. And of course our father wasn't around."

In Tucson, Arizona, Darrell Munson, now sixty-four, heard the news when a neighbor came by and told him. "I don't read newspapers or watch television because I just don't like the news—it's all bad," he would say. He had last seen his family five years earlier.

In this case, he was right. The news was all bad.

In Chicago, Bobby Murcer took a phone call from his friend Jimmy Lindstrom in New Jersey telling him the news. Lindstrom, along with his sister Candy, were old friends of the Murcers. The friendship had begun when they were running the Bobby Richardson Fan Club in the sixties. Richardson had introduced them to Murcer, then nineteen, as someone they would like.

By coincidence, I, as a youngster, was in that fan club! Richardson had been a special player to me and we had maintained a friendship after I joined the Yankee PR department, one that continues to this day. (I call him each year after the World Series to "celebrate" his 1960 Series RBI records lasting another year.) So Richardson, Murcer, the Lindstroms, and I were all linked through this strange circle of connections.

With no hesitancy, Bobby called Diana's house. Her friend Joanne answered the phone and Bobby told her they would be there as soon as possible. Kay hurriedly got her two children settled with neighbors while Bobby arranged a flight from Chicago to Canton. And they arrived Thursday night, hours after the crash.

Heading straight for the house, Kay remembers it being "full of family and friends, with lots of hugs, tears, and stories throughout the night. We gathered around the kitchen table and just told Thurman stories. There were many laughs too as the night progressed. Everyone was drained and sappy, but just too emotional to know any other way to react. No one was hysterical, mostly we were just operating in disbelief."

The Murcers went to an upstairs bedroom at around three in the morning, had a little sleep, and returned to Chicago on Friday, gathering the kids and clothing for a trip to New York. Bobby phoned Billy Martin to tell him that Diana wanted the games played, but that he himself would have to miss the Friday game, and would be back Saturday.

They arrived on Saturday at the home of the Lindstroms in Wayne, New Jersey, where they would stay for the weekend. Kay and the Lindstroms went to the game on Saturday night, in which Bobby played.

"They were our port in the storm," says Kay. "Our kids always knew them as relatives."

Prior to his arrival, Bobby asked Jimmy Lindstrom to help him prepare a eulogy. Diana had already asked him to be one of the speakers at the still-being-planned funeral. Bobby was just too emotionally drained to focus on it.

When Bobby arrived in New Jersey, there were Jimmy and Candy at a table working on the eulogy. They showed Bobby a quotation from Angelo Patri, an American educator, that might work as the opening of the eulogy.

Together, Bobby, Jimmy, and Candy worked out the final draft, although Bobby would still be tinkering with it when I met up with him on Sunday night in Canton.

By six o'clock, the bulletin was being reported from coast to coast on television and radio. Five minutes earlier, the Mets had posted the news on the Shea Stadium scoreboard before 15,319 fans watching them play a Thursday doubleheader against the Phillies. Lee Mazzilli was at bat when the news went up and it caused a strange murmuring from the crowd.

"Usually when you hear something you look at the crowd," said center fielder Gary Maddox. "When I didn't see anything I turned to the scoreboard. I just felt grief-stricken."

Tim McCarver, a catcher for the Phillies then, said, "I've never heard a ballpark that was any quieter than that."

Arthur Richman, the Mets' PR director, made the decision to put the announcement on the scoreboard. "We could do that, do it with a PA announcement, or do nothing," he said. It was not an easy call.

Mickey Rivers, a teammate of Thurman's just days before, was in Cleveland with the Texas Rangers, playing cards in his hotel room with his new teammates. He was confused. He wanted to go to Canton to pay his respects, but couldn't get an answer at the house. He wanted to stay for the Monday funeral, but thought the Rangers wouldn't let him. In the end, he just said, "Look, I've got to go to the funeral." And he would go.

Keith Olbermann, who earned national fame on ESPN's *Sports-Center* and became a prominent newscaster and commentator, was just beginning his career in journalism at UPI radio, where he had taken his passion for baseball cards and baseball history and turned it into a daily sportscast.

I'd graduated somehow from Cornell and begun work for Sam Rosen at UPI's old radio network in the Daily News Building on East Forty-second Street in New York. At twenty, I was thirteen years younger than the next youngest radio staffer, and among my UPI colleagues were Milton Richman, Joe Carnicelli, and Bill Madden.

I had been entrusted with maybe ten shifts of my own by August 2, starting with a 5:45 sportscast. I was then on, hourly, through 10:45. The UPI sportscaster had to take in and edit tape from games, do occasional enterprise interviews, write and voice a two-minute commentary, and do those six sportscasts.

I prepped them in the backup air studio, then crossed the tiny radio newsroom past a bank of teletypes, our means of interaction with the various bureaus and desks around the world. (There was one computer for all of radio and it was used only to prepare the radio "billboards" and such that went out on the clackety-clacking machines around the country.)

I grabbed my copy at about 5:43 and started to move toward the main air studio, and just as I passed the ten or twelve thermal printers, the bells went off as if the thing were about to explode. It was the "abstract" wire—the intra-UPI method bureaus used to send messages to New York. For some reason I stopped and read it: CLEVELAND BURO URGENT TO NY; THURMAN MUNSON YANKEES DEAD CRASH PILOTING PRIVATE JET CANTON-AKRON ARPT.

I got woozy. Not ten months earlier I had been a pure Yankee fan watching him bully and cajole his pitchers into a second straight world championship. Now I had to go on a thousand radio stations and kill him. And I had sixteen words to work off.

I rushed into the booth and scribbled something on my script and basically started to wing it. I recited Munson's Rookie of the Year Award, his leadership of the Yanks back to respectability, the 1976, '77, and '78 World Series. The sportscast was only two minutes long. Somehow I finished it.

The rest of the night was people grabbing me and telling me what to do next. The moment the 5:45 newscast was over, the news editor, Frank Raphael, burst in and pulled me out of the chair. "Write a forty-second bulletin on him! As quickly as you can!" A friend of mine from college said he heard it on the air on a Buffalo station at about six o'clock. He said he nearly drove off the road half because of the tragedy and half because it was me telling it.

Within minutes, Sam Rosen was on the phone. "Call every stringer you can get, get them to get reaction from any player they can before the games are over. I'll get there as soon as I can!" I was not utterly numb. It seemed I'd just put the phone down when Sam walked in. "Here. I hate to do this to you, but I have to work on a special about him. These are the home phone numbers for Roy White and Lou Piniella."

I haven't gulped much in my life, but cliché that it is, I gulped then. Roy White had been with the Yankees since the day I became a fan. I tried him first. My memory's hazy—either he or Piniella wept, but the other begged me to tell them it was a horrible mistake. But both of them—and I'll never forget this—actually spent five minutes expressing their emotions eloquently and honestly. I could only thank them by telling them that I'd make copies of the interviews for the other networks and New York stations so they wouldn't be barraged any further. I remember a stringer ap-

pearing within an hour and to our credit, we really did it—
we made copy after copy for the other stations.

At that time, of course, the details and the interviews and
the memories kept flooding in. I suddenly got the picture in
my mind of Thurman from the Yankee Stadium fiftieth anniversary book, back in 1973, carrying his infant daughter in
his glove. He was dead because he wanted to see her, and
the rest of his family, more often. It was suddenly a world
filled with the potential for bitter, heart-rending irony. I
think I started one of the sportscasts, or maybe the morning
commentary, by describing that photograph and the tragedy
it unknowingly portended.

And suddenly it was one a.m., two hours after my shift
should've ended. Sam was tapping me on the shoulder.
"They're killing our team. We should go to Mexico and
smoke ourselves blind," he said. "And you should go home
before you miss the last train to Hastings."

I remember riding it, staring out at the inky blackness of
the Hudson River. I couldn't figure out why I heard somebody laughing elsewhere in the car. How could they be
laughing? Munson was dead. He was the first man I remembered the Yankees drafting. I saw him play when they
brought him up at the end of 1969. He was the hope of the
future. The reality was even better. Sure he was tough on the
media, but not on the kids like me. And he was there from
my days as a novice fan through the start of my career. How
could they laugh? His life was over—and so was my childhood.

Dennis D'Agostino, later a publicist for the Mets and the Knicks,
was working the dayside shift at the Associated Press in New York.
"Between the shift supervisor and the wire filer we had several print-

ers, including a 'message' printer in which other bureaus around the nation could instantly message us. In midafternoon, we got a few messages from the Akron bureau saying that the local FAA there was reporting that a plane had gone down and one of the victims may have been Thurman Munson. Not long after four p.m., Dick Joyce had me call the Yankees just to ask if they had heard anything.

"I got Mickey Morabito on the phone and said, 'Mickey, I don't want to alarm or scare you, but we've been getting a few messages about a plane that has gone down in Akron and that Thurm might have been on it.' Mickey said, 'We know. We've heard the reports too, and we're checking them out.' And that was it. A little while later, obviously, the word started getting out."

At the city desk of the *Canton Repository,* the paper Thurman had delivered as a boy (with Diana in pursuit on her bicycle), city editor Jim Weber got the first call soon after the accident. "We didn't know it was Munson's plane with the first call, but we knew soon after," he recalls. Reporter Diana Rossetti raced to the scene on her Yamaha motorcycle, knowing roads would be blocked. A second reporter, Jim Clark, headed out there from the newsroom. Bob Rossiter, a staff photographer, had trouble getting to the site, so he abandoned his car and walked a mile carrying his gear.

"You could smell it before you could see it," says Rossiter. "My nostrils burned from the acrid odor of the fuel-fired blaze and the molten asphalt beneath it."

Clark says, "What sticks with me is all the dumb stuff I did trying to get the story. I drove up to the airport and went to the terminal. I had no idea where it happened. I finally went to the north end of the airfield. The first fireman on the scene was the guy I wound up talking to. I didn't even have change to call Weber and tell him what it was and what was happening. When I got back, everyone said, 'What did the witnesses see?' I didn't have a clue."

Sports editor Bob Stewart, who had covered Thurman's scholastic career, was clicking away at his typewriter. It was a night to re-member for the small city newspaper, where "stop the presses" sto-ries were few.

The first New York reporter on the scene was Dan Lauck of *Newsday,* who got there after sunset, and after the body had been removed. "I hadn't been driving five minutes when I came up over a rise in the road and there it was," he said. "A hulk of metal and plastic and rub-ber—a Cessna Citation—twisted, flattened, and still smoldering, smack in the middle of the road. I got out of the car as quietly as I could. Would have whispered if there had been anyone around. But there wasn't. No security, no investigators, no celebrity ghouls, just me and one other soul. Thurman Munson's. I found myself circling the wreckage, as you would a casket, though Munson's body already had been pulled from the plane. It was the smell that struck me. I told myself I would never forget it. Maybe it was a combination of the rubber and plastic and paint, still cooking, that gave the scene its pungent scent."

The *New York Times* jumped into action, typewriters clicking away, wire copy machines screaming with bells alerting the newsroom to a breaking bulletin out of Canton. Sports and metro needed to di-vide coverage. Jim Tuite called Murray Chass at home, and Chass volunteered to write the "Man in the News" feature. "My wife was in the hospital at the time," he says. "I could do 'Man in the News' from memory. I'd covered his whole career. The news story would require a lot of phone calls to local authorities and to teammates for reac-tion. I was better suited that day for the bio."

"We mobilized at once," recalls Arthur Pincus, the Sunday sports editor. "I was on the fifth floor when we got word, working in the art department with Gary Honig, the photo editor, and Pat Flynn, the art director assigned to sports. We were starting to plan the Sunday paper. Joe Vecchione, our Sports Monday editor, called us, looking for Gary, who said, 'We gotta go; Thurman Munson's been killed in a plane crash.'

"LeAnn Schreiber was our sports editor, about six months into the job, which was pretty historic—a woman sports editor at the *Times*. We had a conference with me, Vecchione, and Harold Claassen. Tuite captained the assignments. Jim Naughton wrote the main news story, and Dave Anderson did about four columns."

The *Times* was used to crisis. "Aside from momentary disbelief, and an effort to make sure we had the facts right, we had things well in hand fairly soon after we heard the news," says copy editor Paul Winfield. "His death occurred early enough for us to put together a complete package. And the circumstances turned the news piece into his obituary; there was no discrete obituary as a result."

Art Toretzky is a talent agent in Hollywood who was still learning his craft and living in New York in 1979. He went to high school and college with me and I had given him a copy of the Munson autobiography. That night, the *New York Times* needed a copy of the book quickly, from which to run excerpts in their coverage. "I was living a few blocks from the *Times* on the West Side of Manhattan," says Toretzky. "The *Times* had a messenger at my door within thirty minutes to pick up my copy of the book. So in my sadness over the story, I also felt that at least I was doing something, and when the book was quoted in the *Times,* I felt I played a small part. I was a big Yankee fan, and this was a big, big loss."

"When I received the call that he was killed, I was stunned," says Phil Pepe of the *Daily News*. "Before I could call my office, the phone rang and it was the office calling me, and we discussed what my role would be in covering the story. I was to call as many players as I could reach. I was the one who broke the news to Roy White because he hadn't yet been called. He couldn't speak after I told him what happened. He put his wife on the phone."

Artist Bill Gallo drew a memorable drawing of Munson, looking down from heaven at two sad youngsters who regularly appeared in his cartoons, with one saying, "NAW, YUCHIE—I JUST DON'T FEEL LIKE PLAYIN' BALL TODAY . . ." He titled it "No Game Today."

In his memoir *Drawing a Crowd,* Gallo wrote:

> The word of Thurman Munson's death . . . reached me while I was delivering the sports segment of the *Daily News'* old radio show. In the middle of my spiel, *News* sports columnist Mike Lupica dashed into the studio with the report that the Yankees catcher and captain had been killed in a plane crash. I gave this information to the listeners live, wrapping up the radio segment and got out of there thinking, "I've got to replate my cartoon."
>
> I had already completed the next day's drawing: it celebrated the pending induction into baseball's Hall of Fame of Willie Mays and my close friend *News* columnist Dick Young. But that drawing would not see print. By the time I was in the News Building elevator, heading from the fifth-floor studio to the seventh-floor newsroom, I knew what I was going to draw. When something big happens, I work that way. My mind works very fast; it sharpens under pressure.
>
> In this drawing I wanted to look like he's gone, but still looking at the symbol of baseball, which is kids. Maybe the symbol has changed now, maybe it would be a dollar sign, but in my mind at that time it was always kids. Baseball definitely starts with kids. Kids playing in the sandlot.
>
> Munson is watching over the kids that he left behind. That was my immediate thought, that he must be looking down, that he's away now but . . . it gets kind of corny I guess. Maybe I think that way. It's a sentimental thing, and why not? I think I was right because I've had so many requests for copies. Twenty years later, I still get requests for this drawing.

Rupert Murdoch had purchased the *New York Post* in 1976, and this was a story made for his tabloid style of journalism. Across page after page in the coming days, both in the news and in the sports sections, would appear a banner called DEATH OF A YANKEE, with a photo of Munson and sensational coverage. Reporter Bob Drury was rushed to the scene. It was a style that the paper would repeat a year later for John Lennon, and then again through the years whenever a celebrity died under tragic circumstances. In many ways, the Munson coverage helped to define the *Post* in its burgeoning tabloid war with its rival, the *Daily News*.

Sports Illustrated made Munson's death the lead item in its Scorecard section a week later, but because so many days had passed, the editors looked at it as not current enough in their news cycle, and did not choose to provide a full story. A photo of Thurman's empty locker accompanied the article.

At WPIX, the Yankees' station since 1951 (and based in the same building as UPI and the *Daily News*), the news was first reported on the 7:30 *Action News* anchored by Tim Malloy and Christy Ferrer, featuring early film from Cleveland's "Chopper 5" over the crash site and a report that two people had been killed. (Ferrer would later lose her husband on 9/11.) They threw to sportscaster Jerry Girard, who called Munson one of the greatest catchers of all time, who performed at his best when it really counted. "He had a passion to win and the ability to do it."

The ten o'clock newscast was expanded to an hour, and Frank Messer and Bill White joined anchorman Steve Bosh and Girard. Jerry called him "the guy you wanted up there with the game on the line."

While the media professionals were going about their business, hearts were breaking. The baseball community and its fans were in shock. The story hit hard with nonfans who just cared about the widow and her three young children.

On film, WPIX had teenage Latino fans seated at the Yankee office entrance steps because it was a place to gather. One was almost argumentative. "Everyone is saying he was the catcher, but he was the *captain*," he kept saying.

Girard played film of an interview he did with Munson, wearing a windbreaker, in March. He asked Thurman why he was now talking to the press, but hadn't the previous year. "I was hurt a lot last year," Munson said. "This year we're just going to have fun. No rock stars this year." Then he mentioned a reporter (Bouton, unnamed) whom he had refused to talk to three times. He said he liked "Mickey, and Ellie, and all."

Said Messer: "I put Thurman Munson in the same class as Mickey Mantle and Johnny Unitas, whose games I broadcast. All three of them were superstars who played in pain."

Added White: "We talked about Ohio a lot. I played for Warren Harding, he played for Canton. We were friendly rivals. An infielder or an outfielder can play with pain; a catcher can't do that if the hinges don't work."

In response to a question about whether there could be any sort of positive effect on the Yankees for the season, White said, "I don't think it can have any kind of a positive effect. This is all about thinking about Diane and his kids. The players aren't going to say, 'Let's win one for Thurman.' That's not what this is about."

Jerry asked Messer why there had always been such a barrier between Thurman and the media. Said Messer: "I think he felt he'd been misused by some members of the media. But he had a friendly, warm side. Just Tuesday when we did a radio interview, I was sitting by his locker, which was next to Reggie's, and he teased Reggie to go on out to the field so the reporters would follow him and we could be alone. We talked about how barometric pressure could affect joints. I had knee replacement surgery a few years before, so we had knee pain in common."

Steve Bosh talked about the side of Munson fans didn't see. "A priest had called the station and asked if Thurman Munson could visit a very sick eleven-year-old in the hospital. They played a film that Munson made, addressing the child, wishing him a quick recovery, telling him to come up to the stadium and visit the clubhouse and shake hands with the guys when he's better."

Added Girard: "I never got to know Munson well; there was always a barrier. I think it was a sense of insecurity on his part. He was so hurt at talk that Jackson was the real leader. He was hurt when a writer said that Rivers deserved the MVP award in 1976. And he wanted assurance from George Steinbrenner that he would always be the highest-paid Yankee. I never really knew him, but I miss him already."

Over at WABC Channel 7, Roseanne Scamardella (yes, she whose name had been mocked on *Saturday Night Live*) said the city was in a state of shock, and she turned the report to Chee Chee Williams, who had gone to Norwood, New Jersey, where Thurman had lived, and visited the homes of Nettles and Hunter. Nettles spoke with her on his front porch, dressed in a T-shirt. He said, "He was like a kid with a new toy. I flew with him a couple of weeks ago, the same plane. I'm just in a state of shock."

Hunter was on the couch in his living room. There were no baseball items on display; it had obviously been rented furnished. There was a floral pattern on the sofa, and a large painting of a bouquet of flowers on the wall. Hunter, in his final weeks as a player, was dressed in shorts and a Puma T-shirt. "He wanted people to like him for what he did, not just for being a ballplayer," he said. "He didn't want praise, he just wanted what was due to him, that's all. If he did something good, put it in the paper, something bad, put it in the paper, and leave it at that. He was my best friend on the team."

Said Chee Chee: "Even those of us who didn't know him personally feel a sense of loss."

She sent it back to anchorman Bill Beutel, who tossed it to sportscaster Warner Wolf. "The key word for Thurman was consistent," he said. "He seldom gave you a bad game. If he wasn't hitting that day, he was still an excellent defensive catcher, and one of the best clutch hitters in baseball. He was the first Yankee to win Rookie of the Year and MVP, an All-American at Kent State, a .529 hitter in the World Series, and he batted over .300 in five of his nine years."

"He was a wonderful guy," said Gabe Paul, now the Indians' president. "He was very misunderstood. I don't think most people understood what a fine fellow he was because he was a little gruff. He loved to play baseball and he played hurt. You couldn't keep him out of the lineup. He was a great player and a great person."

Back at home, Thurman's high school coach Don Eddins said, "He was a fantastic competitor. He had extreme confidence in himself and he could have excelled at any sport he desired."

Governor James Rhodes of Ohio said, "He played the game he loved hard and with unmatched skill. He was a fit hero for young people, a man who put family first and who stood for the highest principles of family life. It is ironic he died while learning to fly so that he could spend more time with his wife and children. Thurman was also a personal friend and it was a privilege to know him. I extend my deepest sympathies to his wife and family during this difficult time."

The *Repository* caught up with Munson friends Bill James and Chuck Gelal, who were at the crash site to view the wreckage. Both were pilots. "I guess he got interested in flying through Bill and me," Gelal said. "He was so excited about that jet."

Tom Villante was working in the commissioner's office late that Thursday afternoon when the news came in. He had worked for the Brooklyn Dodgers (through the ad agency for Schaefer, their beer sponsor) in the 1950s and was also a former Yankee batboy, circa 1945.

He had to walk from Rockefeller Center to Grand Central for his train to Harrison, New York. "I was walking, and I was in a daze," he recalls. "This was such an enormous story, but it was before e-mails and cell phones, and back then, it took hours for stories to get around. So I walked those seven or eight blocks to Grand Central and I could tell no one knew. The papers no longer turned out 'extra editions' (read all about it!) and this was too soon anyway.

"I had this urge to stop and tell everyone as I walked along Fifth and Madison avenues," he says. "It was like I was holding this secret, this enormous news, and I was being selfish with it. I had the need to stop people and say, 'Thurman Munson is dead,' but on Manhattan streets you don't make eye contact and don't talk to strangers. So I didn't stop anyone. I went home on the train and thought about the tragedy to the game and for his family. It was such a sad thing.

"I thought about Roy Campanella and his car accident in 1958. Another great New York catcher, another MVP. Very different personalities, of course. And as it turned out, had the plane not caught fire, Thurman would have lived out the same life as Campy, paralyzed and wheelchair bound. I guess it was a blessing, in its own way. Not many people out there like Campy who could have adjusted to thirty-five years in a wheelchair and kept a sunny disposition. Not many."

19

The Murcers sent a message from Diana in Canton on Friday expressing the hope that the team would play all the scheduled games, because "that's what he would want the team to do." And so the Yankees pressed on, making plans for the pregame ceremonies on Friday night.

"I'm in no frame of mind to play at all," said Piniella, who added, "It took me until my second season here to get through his hard shell. I got to know him probably as good as any player on the club or better. He really had compassion. He didn't want everyone in the world to know it, but he had compassion and tenderness."

Roy White's locker had been next to Thurman's for ten years. "It'll be tough to concentrate on what you have to do as a ballplayer," he said. "I was hoping they'd call the game off. The games seem very insignificant after what has happened. It doesn't seem so important to go out and play. I'll always remember being out with him in spring training. We'd go to the dog races at night and he'd handicap the races. This is tougher than anything I've gone through in my life. It makes me think about my own life. Do I have my life in order? Am I too selfish? You never know how close you are to death. It's so simple. Here you are with him one moment, then he's gone. Forever."

"I'll always remember all the laughter we shared," said Guidry. "Even when we were trying to be serious, we couldn't."

Early in the morning on Friday a carton of a dozen Louisville Slugger Munson bats were delivered from Hillerich & Bradsby and quickly put away in a storage area by a grieving Nick Priore, Pete Sheehy's clubhouse assistant. Nick was crusty and cantankerous like Munson, but also like Thurman had a soft side that he didn't necessarily like people to see.

A delivery from the New Rochelle–based dry cleaners used by the Yankees included all of their home jerseys with black armbands added to the left sleeve.

"I got a call from my wife about seven p.m. on Thursday saying the Yankees were urgently trying to reach me," says Joe Fosina, whose company, Raleigh Athletic, handled the Yankees' cleaning needs. "I called Pete Sheehy and he said, 'You heard the news?' I had only heard it moments before, on my car radio. Pete said we had to do something for the uniforms in time for the Friday game. I went to the stadium and picked up one full set of home uniform jerseys. At the factory in New Rochelle, we created several ideas: the armbands, a number 15 patch, and some other things.

"At seven a.m. on Friday I went to the ballpark with my samples. Pete was there; he had slept overnight in the clubhouse. He took the samples up to George Steinbrenner. In the meantime, we brought in a half dozen seamstresses to be prepared for this rush project. Finally, the decision came down to go with the armbands. I raced back and everyone went to work.

"I returned to the stadium later that day with one full set done; we would have time later for the backup and road versions. At the entrance, after I was photographed walking in with them, I was stopped. I was told no one could go to the clubhouse except players and coaches. So I'm standing there, a regular visitor, holding an armful of about thirty-five uniform jerseys, and finally Bill Bergesh, the Yankees' scouting director, came by and authorized me to go downstairs. I walked in with this awful delivery and all the players were staring at me. Pete took them from me and began hanging them in the lockers, silently, one at a time."

Fred Stanley had been the first player to arrive. There were TV crews waiting to get reaction.

Larry Sacknoff was there from WNBC Channel 4. An unshaven Piniella stopped to talk to him as he walked from his car.

"He was witty, charming, compassionate; he was a good human being," said Sweet Lou. "He was liked by the kids here at the ballpark and in his community back home in Ohio."

Tippy Martinez, in town with the Orioles, said he was "amazed and shocked. I turned to my wife and said Thurman's been killed. It was a weird time because we were praying at the time, so we continued to pray. We know he's with the Lord right now."

Hunter and Nettles also spoke to the waiting TV crews as they prepared to enter the stadium.

Rick Cerrone, later one of my successors as the Yankees' PR director, was at that time the publisher of *Baseball Magazine,* a monthly that had revived the name of a classic baseball publication from the game's first half century. He brought a large floral arrangement to the outside of the clubhouse, which Sal, the guard at the door, took and gave to Pete. Sheehy placed it at the locker, and decided one was sufficient and there would be no others.

The other bouquets were arranged in the reception area at the Yankee office entrance.

Pete hung Thurman's uniform shirt in his locker with the "NY" facing out. "I just thought it was the way to do it," said the man who had been hanging uniforms in lockers for the Yankees since 1927. "I've never had this happen before."

The early newscasts were all leading with the story of the activity at Yankee Stadium. For veteran New York publicist Joe Goldstein, the horrific news from Canton had knocked him cold. He had organized a visit to the site of the old Polo Grounds with Willie Mays, prior to Mays's departure for Cooperstown and his Hall of Fame induction on Sunday. He now had no media available to work with and no event to stage, as the attention of everyone in New York's press corps turned to Canton and to Yankee Stadium.

This was still a time when cable TV was in its infancy. CNN didn't launch until the following year. ESPN's *SportsCenter* would not debut until September 7, 1979, about four weeks later. The burden of coverage was on local news.

At Channel 4, Marv Albert, his hair long and untamed, said, "Thurman Munson was a paradox—well liked by his teammates and opponents, but little rapport with the media, and this by his own choice. He was the heart of the Yankee ball club and one of the most gifted clutch hitters of all time." Then he played Sacknoff's filmed interviews from the stadium.

Also shown was film of groundskeepers preparing for the game, with Thurman's face on the scoreboard. The AT BAT part of the scoreboard showed number 15, .298, while work went on.

Marv concluded his report by showing that business was continuing. He said, "Meanwhile, the Yankees today brought up Brad Gulden and Bobby Brown, put Ed Figueroa on the disabled list, and obtained former Met infielder Lenny Randle from the Pirates."

At WCBS, Channel 2, anchorman Jim Jensen reported that all flags would be flown at half-staff on order from Mayor Ed Koch and Governors Hugh Carey of New York and Brendan Byrne of New Jersey, and then threw it to Sal Marchiano, who was outside Gate 4, behind the home plate rotunda, reporting live.

"None of the joy normally associated with the scene outside Gate 4 is visible," he said, describing the scene.

Jensen asked Marchiano, "Is this the sort of thing that can ignite a club and help them to win?"

Marchiano replied, "No one will discuss anything like this."

Channel 2's Carole Simpson introduced the spring training film of Thurman, in which he talked about flying with Tony Kubek. NBC Sports had made it widely available to all stations. Thurman had said, "Just the feeling of being alone for an hour or two by yourself, no one asking any questions, you don't have to put on any kind of an act, you just have to be on your toes and it's just a relaxation where you spend time by yourself and I need that. I also need to get home a lot, so I love to fly."

Jensen called him an "aging baseball player, but too young to die."

Bill Mazer caught up with Yogi Berra and filmed an interview for Channel 5's *10 O'clock News*. Yogi had "seen it all" during his thirty-four years in the majors, including the death of Gil Hodges, the manager of the Mets, six years earlier when Yogi was a coach there. No one went to Yogi for eloquence. He just delivered it straight: "He played the game hard, a real competitor, I'm gonna miss him."

Channel 2 also had Jerry Nachman by Gate 4, who reported, "Some fans are wearing armbands with the number 15, similar to what we saw in Los Angeles last year when Junior Gilliam died. The mood here is much more of a wake than a baseball game."

Nachman also caught up with Piniella, who said, "It's a shame. Thurman was a very good friend of mine. He loved to fly . . . had that accident yesterday . . . I just feel sorry that something like that had to happen."

Frankie Albohn, a likable longtime member of the stadium grounds crew, was interviewed and said, "He was a special guy to us, we're all going to really miss him. It's a sad thing."

Nachman, then on film speaking from Monument Park, said, "A

plaque will be placed here, and his number will be retired, and no one will ever use his locker."

Frank Duca, a runty grounds crew member whose job was to paint the lines around the catcher's box, wore an open shirt and a Yankees cap that looked like it was from the 1920s. He said, "The poor guy, not going to be here tonight and I'm painting it for somebody else."

Nachman reported that there was a sign by the Yankee clubhouse that said, "Please bear with us, give us tonight, only tonight, to be by ourselves."

Mickey Morabito released a statement from George Steinbrenner that said, "There's very little I can say to adequately express my feelings at this moment. I've lost a dear friend, a pal and one of the greatest competitors I've ever known. We spent many hours together talking baseball and business. He loved his family. He was our leader. The great sports world which made him so famous seems so small and unimportant now—and therein lies a great lesson for all of us."

Before going down to the clubhouse, Steinbrenner met Dave Anderson of the *New York Times* in his office overlooking the field. "I don't think most people knew how close we were," the owner said. "Nobody knew how much time we spent together. He used to come up here and talk with me, sometimes before the games or sometimes even after batting practice. He would be wearing his uniform pants and a T-shirt and sandals and he'd put his feet up on the desk and have a glass of orange juice and we'd talk. He liked to talk to me about business because he had all those deals going in Canton, where his home was.

"I remember telling him not long ago to get liquid, that we were going into a recession, and to get fixed interest rates for his money rather than floating on prime. As a businessman, he was the same way he was as a player—a hardworking, smart guy."

I smiled to myself when I read this. Thurman's version of the story was that he wore his spikes, not sandals, and that the clumps of mud that dropped onto Steinbrenner's desk gave him a kick. George didn't remember it that way, or chose not to.

Steinbrenner also revealed that he had said to Thurman, "Would it make any difference to you if we traded you to Cleveland like you always wanted?" And Thurman had told him, "It might. If you got a deal for me with the Indians, maybe I'd consider playing a couple more years." And so Steinbrenner had phoned Gabe Paul, now at Cleveland, and the two had agreed to discuss this possibility after the season.

Some fans put floral arrangements near the player entrance. The gates mercifully opened at six p.m. Eddie Layton played somber music on the organ for nearly the full two hours leading up to game time, setting the tone in the ballpark. He made it feel like a church. There was an unusual stillness as the fans entered and headed for their seats. A misty rain was falling—a baseball rain—not enough to call off the game, but appropriate weather for everyone's mood.

At 6:30, Steinbrenner went into the clubhouse and the full team met. He wanted to talk about playing the game. "Nobody wanted or felt any desire to play baseball," said Figueroa in his book. "Murcer conveyed to us that Munson's wife had said that we should play the game, as that would have been her husband's wish. Then George Steinbrenner talked to us. He could not contain his tears and began to cry, as did the rest of us, joining him in shared sorrow. It was a very sad night for all of us, the players and the Yankee management."

"Billy had to talk to everybody and he couldn't hold himself from talking about it," said Chris Chambliss. "Everybody was crying in there."

Emerging from the clubhouse after the meeting, Steinbrenner talked to the waiting press. He was wearing a white shirt with a red tie, and no jacket. Said Steinbrenner: "We had a meeting. We talked about the untimely passing of Thurman, and I'd just rather not discuss what took place in there. Everybody was there and a few fellows spoke and it was a tribute to Thurman and that's all I can really say."

But in answer to a question, he added, "Bobby Murcer said he talked to Thurman's wife last night. Diane said he would want them to play and that she felt that's what he would want and therefore she would appreciate it if the fellows went out and played . . . We're gonna play tonight, Monday we're all going to the funeral and if we don't get back, we don't get back, we'll forfeit."

And with that he turned and walked away.

20

The field was covered after what Frank Messer, on WPIX, called "desultory batting practice." But the tarp was removed just after eight p.m. In pregame remarks on WPIX, coming toward the end of Channel 11's 7:30 *Action News,* Messer revealed at once that number 15 would be retired, joining 3 (Ruth), 4 (Gehrig), 5 (DiMaggio), 7 (Mantle), 8 (Dickey and Berra), 16 (Ford), and 37 (Stengel); that Thurman's locker would be retired and never again used; and that there would be a plaque hung for Thurman in Monument Park.

Further, Mrs. Diana Munson would join Mrs. Eleanor Gehrig as the "First Ladies of the Yankees."

Ordinarily those might have been separate ceremonies, perhaps even the following year. Now it was done at once and announced at the top of the broadcast. It was included in the day's press notes so that the writers had it by six p.m.

WPIX did not use its upbeat opening animation. Don Carney, the veteran producer and director of the game, knew he had an unusually difficult telecast ahead of him. Messer and Bill White appeared on camera together, live, as they had the night before in the WPIX news studio on East Forty-second Street. There was no pre-taped opening segment, as was usually the case.

"We never know how the team will react," White said, as the tarp began to be removed from the field at 8:02.

Phil Rizzuto and Fran Healy were on WINS radio and the vast Yankee radio network. Listeners heard the familiar opening Yankee theme song, but then the somber voices of the announcers began filling time until the ceremony began.

Healy talked about his becoming a teammate of Thurman's in 1976, and how soon thereafter, when the Yankees were playing in Cleveland, Thurman had invited him to spend the night at his in-laws' home in Canton. The two had been opponents as far back as 1968 in the Eastern League.

"We were there, and he pointed to a house in the backyard and said, 'That's where you'll sleep.' And I looked at it and said, 'No way!' Thurman said, 'Well, what do you want me to do?' I told him he has to stay there too; he could sleep on the floor. And that's what he did!"

The two talked about how Munson had actually done something few players managed during their careers: he *had* "stopped to smell the roses"—had been there more than most players for his kids as they grew up.

Rizzuto said he didn't "know how I even got to Yankee Stadium to-day. Every few minutes my mind just went blank. But today is easier than yesterday, which was the longest night I can remember. At least today we're surrounded by teammates and friends, and the players can go out and spend some energy, hitting and catching the baseballs.

"Thurman used to tell me a little prayer," said Phil, "something that can work for everyone, whether you are Jewish, or Catholic or Protestant . . . 'You've got to live for today because tomorrow may never come.' And how true that is, and how much we feel that now."

On this night, Yankee Stadium would indeed serve as a cathedral.

There were signs all over the stadium: "We'll Love You Always Thurman," "Thurman We'll Miss You," "15 Thanks," "NY 15 is in Our Hearts Forever." White talked about Jerry Narron, "who will hit with power, and I wouldn't be surprised if he hits as many as thirty home runs a year." It was mentioned that catcher Brad Gulden was also called up to take Thurman's spot on the roster.

Reggie Jackson was alone, stretching in the wet outfield grass. Don Carney called for frequent shots of him from the "low third" camera. Reggie had been in Connecticut on Thursday and hadn't been reached by any news media for comment. His agent Matt Merola said he "was in a state of shock."

The lineups were taken to home plate by coaches Cal Ripken Sr. and Mike Ferraro, not by the two managers, Earl Weaver and Billy Martin.

The whole Yankee team was in the dugout, end to end, with no one in the bullpen.

The Yankees and Orioles emerged from their dugouts at 8:05. Figueroa, on the disabled list and in street clothes, stood out. The only one missing was Murcer, who had called Martin to say he wouldn't be at the game and would stay in Canton with Kay Friday night. The Yankee starters went to their positions, with Luis Tiant dabbing tears from his eyes on the pitching mound, and Reggie Jackson doing the same, wiping his glasses, in right field.

Carney called for frequent cuts to Reggie in right. No doubt fans were wondering what he was feeling. He had been Munson's foil. Were they staring at him, thinking he was being insincere? All of this had to pass through Reggie Jackson's mind. The fans had little knowledge of the peace they had forged; how Reggie had flown with Thurman just a few weeks before.

The umpires lined up by the third base fungo circle. Still photographers gathered behind home plate.

Home plate stood empty. It was for many the single most memorable thing about the evening. The empty home plate. Jerry Narron, who would catch that night, stood between Yogi Berra and Art Fowler at the top of the dugout steps in his shin guards and black chest protector. (He wouldn't wear Munson's orange protector.) For many, it was a visual moment that evoked memories of the riderless horse in the funeral procession of President Kennedy sixteen years earlier.

Bob Sheppard, the already legendary PA announcer, commanded the crowd to "direct your attention to the microphone behind home plate, where Terence Cardinal Cooke will address us."

And the formal program began.

"O mighty Lord and father of us all, we pause to pray for Thurman Munson," the cardinal began. "Our brother and your faithful son. He was a good family man first and foremost, and you blessed this captain of the Yankees with skills and talent and a great dedication to the game of baseball and the many fans he touched because of it. We offer a moment of silent prayer in his memory. Strengthen and console his loved ones and give him light and joy in heaven with you forever and ever."

Robert Merrill, who had been standing a few feet away, walked to the microphone and sang "America the Beautiful" with his eyes closed.

The scoreboard, with some bulbs out, carried the image of Thurman's face, alternating with a message written by Steinbrenner that said, "Our captain and leader has not left us—today, tomorrow, this year, next. Our endeavors will reflect our love and admiration for him."

"I never really felt as close or as one with the team as I did at that particular moment," remembers Willie Randolph. "The feeling of togetherness. Knowing that here we are at a tough time, but we've got to go out tonight and play, and play for the man because when we looked up at the scoreboard and we saw that picture of Thurman, we knew that he was on the field with us. And in essence, he was."

Over the PA system, Sheppard said, "Thank you for your complete cooperation."

No one knew what to expect at this point. The ceremony had lasted for six minutes. Was that enough? Was it over? Do we now play ball without our captain?

The silence turned to applause and cheering.

Great cheering.

And then came a chant of "Thurman, Thurman, Thurman." And on it went, and louder it got.

And it was to be a moment that would refuse to be just a moment. It needed to be the last great cheer for this immortal Yankee, this hard-playing, hard-driving presence who took this team on his back and restored the Yankees to greatness. How could this possibly end in six minutes? On went the cheers, the fans calling his name, crying, yelling, being the way fans are supposed to be at a ballpark in the Bronx. Anything but silent.

The image of Thurman on the scoreboard would alternate with the "Our captain" message. Whenever the image would return, the applause and cheering would increase.

And then, finally, finally, nine more minutes later, the voice of Bob Sheppard rang out again.

"Thank you, ladies and gentlemen, for your wonderful response."

This time, it felt right. The Yankee fans—a full house—had made themselves part of this moment, part of the ceremony. They had taken command of the event.

Narron, number 38 on his back, moved to the catcher's position at last to start taking Tiant's warm-up tosses.

"All year long Thurman helped me out," Narron had told reporters. "He told me I would have to do most of the catching this year, and that if he did come back next season, he would probably play a different position, and definitely not catch as many games as he had."

On TV, Bill White said, "A great tribute for Thurman Munson, a great amount of respect and love."

Added Messer, "You can't describe what just went on here."

On radio, Rizzuto said, "I can't ever remember when I've ever been so emotionally touched by the way these fans reacted."

Healy said, "This is amazing. Two days ago we were in Chicago talking about how much easier it was to play the outfield or first base . . . two days ago."

Among the mournful fans in the ballpark that evening was Juliet Papa. Just embarking on a career with local radio station WINS (the Yankees' station), she was here not as a reporter, but as a lifelong fan. She grew up in an Italian family in the Bronx that lived and died by the Yankees. Now, with her brother at her side, she felt she needed to be there that night. It would be her way of paying respect, of being in the company of fellow fans, who had come to say good-bye in this unusual setting. She was one of more than fifty thousand in the house that night, but she well represented the overwhelming feelings they all shared.

"There was that ovation," she recalls. "Oh my God. As a fast-learning newsperson, I looked at my watch. It had to be a good ten minutes that the packed house stood and applauded in a continuum that to this day sends a chill up my spine and puts a tear in my eye. It reverberated through the air and through the soul. It was perhaps all you could do, but the best thing to do. The people just didn't want to sit down."

The Yankees lost the game 1–0 to Scott McGregor and Tippy Martinez, two former friends and battery mates of Thurman's. Reggie said, "I wanted to hit a home run, but I couldn't do it. I was thinking of him every time I came to the plate. I'll do something for him and it doesn't have to be on the baseball field. I'd like to do something for his family, his son."

The announced attendance was 51,151. George Steinbrenner decided what the attendance figure would be and told Mickey Morabito to announce it in the press box. It was not uncommon for a team to cheat a little bit with an attendance figure if they could make it up the next day with the same team—no harm, no foul. It gave them the ability to turn a 19,000 crowd into a 20,000 crowd, and it looked better. The Boss took artistic license with this one. Good for him.

The Yankees lost 5–4 on Saturday and won 3–2 on Sunday before full stadiums as well. The signs didn't go away. In Cooperstown on Sunday, flags were at half-staff on what should have been a more joyous New York event: the induction of Willie Mays into the Hall of Fame. Instead, 466 miles away, people were filing past Thurman's casket at the Canton Civic Center. Thurman's death had diverted the attention of baseball fans.

Thurman Munson was all that was on everyone's mind all weekend at Yankee Stadium. If there were games going on down there, it was the players going through the motions. It was almost too painful to see Narron and Brad Gulden catching.

"Toughest games I ever had to broadcast," said Rizzuto.

21

And so the baseball world descended upon the football town of Canton to grieve and mourn the local hero who never moved away.

The Pro Football Hall of Fame ceremonies and exhibition game in Canton had been held on Saturday, July 28, and the town had returned to normal. Now there was this.

Canton had not seen an event like this since President William McKinley's memorial service in September 1901. McKinley had been assassinated in Buffalo, and the funeral service was held there. Then, after the body was taken to Washington, he was brought home to Canton, where a memorial service was held prior to his burial. If there were any people who attended that one, seventy-eight years earlier, and who filed past Thurman's coffin on Sunday, it went undiscovered.

The Thurman Munson funeral, in fact, would be held in the McKinley Room of the Canton Memorial Civic Center. It was scheduled for 9:30 on that Monday morning, August 6. The original plans called for it to be at the Rossi Funeral Home, but when the size of it became clear—with the entire Yankee team coming—it was moved. The Yankees were scheduled to play the fourth game of their four-game series with Baltimore that night in Yankee Stadium and would return to New York after the service.

Rossi nevertheless handled the arrangements in cooperation with Diana. "When you have a burn victim, that's a horrible thing," recalls Marion Rossi. "But Thurman's body was recognizable. His face was virtually unharmed. Diana was on top of all the details; very composed, despite the enormous tragedy that hit her. The arrangements like the music to be played, the order of speakers: that was all her planning."

On Sunday, starting at two p.m., about three thousand people filed past Thurman's bier paying last respects at the Civic Center. Piping and drapes had been set up to create a walkway entering and then exiting the casket area. In between were scores of floral displays. Youngsters wore their Little League uniforms. Diana, Tracy, and Kelly visited in the afternoon. Diana kept up with New York newspaper coverage, as visitors from New York had brought the papers to her.

In New York, a larger-than-usual number of players attended Sunday morning chapel service in Yankee Stadium, conducted by Tom Skinner. "We should remember the privilege of knowing a man like Thurman Munson," he told the Yankee and Oriole players. He also talked about not carrying grudges. Reggie Jackson, who had not been speaking to Moss Klein of the *Newark Star-Ledger*, then went to Klein and said, "Are you going to the funeral?" When Klein said he was, Jackson said, "That's good; I'm glad," and their feud was over.

Marty Noble of the *Bergen Record* was not as impressed. "I liked Reggie, perhaps more than most newspaper guys," he said. "But not that weekend. I didn't like him wiping his eyes on Friday night while everyone else was standing at attention, and I didn't like the oversized Bible he carried with him to the funeral, with gold fringes. He just had this need to call attention to himself."

Friends and family, filing into the spectacular two-year-old Munson home, had kept Diana going, along with her motherly responsibilities. On Saturday, she allowed a photographer from the *Repository* into the house to take a picture of her looking at Thurman's MVP plaque on the wall. Flowers, cards, and telegrams were pouring into the home, some just addressed to "Mrs. Thurman Munson, Canton, OH." The curious simply drove by the house slowly. Police were outside keeping the sightseers from stopping and controlling access to the home.

"She's not ready to talk to the press," said her closest friend, Joanne Fulz. "The family is holding up, but they're still not ready to discuss it. The kids are doing well. They'll go through periods of questioning what happened and times of sadness, but you know kids, they bounce back."

Canton was always more of a football town, in the pocket of the nation where Friday night high school football, like McKinley versus Massillon, felt as big as the Super Bowl. But on this day, Canton, population 93,000, turned its attention to its favorite baseball son.

I flew out on Sunday night, landing at Cleveland and renting a Lincoln Town Car because I was to pick up Commissioner Bowie Kuhn, American League president Lee MacPhail, and my old boss Bob Fishel (now the league's PR director) early Monday at Akron-Canton Airport, in order to take them to the funeral. For MacPhail, of course, it was full circle. As Yankee general manager, he was in the Munson home the day Thurman had signed his Yankee contract eleven years earlier.

Kuhn had weighed whether it was his place to be there. I was part of that discussion in his office on Friday afternoon. It was a question of whether a commissioner should be attending a player's funeral because he was a star player. He had not, after all, attended Lymon Bostock's funeral the year before when the Angels outfielder had been shot to death. He didn't want to do the wrong thing by the Munson family, or by his office, or to send the wrong message, particularly along racial lines, as Bostock was black. Kuhn was often the subject of ridicule for his stuffed-shirt appearance and seemingly endless string of losses to the Players Association, but I found him to be a decent man with a great love for baseball and a keen intelligence. (I later coauthored *his* memoir with him, putting him into a small club with Munson.)

I was straightforward about it. "He was the captain of the reigning world champions," I said, painful as it was now to use the word "was." "You presented the World Series trophy to him in the clubhouse ten months ago. I think the commissioner should be there."

When I landed in Cleveland, I ran into the Piniellas and the Murcers, who had flown out after the Sunday game to be with Diana. I offered them a ride; Bobby, Lou, and Anita sat in the back, with Kay in the front along with Mike Heath, who now played for Oakland and happened to run into us. Heath was one of a number of former teammates who had come in at their own expense for this. Murcer navigated the route to the Munson house, and he and Lou talked in the backseat about what each would say at the funeral. Diana had asked them to be the two eulogists. It was raining, and in the dark it was hard to find the house, but Bobby had managed to remember the turn off Market Avenue.

Heath was uncomfortable going to the house, not really knowing the family, but Murcer had told him he would absolutely be welcome. Mike had been a Yankee catcher behind Thurman in 1978 and had flown in from Seattle.

I had little idea what to say to Diana, because "I'm so sorry" seemed so insignificant. But she gave me a warm hug and she took the lead.

"I want you to know how much that book you did with Thurman means to us all now," she said to me. "We will always have that."

I said what I hoped were a few appropriate words, and remember ending with "I'll always be proud of being linked with Thurman."

I was so amazed by her presence. She was thirty-one years old and about to become a very public figure. In 1979, many of us were still judging "funeral behavior" by the example set by Jacqueline Kennedy sixteen years before. No one who lived through that would ever forget her dignity. What many had forgotten, or never stopped to contemplate, was that Jackie Kennedy was only thirty-four at the time of her husband's death.

I told Diana that I would be bringing the commissioner to the funeral in the morning. She seemed pleased.

And then she asked about my upcoming fatherhood. I couldn't believe she could think of that or ask it at that moment. What a lady she was to have asked at a time like this.

Tracy and Kelly, nine and seven, were such sad figures for those of us in attendance. Gene Michael, Thurman's fellow Kent State alum and Yankee teammate, and now manager at Columbus, remarked to me that they must be in such shock they couldn't possibly understand all of this. Michael Munson, four, was scampering around the house. Diana's mother, Pauline, was helping with him. Ruth Munson, Thurman's mother, sat quietly by herself, visited every few moments by one of her daughters. There was talk at the house about whether Darrell Munson would have heard the news, whether he was even alive, where he lived, and whether he might attend the funeral. It was all quite mysterious. The Munsons and the Dominicks were not getting along well at this time and this event failed to bring them closer.

This was my first time in this house, a fourteen-room mansion set back about 250 feet from the street, behind a circular driveway and a big lawn. White pillars marked the front entrance. It was magnificent, drawn from a similar plan that had been used in constructing the home in Norwood where I had worked with Thurman on his book. It was light brown, two and a half stories high. Stone from as far away as Alaska and Hawaii had been hauled in, as Thurman supervised the construction down to the smallest detail.

Thurman's office, through double mahogany doors, included the model of the Citation on his desk and the 1976 MVP award on the wall. And there was the framed photo of the four great Yankee catchers together: Dickey, Berra, Howard, and Thurm, which I had set up with tough cooperation from Munson himself.

I left to go back to my hotel around eleven p.m. The next morning, after a five a.m. wake-up call, I headed for the airport to pick up Kuhn, MacPhail, and Fishel.

Back in the Bronx, traveling secretary Bill Kane had arranged for three Carey buses to take players, their wives, and front office people to Newark Airport for the charter flight that was to depart at 8:15 a.m. For most of those who would make the trip, the day also began around 5 a.m., with the players and wives instructed to be at Yankee Stadium by 6:45. There was a flight delay and the Delta 727 arrived about a half hour late, touching down at Akron-Canton at 9:27. The last-minute charter cost about $20,000 to book.

Fortunately, the wreckage had been removed to a remote hangar by the day of the funeral, but no one in a window seat could avoid looking down during the landing and feeling heightened emotion at being so close to the spot where Thurman had died. There were a few floral wreaths at the site of the accident on Greenburg Road, and it was reported that some scavengers had been by to remove scrap metal, perhaps as souvenirs.

"Landing at that airport was one of the worst parts of that terrible day," said Gene Monahan.

The Yankee players and wives boarded three buses leased from A&M Transit Lines and sped down I-77 under police escort. They got off the highway and headed down Market Street, passing construction workers who stopped to watch the buses pass.

Inside the Civic Center, some seven hundred people were gathering for the private funeral, sitting there staring at the American flag–draped coffin, with some two hundred floral wreaths around it, with an oil painting of Thurman in his Yankee uniform, framed in gold, hanging above it. The music of Neil Diamond played softly. Outside, a local color guard was assembled to form a path for arriving dignitaries.

"I had no idea that Neil Diamond was Thurman's favorite," says his sister Darla. "I had once heard a tape and asked what it was and was told, 'That's *Hot August Night* by Neil Diamond,' and I said, 'Oh, I love that so, I have to get it.' So it was my favorite album, and there I was sitting in the Civic Center, and they're playing it, and someone says to me, 'Neil Diamond was his favorite.' We had that in common and I didn't even know it. And of course, a hot August night was when he crashed."

Besides Diana and her three children, besides Piniella and Murcer, besides Duane and Janice and Darla and their mother, Ruth, plus so many friends and neighbors from the Worley School and Lehman, were the mayor of Canton, Stanley Cmich; the young Cleveland mayor, Dennis Kucinich; Gabe Paul, now back as the Indians' president; Phil Seghi, his general manager; and Bob Lemon, so recently deposed as Yankee manager, attending another funeral nine months after he buried his son. Herb Score, the Indians' broadcaster, was there, as was Al Rosen, who had just recently resigned as president of the Yankees. Sports agent Bob Woolf was also there.

Duane wore a short-sleeved yellow shirt with a tie and no jacket. Janice was in a black dress, her hair up in a bun. Darla, her hair shoulder length, wore a blue-and-white short-sleeved dress and large glasses. Duane kept his arm around her throughout.

Ruth Munson, heavy, moving awkwardly with an unsteady gait, was in a striped shirt and vest over a long dark skirt. Her children stayed close to her. She was experiencing the worst loss a mother could possibly feel, and the expression on her face showed it.

Gabe, ever the glad-hander, spent time introducing Kucinich to everyone. "Say hello to Mayor Kucinich," he'd bellow. He was "working the room," working to score some points with the mayor by introducing him to all the celebrities. Kucinich, later the U.S. Congressman who twice sought the Democratic presidential nomination, was also the son of a truck driver.

As for me, I had no calling as a Secret Service agent; that was for sure. I screwed up my only assignment, picking up Kuhn, MacPhail, and Fishel.

I had parked at the small airport and gone inside to await their arrival. In the age before cell phones, this was no easy task. There was no posting of a landing time for their private jet. Since the lobby area of the airport was small, I figured I would just wait there and see them. But they had somehow expected me to be waiting on the tarmac for them with the car, as perhaps someone more experienced at such things would do, and when I failed to appear, another car was summoned and they left for the funeral without me. I was now in deep panic. They had landed at 8:51 and I was totally unaware of it.

After what felt like an eternity, I went to the office of the airport manager, who told me that they had landed and were being driven to the funeral home. I raced to my car, and somehow arrived at the same time they did, pulling up alongside of them in front of the building, a few minutes ahead of the team. I felt so foolish, but there was no problem whatsoever. We parked, shook hands, and entered. I sat to Kuhn's left, about twelve rows back, with Fishel on my left. The front rows were reserved for the team, which arrived, with wives, in the three buses. Diana met them in the lobby; that morning was the first time she broke down in front of people.

All the players and their wives entered a separate room, where they individually hugged Diana and pledged their love and help. Reggie Jackson carried his oversized Bible with gold fringe.

Tracy and Kelly sat quietly with their grandparents, while Michael, in his little number 15 uniform, scampered in and out of the room. It was very comforting for the team that Diana had made herself available to them, rather than removing herself and sitting in the front.

Billy Martin, wearing sunglasses, then led the team into the McKinley Room. He had sought assurance before leaving New York that the casket would be closed. It was.

He hugged Diana, but it certainly seemed that someone was going to have to get the emotional Billy through this day. He was not going to be the one providing moral support. George Steinbrenner, also in dark glasses, embraced her.

Everyone received a two-sided, mimeographed "program," titled "Funeral Service for Thurman Munson, McKinley Room, Canton, Ohio, August 6, 1979, 9:30 a.m." On it, I jotted down names of former teammates or opposing players who had gone to the trouble of getting to Canton on their own: Bobby Bonds, Mickey Rivers, Dick Howser (then the baseball coach at Florida State), Dell Alston, Jay Johnstone, Paul Blair, Sparky Lyle, Fritz Peterson, Gene Michael, Mike Heath, Dave Rajsich, Duane Kuiper, Scott McGregor, Rick Dempsey, Cliff Johnson, John Ellis, Toby Harrah, Mike Hargrove, Buddy Bell, and Wayne Garland. Two umpires were there, Rich Garcia and Bill Haller.

Blair, who went to Cincinnati early in the season, expressed what many of the old teammates were feeling. "I expect somebody to say 'Thurman's alive.' I can't believe the man is gone."

The manager of the Mets, Joe Torre, was there, little knowing that he would one day be a big part of Yankee history too. With the Mets he was enduring a third straight last-place finish. But there was the New York connection, and he was delegated to represent the crosstown rivals. Torre, McGregor, and Dempsey flew on the Yankees' charter.

The Yankee teammates and staff present that day included manager Billy Martin; coaches Yogi Berra, Mike Ferraro, Art Fowler, Jim Hegan, Elston Howard, Charley Lau, and Jeff Torborg; bullpen

catcher Dom Scala; batting practice pitcher Doug Melvin; trainers
Gene Monahan and Barry Weinberg; traveling secretary Bill Kane;
clubhouse men Pete Sheehy and Nick Priore; PR men Mickey Mora-
bito, Larry Wahl, and Marsh Samuel; general manager Cedric Tallis;
administrative assistant Gerry Murphy; broadcasters Fran Healy,
Frank Messer, and Phil Rizzuto; and players Jim Beattie, Juan
Beniquez, Bobby Brown, Ray Burris, Chris Chambliss, Ken Clay, Ron
Davis, Bucky Dent, Ed Figueroa, Oscar Gamble, Goose Gossage, Ron
Guidry, Brad Gulden, Don Gullett, Don Hood, Catfish Hunter, Reggie Jackson, Tommy John, Jim Kaat, Bobby Murcer, Jerry Narron,
Graig Nettles, Lou Piniella, Lenny Randle, Willie Randolph, Jim
Spencer, Fred Stanley, Luis Tiant, Dick Tidrow, and Roy White. Gam-
ble, Randle, Beattie, Brown, and Gulden had been added to the ros-
ter just days earlier, as had Torborg as a coach.

Rizzuto was, of course, the "senior Yankee" present. It was during
his rookie season of 1941 that Lou Gehrig had died. He hadn't attended that funeral; the Yankee team was playing in Detroit and
didn't come home to New York for it. Only Bill Dickey and manager
Joe McCarthy had left the team and come back.

For Brad Gulden, a squatty catcher nine years younger than Thurman, it was more painful to be there than most people knew. Most
people didn't even know him. But Thurman had called him the "Little Midget" and told him to hang in there because he was going to
be the next Yankee catcher.

"I only knew him less than a year, but he really got to me," says
Gulden. " 'C'mon, Stumps,' he'd say, 'Just watch me.' He told me I
looked just like him when he was young. We talked baseball and
business and flying and spent more time together than a rookie and
a big star should. I really loved him."

He had played his first big-league game on Saturday night. He
didn't want it to be this way, not under these circumstances.

Nettles, who had flown with Munson twenty-five days earlier, said,

"I thought we'd be friends for life." Nettles was now weeks shy of turning thirty-five, and attending his first funeral.

Off to the side stood a forlorn, slim figure in an out-of-place straw hat, a small version of a Mexican sombrero. He wore a long-sleeved white shirt, brown pants, brown shoes, and a brown-and-black-striped tie. He had no jacket.

It was Darrell Munson. He had last been seen around the time that Michael was born, four years earlier.

"He saw my mom and went over and said, 'Hi, Mama, how the hell are you,'" recalls Darla. "Then I heard him say, 'This is a fucking zoo!'"

Several reporters made their way to him, and when I pointed him out to Dave Anderson of the *Times,* he discovered his column for the next day. All the New York papers had sent reporters and columnists to Canton. TV stations from New York had crews there as well.

"When was the last time you saw Thurman?" Darrell was asked.

"Quite a while," he said. "Thurman never found himself."

"Why did you leave Canton?"

"The idiosyncrasies of life" was his reply.

"What do you do in Tucson?"

"I work in the parking lot at the University of Arizona."

"Were you hoping he'd get traded to Cleveland, since they train in Tucson?"

"No, he belonged with the Yankees."

The questioning began to cause an embarrassing disturbance in the crowded room. Darrell was speaking too loudly and showing no respect. He finally sat down by himself, near the back.

22

The media representatives sat near the back as well, behind the players. There was audio from the room that was played to those outside. It was estimated that seven hundred people were in the room, with an additional thousand waiting outside in the summer morning.

Aftér the Neil Diamond selections on the organ came the entrance hymn, "Amazing Grace."

Mayor Cmich, whom Thurman knew, made some opening remarks and then turned it over to the pastor of St. Paul's Roman Catholic Church. The Reverend J. Robert Coleman had married Thurman and Diana eleven years earlier.

There was a reading from the Old Testament, from Ecclesiastes and a Psalm, and a New Testament reading from Matthew.

Michael Munson, in his little Yankee uniform, was restless now, and Diana's mother took him outside for a walk. If there was a focal point for the grief everyone in the room was feeling, it was seeing Thurman's young son scampering around, unaware of what was happening.

Many telegrams had arrived, and Diana selected four for Reverend Coleman to read.

"I want to express my sincere sympathy. Thurman was a credit to baseball and to the All-American way of life. My prayers will be with you." Muhammad Ali.

"Deepest sympathy to you and the children." Eleanor Gehrig.

"My deepest sympathy and prayers. Please let me know if there is anything I can do. Give me a phone call." Reggie Jackson.

"Diana, we are grief-stricken and our hearts ache for you. We know how you loved each other." Anita and Lou Piniella.

The fact that Diana selected Reggie's telegram from the many to read indicated a desire in her heart to show that her husband and Jackson had come to peace with each other. This was, of course, a day for peace.

"Thurman Munson was someone special," said Reverend Coleman. "He was not just an ordinary Lehman High School graduate. He was not just an ordinary ballplayer. He was not just an ordinary card-playing buddy. He was not just an ordinary husband or father.

"He spent quality time with Diana and the children. He loved his wife. He built her a castle, a large home in Plain Township. He learned how to fly for her because he loved to be with her and share all that they had in common.

"Thurman loved his Yankee teammates too," said the pastor. "In the last three years, while they were winning their championships, the Yankees grew to love one another as persons. They loved one another despite, and perhaps because of, the pressure cooker they were in."

He even touched on Thurman's stormy relationship with the press. "The media and Thurman didn't always get along," he said, mentioning Jim Bouton by name. "How many times can you answer the same questions? And beyond that, how many times can you give up time with your family to answer these questions for the sake of a headline that by cheap sensationalism causes the other ballplayers grief?"

Reverend Coleman mentioned that Thurman liked to read, and that *Jonathan Livingston Seagull* was a favorite of his. He noted his friendship with Wayne Newton, who also flew a Cessna Citation, and who may have helped influence his decision to get one. He mentioned Roberto Clemente and noted that "he went right into the Hall of Fame. Perhaps for Thurman Munson an exception can be made also.

"Thurman Munson died because he loved his family. He loved to fly. He was fascinated by how he could move home so quickly, saving precious time to be spent with his family. He also loved flying because he could be alone with himself . . . alone with God.

"Thurman Munson was proud to be a Yankee."

The organist, Bill Roden, played Neil Diamond's "Holly Holy" as Reverend Coleman took a seat. He had spoken for twenty-five minutes. He said that the St. Paul's Day Care Center on Fourteenth Street NE would be renamed the Thurman Munson Center.

Kuhn, stiff-lipped, towered over me on my right, but now I was filling with tears. I had spent nine great seasons with the team, and although I now was working in the commissioner's office, where the daily attendance indicated in the box scores seemed to be the most important thing, I felt reconnected to my organization and proud to have been a part of it. The events since the Friday night "moment" of silence had sent me to tears several times. This was going to be another one.

Piniella walked to the front, taking a last drag on his cigarette. He'd been nervous about this, chain-smoking and pacing. He read the passage from Ecclesiastes that begins "To every thing there is a season."

"I knew him better than most," he began in his own words, tears already visible on his cheeks. "He played hard. He played tough. He played fierce. He played to win. Thurman was unselfish. He was a winner. As a baseball player he was one of the best competitors.

"I found Thurman affectionate, very friendly. He was my friend. We don't know why God took Thurman away. We'll remember him as long as we live. Diane and the children, I hope God gives you the strength and conviction to carry on. I hope you have the strength to carry on the way Thurman would have wanted you to."

Now it was Murcer's turn. He'd worked a little longer on his remarks and the Lindstroms had helped craft them.

To Diane, to Tracy, to Kelly, to Michael, to Tote and Pauline, relatives, friends, to the millions of fans across the country who have cheered and now mourn our tragic loss, to the special New York fans who knew him as their idol, to Mr. Steinbrenner and the entire Yankee family, to Billy Martin, the coaching staff and to the twenty-five of us who had the honor of saying we are teammates, I quote these words of Angelo Patri that, to me, reflect Thurman so well:

"The life of a soul on earth lasts beyond departure.

"You will always feel that life touching yours.

"That voice, speaking to you, that spirit looking out of other eyes, talking to you in the familiar things he touched, worked with, loved as familiar friends.

"He lives on in your life and in the lives of all others that knew him."

And live he did . . . He lived . . . He led . . . He loved. Whatever he was to each one of us . . . catcher . . . captain . . . competitor . . . husband . . . father . . . friend . . . He should be remembered as a man who valued and followed the basic principles of life.

He lived . . . He led . . . He loved . . . He lived blessed with his beautiful wife, Diane . . . his daughters Tracy and Kelly, and his son Michael.

He led . . . his team of Yankees to three divisional titles and two world championships.

He loved . . . the game . . . his fans . . . his friends . . . and most of all, his family.

He is lost, but not gone.

He will be missed, but never forgotten . . .

As Lou Gehrig led the Yankees as the captain of the thirties, our Thurman Munson captained the Yankees of the seventies. Someone, someday, shall earn the right to lead this
team again, for that is how Thurm—Tugboat, as I called
him—would want it. And that is how it one day will be . . .
five years . . . ten years . . . whenever . . . if ever . . . No
greater honor could be bestowed upon one man than to be
the successor to this man, Thurman Munson, who wore the
pinstripes with number 15 . . . number 15 on the field . . .
number 15 for the records . . . number 15 for the halls of
Cooperstown.

But in the Living . . . Loving . . . and Legend . . . history
will record Thurman as Number One.

Murcer, now tearful, his voice breaking over the final sentences,
was glad it was over. He took his seat next to Kay.

The Lord's Prayer was sung. Two verses of "America the Beautiful"
were sung. "Let There Be Peace on Earth" was sung. The service had
taken an hour. The room was slowly cleared except for family and
teammates.

The six pallbearers were local friends: John Biskup, Bill Crocker,
Jim Althouse, Dick Lombardi, Paul Scurre, and Dave Teitel. Biskup
had told the *Repository,* "He was a true friend in the truest sense of
the word. And Thurm was a realist. We talked of the risks of flying.
It was his turn to go and he went. We'll really miss him."

They escorted the casket out to the waiting hearse, elegant in sil-
ver with a black top. Diana hugged her father and led her daughters
by the hand to the waiting black Cadillac limousine. She herself had
to be helped in. She wept and bit her fingers as she headed for Sunset Hills Burial Park in nearby Jackson Township.

I was wiping my eyes during the service. I was now supposed to drive the commissioner back to the airport. But he leaned over to me and said, "Do you want to go to the cemetery? It's all right if you do."

I thanked him. Yes, I needed to go.

But so too did the entire Yankee team. That had not been the plan. They were supposed to attend only the funeral service in order to get back on the charter and make it to Yankee Stadium in time for the game. Reggie Jackson was seen wiping his eyes as the players exited. He hugged Jody Anderson, Jerry's wife. Martin, though, became inconsolable, and was comforted and led by Paul Blair, his former player. Rivers, White, and Dell Alston held on to one another, openly crying, forming a triangle, letting free their emotions.

"You never see players in such an out-of-character moment," said Noble. "To see Rivers, who was always so happy-go-lucky, and White, who was always so stoic and unemotional, was an amazing sight."

Rivers broke free and embraced Steinbrenner, who had traded him away days before. Mickey became overwhelmed by tears and was helped by White.

George Steinbrenner made an executive decision. "We're going to the cemetery," he said. "We're going to be with him till the end."

The team got back on the buses, passing by Marv Albert of WNBC and Chee Chee Williams of WABC, who had come to Canton to file reports back to New York.

The route was about seven miles, ending up at the cemetery entrance on Everhard. Along the route, people stood, some with hats or their right hands over their hearts. Many knew what was happening and what this cortège represented. Some just seemed enthralled that the New York Yankees were passing through town. Some kids rode their bikes alongside, oblivious to the meaning of it all. Others seemed to know that this was the Thurman Munson funeral procession. At one point the procession passed a row of fast-food restaurants.

"Only Thurman would get buried next to a Burger King and a pizza parlor," said Nettles.

One image rolled through Nettles's mind. After the 1976 World Series the Yankees and the Royals went to Hawaii to compete in a "Super Teams" competition for ABC television. In the swimming relay, "Thurman got about halfway through the second lap of his two laps and he started rolling around in the water like a big walrus. He started laughing and we all started laughing. We lost the relay because he ran out of gas. It was hilarious. I was smiling to myself as I thought about him while I was sitting in the bus."

The three buses parked by the entrance, and all the other cars parked behind them. I was somewhere near the end. We walked into the cemetery and headed right toward the mausoleum where his casket would be placed. I walked with Mickey Morabito, my onetime assistant and now the team's PR director. Mickey wanted to stay close to Billy for support.

It was at this point, according to Diana, that Darrell Munson approached the coffin and said, "You always thought you were too big for this world. Well, you weren't!"

"Look who's still standing, you son of a bitch!" he added, according to *Esquire* magazine's Michael Paterniti.

With this, Tote Dominick came by and took him by the elbow and escorted him away.

"Got to get back to Tucson right away," he said over his shoulder. "Got somebody meeting me there."

Duane, driving back to Maryland, would drop his father off in Pittsburgh to catch a plane home.

We all assembled at random, Reverend Coleman delivered another blessing, and it was over very quickly. But it felt very right and proper that we were all there for this final moment.

The players and some of the wives reboarded the buses and departed for the airport, now back on schedule to play their game against the Orioles.

About nine of the wives returned to the Munson home to spend the rest of the day with Diana. Among them were Kay Murcer, Audra Chambliss, Helen Hunter, Ginger Nettles, Juanita Gamble, Anita Piniella, Linda White, and Lynn Stanley. "We sat in Diana's bedroom and talked about the loss," said Audra. "Diana described the details of the accident as she knew them at that point. She had to be a strong woman to be married to such a strong man, and she was."

Steinbrenner had ordered two small planes to take the wives back. When they arrived in New York, they went to Yankee Stadium and joined the game in progress. Larry Wahl and Gerry Murphy, there to assist Diana even beyond the team's departure, finally departed for Cleveland for a late flight.

I drove to Cleveland for a late-afternoon flight and was back home in Westchester by six. I was exhausted and had no desire to go to the stadium for the game. It was hard to imagine that the players could take the field after such a day.

23

What had been an emotional day would soon end with a unique game, one of the most memorable in Yankee history. In a franchise built as much on sentiment as it had been on championships, there was one more act of drama left.

In the still-dazed Yankee clubhouse, Graig Nettles reached into a bag and pulled out a tape. It was Neil Diamond's *Hot August Night*. It just was. And the song that played was "Done Too Soon," about departed celebrities. He looked at sportswriter Marty Noble and they both made the sound of a *Twilight Zone* moment. It was all too creepy.

In the WINS radio booth, Rizzuto was letting his emotions out in his own inimitable way. Authors Tom Peyer and Hart Seely would later publish a book called *O Holy Cow!* and turn the Scooter's musings into poetry. This was Phil, speaking to Frank Messer and to grieving Yankee fans that evening:

> *The Yankees have had a traumatic four days.*
> *Actually five days.*

That terrible crash with Thurman Munson.
To go through all that agony.
And then today.
You and I along with the rest of the team
Flew to Canton for the services,
And the family . . .
————Very upset.
You know it might,
It might sound a little corny.
But we have the most beautiful full moon tonight.
And the crowd,
Enjoying whatever is going on right now.
They say it might sound corny,
But to me it's some kind of a,
————Like an omen.
Both the moon and Thurman Munson,
Both ascending into heaven.
I just can't get it out of my mind.
I just saw that full moon,
And it just reminded me of Thurman.
————And that's it.

Billy Martin, meanwhile, now turned his attention to the game.
On the flight home he told Murcer he wouldn't play that night
against the Orioles. But Bobby objected. "I feel like I need to play
tonight," he told Martin. He needed to complete a day that had
begun at five a.m., and which took him beyond any emotion he had
ever experienced.

And so Murcer played left field and batted second, with Ron
Guidry, equally spent, on the mound. One had to wonder whether
the Yankees would go through the motions on this night, or whether
they would "win one for Thurman" before life resumed as normal.

ABC television had received permission from Steinbrenner to lift a blackout that would have limited the viewership of the *Monday Night Baseball* telecast. Earlier, George had gone to the clubhouse to further console his players. He patted Chambliss on the shoulder. He stopped in the training room, where Piniella and Randolph were asleep on tables. Luis Tiant slept on the floor.

Appearing on camera with Howard Cosell during the game, Steinbrenner said: "Well, Howard, I think we're all emotionally drained in the Yankee family, and yes, but Bobby Murcer spoke in the Munson house, Thursday night, and he came to see me Friday morning when we were talking about it and he said Diane asked for one thing—that Thurman never quit when he was hurt, and everyone on that ballclub was hurting and has been for four days, but we're Yankees and they don't quit, and so a determination was made that it was best for the team and we play and we played them right to the wire every game."

"So the trading of Rivers was not a give-up sign?" asked Cosell.

"Not at all, we proved that last year, and we've had more adversity than any team I ever saw this year but they all got up this morning at 5:30—they're drained emotionally, they're tired, but they wanted to be there right to the grave, and right to the end, and that's what the Yankees are."

"I know you wanted Diane to see the Yankees tonight. Thank you for lifting the blackout."

The Oriole players intended to wear black armbands, arranged by Mark Belanger, but couldn't pull it off by game time. Earl Weaver had held a clubhouse meeting before the game to try to spark some life in his team under difficult circumstances. Many of the Baltimore players had hoped not to play. Ken Singleton (born three days after Thurman) recalled Munson's constant behind-the-plate chatter when he would come to bat.

Dennis Martinez started for the Orioles. He struck out Murcer in the first inning, and then got him on a fly ball deep to right and on a liner to short. The Orioles were up 4–0 as the Yanks batted in the seventh.

With two out, Dent walked and Randolph doubled him to third. Suddenly, Bobby found the power that used to keep him among the league leaders in his younger days as a Yankee regular. He swung at a fastball and lifted a three-run homer into the right field seats for his first Yankee home run since September 1974, and his first in Yankee Stadium since September 1973. It had been one hundred at bats since his last home run, that one with the Cubs.

"That's for Thurman," Bobby said to Billy Martin as he reached the dugout.

"Suddenly," said Guidry, "we were back as a team, professionals playing the game. It changed our focus. Until then, we were just going through the motions."

In the ninth, Guidry was running out of gas. Martin went to the mound to replace him, but the Gator, like Murcer, had an inner calling.

"No, Skip," he said. "I've got to finish this one."

He retired the Orioles in the ninth.

By the last of the ninth, Tippy Martinez had replaced Dennis Martinez on the mound, with the Yankees still trailing 4–3. Dent led off with a walk, and Randolph laid down a sacrifice bunt that was thrown away by Tippy, putting runners at second and third, with Randolph representing the winning run. A hunch—nothing but a hunch—told Billy Martin to let Murcer hit. It went completely "against the book." Bobby's fellow eulogist, Piniella, was available to pinch-hit from the right side. Martin's gut told him to stick with Murcer.

Now it came down to Tippy facing Bobby Murcer, both filled with thoughts of Munson. Tippy loved Munson, who never treated him like a rookie, and always encouraged him. "Thurman taught me how to pitch inside—he forced me to be there," says Tippy. "I never really understood it before. But he made me understand it. He'd also argue for his pitchers with the umpires all the time in a quiet way. I didn't go to the funeral because I just don't like funerals, but I was feeling badly about not going to his. I was on the mound facing Murcer, who I owned. Lefty-lefty. I could always get him out with breaking balls."

He quickly had him at an 0–2 count.

Martinez looked in at Murcer, rubbed up the baseball, and let his mind flash back.

Years earlier, Ron LeFlore had a 30-game hitting streak for the Tigers. He went 0–3 against the Yankees, and Tippy, then with an "NY" on his uniform, was pitching in the eighth, leading 9–5. The count was 0–2 on LeFlore, and Munson called for a fastball. He took it for a called third strike and the streak was over. But later, Munson told a reporter from Sports Illustrated *that he'd called for a pitch he felt might be more to LeFlore's liking to give him one last chance at keeping the streak alive.*

Tippy's concentration returned to the moment at hand.

"So I'm facing him and I understand all that's on the line there, and something came over me and said, *Throw one fastball to him—for Thurman.* And I did. It didn't have to be a strike, but it was, and he still had to hit it, and he did."

Murcer connected and lined the ball into the left field corner, scoring the winning runs in a 5–4 Yankee win, giving him all five RBIs for the night. At first base, Bobby leaped into the air and into coach Yogi Berra's arms.

He was rushed by his teammates, with him and Piniella, who had delivered the eulogies, in tears again, leaving the field in an embrace.

As he walked off the mound, beaten, Martinez looked upward and said to himself, *Okay, Thurman, that one was for you.* The ABC telecast followed Tippy, and caught the quick heavenward glance, but was of course unaware of what they had.

The 36,314 fans cheered and cheered for Bobby to take a curtain call, which, embarrassed but euphoric, he finally did. Thirty-six million watched on TV, the second-highest rating in four years of *Monday Night Baseball*. "They won the game for the captain," said Cosell. "Emotion won the game." In his earpiece, producer Dennis Lewin was yelling, "Sign off, sign off," because the eleven o'clock newscasts had to start on time.

"That was Roone Arledge's command," said Lewin, speaking of the man who ran both ABC Sports and ABC News. "I hated to leave that game. We never interviewed Bobby. That's one telecast I think about a lot."

After the game, the crying resumed. One by one, the players stood before Thurman's empty locker, trying to gather their thoughts.

Murcer would give the bat he used that night to Diana Munson. He never used it again.

Of all the great moments in the history of the New York Yankees, this was, perhaps, the most emotional of them all. What else could compete with such a performance on the day they had buried their captain? When had the Yankees ever won a game where everyone filed out in tears?

24

On the Sunday night six days after the "Murcer Game," Channel 5's *Sports Extra* in New York did a lengthy Munson special, with John Dockery and Jerry Izenberg interviewing Steinbrenner, Fran Healy, Mel Allen, Bill White, and me.

"Thurman Munson was a unique individual," said Steinbrenner. "I think people now understand why we made him the captain and what a leader he was by example. As a competitor he was the greatest I've ever known and as a person he had a deep human concern for other people, their families and their lives . . . I don't know what else you can look for in a leader, a man who does it on the field, by example, who plays when he's hurt, who never asks any quarter and gives none in competition and at the same time was a deeply caring human being."

The Yankees paid Diana Munson the remainder of Thurman's contract, some $1.2 million, through 1981, without dispute, since they had removed the no-fly clause after the contract was renegotiated during spring training in 1978. And just a week after the accident, Steinbrenner told Dick Young of the *Daily News,* "One thing that saddens me about Thurman is that he spent too much of his little time growling at people . . . Personally, I'm sorry about Munson's untimely death, but I can't be hypocritical about his character. I can't choke up over guys who glide through life saying, 'I should be making more money than anybody else.' "

That was a tough statement by the Boss, and related directly to Thurman's demand that his salary should be equal to whoever came along as the highest-paid player on the club. No doubt the reality of paying over a million dollars in his remaining salary to Diana was kicking in.

If you could overlook his seemingly endless war with the media, you had in Thurman Munson a guy who came from a troubled childhood, but was still the most regular guy in school, in sports, and on into celebrity. A good relationship with the press might have let that come across better. But he never really "got it" when it came to the media, because in the end, he was a Canton boy from start to finish, and that part of New York, the celebrity part, just didn't work for him. He would not have dealt well with the proliferation of media in the era that was to come, with sports talk radio, cable television, and the Internet. The "Information Age" was not for Thurman.

Maybe Gabe Paul was going to pull off a trade and bring Thurman to Cleveland for 1980. It was always difficult for Yankee fans to view their man as a hometown hero and know that he seemingly had no problem with going to the Indians. It was one of those things the fans tried their best to ignore.

Diana was convinced that Thurman was going to sell the plane; that he'd either seen its dangers or no longer felt he needed it. "He was coming around, I know he was," she told Wayne Coffey of New York's *Daily News,* during a lengthy twenty-fifth anniversary interview. On the twentieth anniversary, she did a long interview with Michael

Paterniti for *Esquire*. She has appeared in most of the documentaries produced on Thurman, including the much-played "Yankeeography" on the Yankee-owned YES Network.

Diana is a wonderful figure throughout this story and remained one after Thurman's death. Little known to Yankee fans, her courage shined in the days after his death, and she wisely limited her public appearances so as not to become overexposed or accentuate her role as the sympathetic Yankee widow.

She made a visit to the crash site some months after the accident, to begin to fully embrace the healing process. She had the expected mood swings of loss, anger, questioning of her faith, and bitterness. But she carried herself with great dignity, as she became a single parent and took on the challenge of raising her three children, keeping them out of the media spotlight, displaying sensitivity and compassion to friends in need, and generally being a role model for anyone thrust into such a horrible position. As a grandmother, she loved attending Little League games and watching another generation—Thurman's grandchildren—fall in love with baseball.

"If there was someone in our circle of friends who had a time of need, you knew Diana would be there at every step," says her friend Joanne Murray.

She pleased many when she went to Old-Timers' Day in New York on June 21, 1980, less than ten months after the accident, allowing the fans to cheer for Thurman as she was introduced.

"I wanted people to know that I'm okay," she said.

She remained pretty and sweet and probably could have dated many men, but she chose to be a mom and to make a full-time job of it. She remained in the spectacular home they had built, answered letters from fans, and made occasional visits to Yankee Stadium for Old-Timers' Days or ceremonial moments. It took more than twenty-five years for her to visit Thurman's empty locker.

"Dating makes you feel more normal," she told the *Repository* as the twenty-fifth anniversary approached. "But there's the whole Mrs. Thurman Munson thing. I think it gets too complicated. I've had people who thought they could get past it and couldn't. At this age, I know Mr. Wonderful might still find me, but I hope he hurries up because I'm getting old and getting tired."

Jerry Anderson kept in touch with Diana Munson for a time, "but eventually she probably said to herself, 'I don't want to sever the relationship, but I don't want to be with him either.' So we kinda lost touch. I was part of a terrible memory for her. Sometimes I'd run into her, maybe just bump into her on the street if I was back in Canton for some reason. We'd exchange pleasantries, but it was shallow. We don't really have any relationship now."

Ironically, with no connection to Munson as part of the equation, Anderson would become partners with Bucky Dent in his baseball school in Florida. He had met Bucky much by happenstance after moving to Boca Raton in 1982. Larry Hoskin had started the school, and he was the mutual acquaintance who introduced Anderson to Dent.

"In 1988 I got a call from Diana," says Jerry. "She said that Michael was now thirteen, and was wondering if he could come down to attend the school. Well, of course he could. Thurman used to say to me, 'That little guy, he's a handful!' I was happy to be able to accommodate this."

With further irony, Jerry's son Jeff played baseball and went to Ohio State on a scholarship. He went on to play ten seasons of Independent League baseball, including a year playing for Ron Guidry on an Independent League team in Lafayette, Louisiana, in 1998, and then at Yogi Berra Stadium with the New Jersey Jackals in 1999. Then Jeff played in Somerset, New Jersey, under Sparky Lyle, where a teammate turned out to be future Yankee Cory Lidle's twin brother.

Dave Hall became an air traffic controller, and eventually moved to Boston, where he worked at the Boston Flight Standards District Office. He politely declined an invitation to speak with ESPN for their 2004 feature, and has chosen to maintain a low profile with respect to his footnote to history. He and Anderson long ago lost touch.

In preparing this book, I asked if he wanted to see the chapter about the accident and to add any comments or correct any facts, but he said he preferred not to. He did confirm some additional facts used in this book and was pleasant and friendly on the phone. He had to check with his wife to recall that Diana had visited him during his hospital stay, saying he remembered nothing from those days. It was clear he had moved on from that tragic event.

How much money did Thurman's death cost the family in baseball earnings? His potential earnings are intriguing to contemplate. His contract took him through 1981. If he had enjoyed continued success in business, continued to enjoy being home, and found his career hobbled by injuries that made his performance suffer, he might have retired.

On the other hand, if he'd enjoyed a new burst of excellence by moving to designated hitter or to outfield or first base, perhaps the lure of big dollars and the enjoyment he got from playing ball might have won out.

There was a long players' strike in 1981, and then he could have declared free agency, and perhaps signed another three-year deal with another American League team (where he could occasionally DH). But here is where it would have gotten interesting.

The Yankees signed Dave Winfield to a ten-year, $23 million deal beginning in 1981, which even included annual cost-of-living increases. Munson, had he decided to stay, would have insisted that he had an agreement which would keep him the highest-paid player on the team. The Yankees might have argued that that agreement was part of his expiring contract and no longer in force. Or, had they felt it was in force, they might have had to think twice about signing Winfield. The contracts would have overlapped at least in Winfield's first season, 1981, a year the Yankees went to the World Series.

It all makes for intrigue as to what might have been. It could have changed Yankee history.

Thurman's death did change things in the future—sometimes in positive ways. A year after his death, representatives from the Association for the Help of Retarded Children in New York visited me at my office at WPIX. I was by then the PR director for the Yankees' home TV station, and would later become producer of their telecasts.

As I'd coauthored Thurman's autobiography, they thought I could help with a special project: holding a dinner in his name as a fund-raiser. Gene Michael would be another of the early organizers.

Thurman had no connection to disabled children, but that didn't matter to those who were visiting me that day. They thought that if they could sell thirty tables and present some awards, they would have honored his name and helped their charity.

Diana liked the idea, and the dinner worked. Thurman's name attracted far more people than they expected, and they decided to make an annual event of it. Not all the honorees were from sports. In the second or third year, James Cagney made one of his final public appearances to receive a "Thurman Award."

The routine always seemed to start in my office, tossing around names of prospective honorees, and working with the local team PR people to secure them. The selection criteria were generally a combination of "Are they good citizens?" and "Are they available the night of the dinner?" Diana, and then sometimes her children, would attend almost every year. I think a snowstorm may have prevented them from coming one year.

She always read a short speech from the dais, and the audience loved her sweetness, her sincerity, and her ability to make everyone remember Thurman with fondness. When I was more actively involved, I had a video produced showing his career highlights, which the audience loved. On into the 2000s, the dinner continued, uninterrupted, with no loss of table sales despite the distant memory that Thurman was becoming for some. Millions of dollars had been raised. Management of the dinner changed, and Gene Michael and I became lost in the shuffle, but it would always be nice to attend the event and catch up with Diana, who was always the focus of everyone's attention.

Tracy and husband Chris Evans had a daughter and two sons. Tracy became a teacher at a Montessori school. Kelly and her husband, Tony Parson, had two daughters and one son. The son, Anthony Thurman Parson, is the one who carries Thurman's name, along with the birth name of his beloved father-in-law and best friend, Anthony "Tote" Dominick. Kelly designs houses, and retains Munson as her last name.

Michael proposed on one knee to his girlfriend, Michelle, in front of his dad's plaque in Yankee Stadium's Monument Park in 2004 when the family returned for Old-Timers' Day. She said yes. Their first child, a daughter, and the first grandchild to bear the name Munson in the family, was born in May 2008.

Michael, because he was only four when Munson died, grew up watching his father's highlights on television having fewer personal memories than his sisters. He grew to be a large man, five feet ten and 240 pounds, much of it from weightlifting. He went to Glen Oak High School and then to Kent State, and in 1995 was signed to a Yankee contract through the good graces of Gene Michael, by then the team's general manager. A catcher, he batted .300 in nineteen games for Tampa in 1996, but he wasn't cut out to be a big leaguer like his dad, and his minor league career would be fleeting.

He wound up briefly playing Independent League ball in the park named for his dad in Canton.

Every bit the Canton guy like his dad, he opened Munson's Home Plate Sports Pub on Dressler Road NW in January 2008. At the finale of old Yankee Stadium in 2008, he represented his dad on the field in pregame ceremonies, receiving a tremendous ovation.

September 16, 1979, was Catfish Hunter Day, as the great Yankee pitcher was preparing for retirement. The team was in free fall after Thurman's death and there were few joyous moments for the fans as the season wound down. Hunter himself was going 2–9 in his final campaign. He told the crowd on his day, "There's three men shoulda been here today. One's my pa"—the crowd burst into cheers—"one's the scout who signed me"—bigger cheers—"and the third one . . . is Thurman Munson." A great ovation rose from the stands. It wouldn't stop. The fans so longed to cheer for Thurman, and this was the first time they could since the days after he died.

After that season, the Yankees would run video on their scoreboard before the games showing great Yankee moments, and one recurring scene would show Thurman, his knees beaten, struggling to rise and continue to play. It was very heroic. And it never failed to increase the crowd's cheering, as though their man had just popped out of the dugout as he had done in the rookie summer of 1970, ready to pinch-hit.

Corky Simpson tracked down Darrell Munson for the interview that ran in the *Tucson Citizen* on October 4, 1979 (and was quoted earlier in this book). In retirement, twenty-nine years later, Simpson remembered it well.

"In nearly fifty years of sportswriting I must have done thousands of interviews and let me tell you, this was not only the strangest, but the most uncomfortable," says Simpson. "Darrell Munson was working in a tiny, corrugated metal shed at the entrance to a parking lot near the University of Arizona. That's one of my most vivid memories—that the father of a magnificent athlete would be working in such a small, telephone-booth-sized structure, collecting change from people parking their cars.

"Mr. Munson was a most unpleasant man who seemed to be angry at the world. That anger and some deep hurt from some unknown cause could be seen in his eyes. He sure as hell was one angry man. It was pretty obvious that Darrell resented Thurman's enormous success. I have heard men say that the toughest relationship of their lives was with their sons—but this was borderline hostility. Over the years, I have asked myself many times if I shouldn't have simply folded up my notebook and walked away from this one. But if I had, maybe an important shred of evidence in a wonderful baseball player's life and times, including his struggle to be great, would have been lost."

Graig Nettles, who would be named the next Yankee captain in 1982, told biographer Peter Golenbock, "For a long time we didn't even bring up his name. Now, when we see a fat guy on the street, someone will say, 'Hey look at Thurman.' Jokes are a way to ease the pain. For a while it was tough to concentrate on playing. When his plane crashed, so did our season. We didn't feel much like playing the rest of the year."

Darla Munson would write a poem, an interest she shared with her brother Thurman, who had written poems many years before to a young Diane Dominick:

Greenburg Road in August

The road I do not travel
The execution site of a ballplayer
Who spent his life in challenge
Until one came along he couldn't master.
Touch and go landings
Up and down, back and forth,

Round and round
Crash to the ground.
Why did he always fly away?
What did he try to prove that day?
What a horrible price to pay
For the possession of a plane;
The thought of it's insane.
Touch and go landings
Up and down, back and forth,
Round and round
An excruciating sound
The crashing to the ground
And all of it went up in smoke,
A pathetic sickening joke.

Thurman's death would cause the 1980 roster to change, with Chris Chambliss traded away to get a replacement catcher in Rick Cerone from Toronto. "With Thurman playing more first base in the end, we thought it might be the end for Chris in New York anyway," said Audra Chambliss. "We hated to leave, but that's baseball."

Billy Martin would get himself fired again after punching out a marshmallow salesman in a bar. Dick Howser would be named manager. Gene Michael became the team's general manager.

In September 1979, the NTSB issued its accident report, based on the investigation of Edward McAvoy. He cited "startling mistakes" by Thurman and concluded:

the probable cause of the crash was improper use of throttles and flight controls, and four gross errors that caused him to undershoot the airport:

1. He made a low approach to the 6,400 foot runway and failed to correct for it, even though there were runway slope indicator lights.
2. He neglected to keep close watch on the jet's airspeed, letting it drop 10 knots below safe speed.
3. He forgot to lower the jet's landing gear, and when he did lower it, he failed to compensate with enough power to overcome the added drag.
4. He was either unfamiliar with or forgot the proper engine procedure for recovery from a low approach.

In addition, he was not using the plane's flaps, which would have added lift to the plane.

"In summary," said the report, "the Safety Board concludes that the pilot's conduct of the flight set the stage for oversight and confusion. His disregard for standard practices, procedures and regulations created an atmosphere in which he could not recognize a worsening situation. Perhaps a more experienced pilot would have recognized the dangerous situation more readily and may have taken proper and timely action . . . Therefore, the Safety Board concludes that the manner in which the pilot conducted his flight was the primary factor which precipitated the accident sequence, not his training and experience."

McAvoy explained, "One employee of A-Flite, an Akron company, taught Munson instrument flying, and another, the operator of the flight center, was the designated FAA examiner. Similarly, one employee of FlightSafety International, Inc., in Wichita, taught Munson to fly his new Citation jet, and another tested him and gave him an FAA jet rating."

"Cessna had a contract with FlightSafety to provide flight training to purchasers of Citation jets and Munson received the flight lessons as part of a purchase package," observes Ettie Ward in the book *Courting the Yankees.* "Although most purchasers were required to get their instruction at FlightSafety's Wichita site and divide their time, on a prescribed basis, between simulator training time and actual flying, much of Munson's instruction in flying his new jet took place while traveling to and from baseball games on the West Coast and the All Star Game in Seattle. At the time of the crash, Munson had just 41 hours of flying time in the Cessna Citation and only six hours as pilot-in-command."

Said McAvoy, "This opens the door to Munson's being a novice pilot."

Despite the findings of the NTSB, Diana was advised to sue Cessna and FlightSafety, the company that trained and certified Thurman to fly the Citation. (Cessna reported that it was the first Citation in the United States to be involved in an accident.) She retained a Canton attorney, Eugene Okey, a former minor league player and amateur pilot himself. Assisting him at trial was Daniel C. Cathcart, who had a long history of litigation in airline accidents, including the 1977 Canary Islands collision between KLM and Pan Am jets, and the 1979 American Airlines DC-10 crash, at the time the worst air disaster in history.

The suit, filed in federal district court in Akron, Thurman's birthplace, in 1980, sought $42 million in damages. Basically, the suit claimed that Cessna and FlightSafety should be liable because of the very findings of the NTSB report—that the sale of the jet and training were a package deal, and that it was in Cessna's interest to grant a license so they could sell the plane.

A claim was also made about design defect in the cabin entry door, which contributed to preventing Thurman's rescue.

The value of the plane, $1,218,900, was part of the claim in the suit. An additional $3 million was sought for Munson's "conscious pain and suffering" while he was still alive. Punitive damages of $9 million were sought, in part "because of alleged negligence in the use of high-pressure sales tactics to induce Munson to buy a sophisticated aircraft, when the company knew he was a pilot of limited experience."

Cessna's lawyers claimed that Munson "crashed not because he should not have been flying a Citation, but because he should not have been flying at all on August 2, 1979. He was fatigued from a late flight in bad weather the night before, and in pain from persistent knee problems, which were aggravated by an injury the night before that necessitated his removal from the game. He was overly complacent in the relatively undemanding circumstances on August 2, 1979, and was under stress from various concerns. All these things together were a prescription for the disaster that occurred."

Leading to the trial, depositions were taken from Billy Martin, Graig Nettles, and Reggie Jackson about Thurman's piloting abilities, and from Yogi Berra and Gabe Paul about his future earning potential in baseball that was lost.

It took four years and approximately $127,000 in expenses for the case to go to trial—five years from the time of the accident. But on May 25, 1984, after only four days of testimony, the parties agreed to settle the case. (Only Cessna was a defendant at this point; Flight-Safety had reached a separate settlement.) The settlement amount was never announced, but it was said that the $1.69 million figure reported in the press was "an understatement."

The Yankees, in an unrelated move, also sued FlightSafety and Cessna, making similar claims through their lawyer, John McCarthy of Cleveland, but suing over their loss of services of their player, whom they likened to property or "unique chattel" in terms of market value. But the district court ruled against the Yankees, noting that their loss was "merely a remote and indirect consequence" of the defendants' actions.

"The accident changed the way aircraft manufacturers, insurance companies, and the FAA look at 'hurriedly training pilots in new aircraft,' " says Jerry Anderson. "Today, it takes twenty-five to fifty hours of flying with a safety pilot before you can move up to a more complicated aircraft and fly on your own. It's ironic that Thurman's death helped change the aviation industry and probably saved many other pilots and passengers from a similar fate."

Despite the findings of the NTSB regarding Thurman's pilot skills that day, three people did survive the crash thanks to the actions he took under emergency circumstances. Yes, Thurman survived the crash, only to die in the fire. He would likely not have lost his life had the plane not hit the tree stump. And when the plane came to a halt on Greenburg Road, Thurman's last words were of concern for his passengers—"Are you guys okay?" He had saved their lives with his actions in landing the doomed aircraft.

"Thurman flew that airplane to the last nanosecond," says Anderson. "He kept it under control and brought us down. He never panicked. He saved our lives."

Ruth Munson died in 1987 in Canton and is buried a few steps from her son. Darrell Munson died in April 1991 in Alexandria, Louisiana, probably on his way to or from Florida, where he alternated stays with his Tucson residence.

Even Thurman's classmates, so loving in their recollections, all seemed aware of the "difficult" circumstances of his upbringing. All things considered, Thurman ended the cycle that began at least with his grandparents, if not earlier. The Munson children are well-adjusted, good citizens of the community, living happy and productive lives.

What ended this cycle and made Thurman the man he was, rather than someone who might have been doomed to a lifetime of psychiatric care, discussing his parents?

Basically, two things saved him. First was his discovery at age twelve of Diana Dominick and his acceptance into her family, giving him a sense of how things should be. He used that to raise his children and to create a family for himself that he never had. Tony "Tote" Dominick, who died in 1985, was both a father-in-law and a best buddy.

Second was his gift of being an elite athlete, which kept him active in sports year-round and provided him with good coaching supervision, good role models, and close friends.

"What saved Thurm was his talent," says his brother Duane. "If he had been just an ordinary ballplayer and fumbled around the league or not made it, nothing would have saved him. And the Dominicks weren't much of a family, but they were Diane's family and she became his wife. The bottom line was that he made some bad decisions, didn't know who his friends really were, and for some reason, gave up on his roots, for whatever reasons. I contributed to that too because I left home and missed his high school years. That hurt me a lot and maybe it hurt him too. I hope not, but I have to believe it may have. Maybe I could have been a more positive influence on his life, who knows. Janice sure wasn't a positive influence on him when she was there and I'm not convinced that any of the Dominicks were either. Things just seemed to snowball and happen for no particular reason. I only ever took credit for making him a little tougher and more competitive. I think I succeeded and have no regrets in those areas, just that I wasn't there at some times when he probably needed an ear and a real friend, particularly a family friend."

"Thurman was a helluva ballplayer. Aside from that I'm not giving him any credit," says Darla. "He wasn't nice to his family. His dad might have been a creep and you wouldn't have liked him, but at least he worked an honest day's living. He took care of us honestly. He didn't go around doing other things to make money."

Thurman's siblings did not manage to maintain a close relationship with Diana and her children, and eventually Janice and Duane settled in Georgia, with Darla the one remaining sister in Canton. As in all cases where families go through such periods, the stories tend to have different interpretations depending on who is doing the telling. Of this there is no doubt: Thurman sought to break free of the Munsons and very much embraced the Dominicks, and later found the happiness of a long-denied family life in the family where he was the dad. And he conducted that part of his life just fine.

One might wish that the surviving siblings had a closer relationship to Diana and her children, and in fact to one another, but perhaps it was their destiny, given the home they emerged from.

An impressive grave site was constructed for Thurman near the entrance at Sunset Hills, not far from what is now Munson Street. It is in Section 1, Lot 6. An etching of Thurman in his home uniform, bat held in his left hand, appears above the inscription

THURMAN LEE MUNSON

CAPTAIN OF THE NEW YORK YANKEES

1976–1979

On a lower section of the grave under and to the left of the word MUNSON (with a space for Diane on the right), it says simply

Thurman Lee

June 7, 1947

August 2, 1979

There is a 15 on the rear of the massive stone.

Munson's uniform number 15 was retired on the spot during the ceremonies at Yankee Stadium following his death, and his locker remained vacant, although sometimes used to store equipment. It isn't glassed in or untouched. Plans for the new Yankee Stadium called for Thurman's locker to be placed in its museum portion.

The plaque for Thurman in Yankee Stadium's Monument Park was dedicated on September 20, 1980, and says:

THURMAN MUNSON

NEW YORK YANKEES

June 7, 1947–August 2, 1979

YANKEE CAPTAIN

"Our Captain and Leader Has Not Left Us

Today, Tomorrow, This Year, Next . . .

Our Endeavors Will Reflect Our

Love and Admiration for Him"

Erected by The New York Yankees

September 20, 1980

The copy on the smaller marker in front of his retired uniform number says:

FROM 1969–1979

THURMAN WAS THE HEART AND

SOUL OF THE YANKEES. HE HELPED

RESURRECT THE YANKEES' GLORY

BY LEADING THE BOMBERS

TO THREE WORLD SERIES.

HIS DEDICATION AND HARD WORK

MADE HIM ONE OF THE

PREMIER CATCHERS AND HITTERS

OF HIS TIME

A 5,700-seat minor league ballpark at 2501 Allen Avenue SE in Canton was built and named Thurman Munson Memorial Stadium in 1989, serving as home to an Eastern League farm team in the Indians organization. Lou Piniella was among those who attended the dedication. A small round number 15 surrounded by pinstripes can be seen on the outfield wall, but the signage for the park was minimal and it wasn't well received by those who rate minor league parks for architecture and ambience. By 1996, the stadium had lost that Eastern League team, and it shifted to use by the independent Frontier League, where Michael Munson played for the Canton Crocodiles (later to be called the Coyotes). He wore number 15, wherever he played.

By 2007 no professional games were being played there, but Malone College, a small Christian college located just blocks away from Thurman's Frazer Avenue home, played their home games there. The home on Frazer is occupied, but unmarked by any sort of marker. "This is a big-time football town," sighs Joanne (Fulz) Murray, Diana's friend. "So, as a professional baseball player, Thurman wasn't so widely embraced and honored locally, nothing close to how fans feel about him in New York."

A senior center was named in Thurman's honor at the Horace Mann School on Grace Avenue NE.

After Thurman died, Linda Fisk, Carlton's wife, sent a sincere, handwritten letter to Diana Munson. She describes the growing respect Carlton had for Thurman and, despite the rivalry and negativity reported in the media, she explains that a real bond was developing between the two men. Speaking for Carlton, she writes: "I don't think he knows how to play without hurt but he told me he felt like he lost family and might as well have stayed in the hotel instead of playing when he heard of the crash—emotional pain can't be iced down."

There is a bronze plaque behind home plate at Veterans Field in Chatham honoring Munson, who played for the Chatham A's before turning pro. The Thurman Munson Batting Award is given each season to the Cape Cod Baseball League's best hitter.

Jorge Posada, the best Yankee catcher who followed Thurman, was a fan of George Brett and Don Mattingly while growing up in Puerto Rico, but after signing with the Yankees, became fascinated with Munson, and would hear stories about him from Guidry, Gossage, Piniella, and Murcer.

"Guidry would talk about his ability to call a game, by being so good at remembering what everyone hit, or missed," Posada says. "He became a role model for me, since he was Yankee catcher, and since I just came to love the way he played the game. I watched him a lot on tape or film—he was always in the middle of everything, whether getting the big hit or making the big play at the plate."

In the weight room at Fenway Park (of all places), Posada saw a picture of Munson hanging on the wall with the inscription, "Look, I like hitting fourth and I like the good batting average. But, what I do every day behind the plate is a lot more important because it touches so many more people and so many aspects of the game. Thurman Munson, 8/25/75." He took it and hung it in his locker at Yankee Stadium.

"I think about him whenever I pass that empty locker," he says. "I really wish I'd known him. He must have been a helluva competitor."

Yankee fans always were passionate about Thurman Munson making the Hall of Fame, and there was a flurry of thought after his death that he might even be named at once, as Roberto Clemente had been. Indeed, he was made eligible for the 1981 election, with the five-year waiting period waived. But he gathered only sixty-two votes that year, his high-water mark for the fifteen years that he remained on the ballot. In his last year of eligibility, 1995, he had only thirty votes. The sixty-two represented just 21 percent, with 75 percent needed for election.

Bill Madden, the national baseball columnist for New York's *Daily News* and a student of the Hall of Fame elections, says, "I used to get periodic letters and e-mails from diehard Thurman supporters, pointing out the three straight .300-average/100-RBI seasons and the fact that how many catchers ever did that? But the bottom line always was only eleven seasons (seven of them All-Star) for Thurman as opposed to twenty-four by Fisk (eleven of them All-Star) and seventeen by Bench (fourteen of them All-Star)—his two contemporaries. There was just no comparison. He didn't play long enough, didn't have nearly enough All-Star seasons, and his lifetime numbers, nice as they were, pale in comparison to the real Hall of Fame catchers—Berra, Dickey, Cochrane, Bench, Fisk, Hartnett. For Thurman to make the Hall, he would have needed the old Veterans Committee that put in Ray Schalk and Rick Ferrell. Against them, you could make the case he was a Hall of Famer."

Others have noted that while Munson's career was cut short, his injuries and reduced playing time at catcher had effectively signaled to voters that they had indeed seen the bulk of his career, certainly his big years, and there was no reason to assume that he would play eighteen or twenty seasons and amass big lifetime numbers.

Time magazine, the week after Thurman died, quoted Munson himself as saying, "I want to play long enough for [Michael Munson] to understand and appreciate what I have accomplished. If I have three or four more good years, I might have the kind of statistics that could get me in the Hall of Fame."

Bill James, the master expert of baseball stats, weighed in thus: "Players in most cases have to be evaluated by what they actually did, not by what they would have done or might have done . . . Munson's situation is an injury, an extreme injury, but an injury. There are dozens of players who would have had Hall of Fame careers if they hadn't been hurt. Hell, there are more of those than there are actual Hall of Famers."

The Hall of Fame did exhibit a glove and a mask of Thurman's. In the 1990s, Jeff Idelson, another former Yankee PR director and then a public relations official with the Hall of Fame, realized a need and persuaded Gene Michael to part with Munson's glove and mask for display in the museum. There was also a temporary exhibit by a New York artist named Steve Linn of a faux Yankee locker made of wood with a carved glass image of Thurman, and bronze casts of his glove, spikes, bat, and jersey, which was on display until 1994 and then moved to storage.

Some fans maintain such loyalty that their stories stand out.

A fan named Terry Fudin started a Web site called Vote ThurmanIn.com to try to spur Hall of Fame interest. "I am a computer programmer and in 2001 I decided to make a simple yet effective Web site which would try to get Thurman into the National Baseball Hall of Fame," he says. "The site encourages people to send letters to members of the Hall of Fame Veterans Committee in support of Thurman's inclusion."

Frank Russo, a fan with a particular interest in "final resting places," maintains a Web site called thedeadballera.com, at which he advocates for Munson being named to the Hall of Fame.

Dewey Wigod has sought to produce a film about the importance of Thurman Munson to the America of the 1970s. He works for a television program distributor, but hasn't yet been able to see this project home. He never quits trying, though. I've been an adviser to him over the years and served as host when he shot a short segment for it at Yankee Stadium. Diana Munson is well aware of his efforts.

"The most important thing to me about Thurman Munson was that an ordinary man with above-average determination led the Yankees back to their former glory," says Wigod. "He was a can-do, up-by-the-bootstraps guy—a quintessentially American story coming at what appeared to be a can't-do time for the country and the world at large."

In 1999, *Newsday* asked me to compose the inscription that might appear on a Munson plaque, not only because I had done his autobiography with him, but also because I had had a hand in writing the Hall of Fame plaques for twenty-one years.

So I gave them:

THURMAN LEE MUNSON

New York A.L. 1969–1979

BECAME FIRST YANKEE CAPTAIN SINCE LOU GEHRIG AND LED TEAM TO 3 CONSECUTIVE PENNANTS, 1976–78. A.L. ROOKIE OF THE YEAR 1970. A.L. MVP 1976. FIRST IN LEAGUE TO BAT .300 WITH 100 RBIS IN 3 CON-

SECUTIVE SEASONS IN QUARTER-CENTURY. NAMED TO SEVEN ALL-STAR
TEAMS. EARNED THREE GOLD GLOVE AWARDS. BATTED .357 IN POST-
SEASON PLAY INCLUDING .529 IN 1976 WORLD SERIES, HIGHEST EVER BY
A PLAYER ON A LOSING TEAM. MADE ONE ERROR IN 615 CHANCES
IN 1971 WHEN HE WAS KNOCKED UNCONSCIOUS ON A PLAY AT
THE PLATE. A PLAYER'S PLAYER.

The year 2004 marked the twenty-fifth anniversary of Thurman's passing, and in addition to marking the occasion at Yankee Stadium on Old-Timers' Day, a panel was held at the Yogi Berra Museum in New Jersey to recall his life. I was the moderator, with Diana, Gene Michael, and Bobby Murcer as panelists, and it was a terrifically "feel-good" gathering of two old teammates, one coauthor, one Yogi, and a hundred or so devoted fans. It was an honor for me to be asked to preside.

There would not be another in-season death of an active major league player until June 22, 2002, nearly twenty-three years later, when Cardinals pitcher Darryl Kile was found dead in his hotel room in Chicago. (Pitchers Tim Crews and Steve Olin died in a spring training boating accident in 1993, and outfielder Mike Darr died in a spring training auto accident in 2002.)

On October 11, 2006, pitcher Cory Lidle died in a plane crash over Manhattan just days after the Yankees had been eliminated from postseason play. He had taken off from Teterboro, Thurman's local airport of choice. Lidle was on the Yankees' roster late in the season, but became a free agent as soon as the season ended. Still, he was treated as a Yankee in death, and of course the nature of his accident had everyone recalling that afternoon in August 1979.

Bobby Murcer died of a brain tumor on July 12, 2008. A memorial service was held in his hometown of Oklahoma City on August 6, attended by, among others, Diana Munson. It was the twenty-ninth anniversary of Thurman's funeral, and of Bobby's magical 5-RBI night.

In 2004, Diana and I both became officers of a now defunct sports auction house, along with Bobby Murcer and the nation's premier collector, Barry Halper. When the National Sports Collectors Convention was held in Cleveland that year, she and I walked the floor together, looking at the many Munson items on sale, marveling at the love people still had for him. And the prices his autographed items brought were astounding.

One of the principals with the auction house met with Diana and encouraged her to consider putting some of her personal effects up for auction.

Rationalizing that she had lived with them long enough and perhaps it was time to let Munson fans take ownership, and perhaps tempted by the elevated prices that things were bringing at auction, she parted with some unique items. Sold at this and then later auctions were a single signed baseball ($13,650), Thurman's Kent State college jersey ($8,041), his last catcher's mitt ($51,518), his 1979 Yankee road jersey ($31,987), his pilot's license ($7,938), the uncashed check from Reggie Jackson for the July 1979 flight from Seattle to Orange County ($2,285), and perhaps most poignant, the bat used by Bobby Murcer to win the game on the night of Thurman's funeral ($16,827). Bobby had given her his blessing to part with it.

At a 2008 auction to coincide with the All-Star Game in Yankee Stadium's final season, Diana consigned additional items of importance to Hunt Auctions, all of which sold at remarkably high prices for someone not in the Hall of Fame.

These include $180,000 for his 1978 World Series replica trophy, $110,000 for his MVP award, $45,000 for his 1974 Gold Glove award, $40,000 for his Rookie of the Year Award, $75,000 for a 1979 home uniform, $32,000 for a game-worn cap, $75,000 for his 1976 World Series ring, $125,000 for the 1977 ring, $85,000 for the 1978 ring, $22,000 for his Mercedes, and $10,000 for the ball from his first major league hit.

Of course part of the reason for the high value of Munson items in the collectors' market—not just these personal items—is that he died before there was a collectors' market. He never participated in mass signings; never had an agent to produce limited editions. And he wasn't especially forthcoming with autographs for fans, often using the trick of carrying something in each hand as he entered and exited ballparks, making it difficult to stop and sign.

He wasn't the most accommodating signer under the best of circumstances. I know of only one copy of his autobiography that he signed, and it wasn't mine. (I never thought to ask.)

In 2007, ESPN presented an eight-hour miniseries based on the book *Ladies and Gentlemen, The Bronx Is Burning,* by Jonathan Mahler. Its central focus was the 1977 Yankees, and actor Erik Jensen played Munson. Munson relatives, fans, old classmates, and others all thought it was a masterful performance and absolutely captured Thurman's look, walk, and personality. I was a consulting producer for the project.

> *"In 2006, I got the call that every actor dreams of," said Jensen. "In spite of having a throwing arm so out of shape I was having trouble getting the ball to home plate while standing up (much less to second from my knees), some obviously misguided unit of directors and producers and writers were offering me the role of Thurman Munson in the ESPN miniseries 'The Bronx Is Burning.'*
>
> *"Okay, so imagine having great sex, eating cake, finishing a marathon, doing a high jump, and meeting one of the Beatles (John, possibly George) all at the same time and that's pretty much how it felt to get that call. I had six weeks to get my skills in shape, find the gait, the stance, the style, the voice and gain 25 pounds. The first day I put on #15, squeezed the orange chest protector and shin guards around my now 204-pound frame, slid my fingers*

into the catcher's mitt, flipped the cap backwards, and shambled out of my trailer onto the ball field, filtering the air through my home-grown walrus mustache, it started to get weird.

"If I were George Clooney or Brad Pitt (my wife chuckles in the background), I probably wouldn't have noticed the staring. I imagine movie stars get that all the time. But as a journeyman actor, not used to getting looked at, it felt a bit like being hunted, or checked out by every girl in the bar (again, laughing wife)— except all the people checking me out were men, most of them were teamsters, none of them wanted to take me home (as far as I know, anyway) and as I walked closer, more than a few had tears in their eyes. One guy in particular, in his mid-fifties, six feet tall, 300 pounds easy, greeted me every day with 'You do Thurman right! Got me?' I think he meant it as encouragement, but I had the feeling I might end up mixed into the cement of the new Yankee Stadium dugout if I blew it.

"Other tough guys came up to me, all choked up, and said things like 'I remember where I was on August 2, 1979...' or 'He was my hero.' 'It means so much to me that you are doing this.' 'You're the first guy, you know that, right?'

"Boy, did I ever.

"And as I read Thurman's autobiography and got to know his co-author who was a consulting producer for the project, watched tape, tried to hit that indelible batting stance over and over again, flopped that lazy glove down and popped it up, got shit from my catching coach for 'stabbing at the ball,' and as I gained that weight—Thurm kinda took over. Mostly because of the people who knew him. From his friends I learned that Thurm certainly could be the 'grumpy' guy he so often projected to the press, but I also learned that he was, according to Goose Gossage, 'one of the funniest people I ever knew.'

"I learned that Thurman quietly offered to fly a cash-strapped reporter's wife and kids in for spring training so that the family could all be together. I learned that as much as he fought with Reggie, there were numerous gestures made by Thurm that were classy, respectful, and hardly grumpy. I learned that he bragged very little about himself and really tried to let the playing speak for itself. I learned that he loved and deeply respected Billy Martin (sometimes like a brother) and that Thurm always kept his word, unless it meant talking to the press.

"I learned that he was, for fans, the guy who worked at the garage next door. I learned that he was a loving father. I also learned that he was like all of us, challenged by the occasional insecurity. I learned that in spite of his numerous accomplishments and awards he sometimes felt like he had something to prove, sometimes to himself, sometimes to others. I learned that he and I both had parental relationships that were complex and sometimes contentious. And I learned that the best tribute I could make to his memory was to play him as a man. Not as an icon. But a man. Not just as the 'grumpy, gruff' Yankee. But as a human being. With the same amounts of difficult, dignified, petty and heroic moments that we all have in this life. And when finally, months after wrapping the series, I met Mrs. Munson at an All-Star dinner, I felt like I'd made the right choice. A two-dimensionally 'grumpy' man would never have been able to hook such a classy, kind, generous woman, to say the least. To walk for four months in #15's cleats was better than just about anything I've experienced short of meeting my wife. It was a very, very close second. And it was an honor.

"I hope to God that teamster thinks I got it right."

Akron-Canton Airport is a busy mid-sized airport with no indication that a nationally covered tragedy once took place there. The field through which the doomed jet bounced is free of trees and free of the stump that prevented Munson from surviving. In the operations office sits a black binder with an index card on the cover that says, "Munson Crash, Aug 2, 1979," containing the NTSB report, photos, and other ephemera from that day. On Greenburg Road, near where the jet came to a halt, the pavement seems discolored and scarred, as though repaired. One can't be sure if this is residue from the awful event.

The Civic Center is much as it was at the time of the funeral.

Thurman's boyhood home on Frazer is occupied by another family that knows of its historic connection, and occasionally deals with people stopping by for a photo. Lehman High is now a middle school but the football field on which Thurman starred is still as it was, extending along Fourteenth Street NW.

There was some talk after Thurman's death of a movie based on the autobiography that we did together, and we did in fact sell an option, but it never came to be. Talk would arise every now and then of what an interesting subject it would be, but it did not materialize. In the meantime, the YES Network produced a series of "Yankee-ographies" in the 2000s, with Munson's being one of the most popular and most repeated. On anniversaries of the accident—the first, the fifth, the fifteenth, the twentieth, the twenty-fifth—there would be columns written about him and television reports about him. Diana Munson was always gracious in welcoming reporters into her home for interviews, and she would drive them to the grave site so that they could see it for themselves. She was always greeted by a thunderous ovation at Yankee Stadium. On the twentieth anniversary in 1999, home plate was again left empty during the national anthem, and then Diana went to the mound, Joe Girardi squatted behind the plate, and to great cheers, she threw him a strike. Coaches Willie Randolph, Mel Stottlemyre, and Chris Chambliss escorted her back into the dugout, while young Jorge Posada maintained a loving applause.

Navy blue Yankee T-shirts with the name MUNSON and the number 15 on the back were always good sellers at Yankee Stadium souvenir stands, and they tended to be found on somewhat overweight middle-aged men.

My son Brian was born on September 18, 1979, about six weeks after the accident. Diana had always asked about how we were doing and sent a congratulatory message despite all that was going on in her life. Coward, McCann and Geoghegan, the publisher of the autobiography, asked me to write a concluding chapter about the accident, and rushed out a memorial edition of the book. The Book-of-the-Month Club made it a featured book almost immediately. It reached best-seller status on a few lists, and a paperback edition, never planned but originally hoped for by Thurman, was issued a year later.

Young fans in the sixties had Mickey Mantle as an idol; in the seventies they had Thurman, and in the eighties, when Brian became a baseball fan, they had Don Mattingly, who became his hero. In the nineties Derek Jeter came along. There was something about the Yankees' always producing just the right man for the times, someone who really connected with their fans.

Bill James, SABR, and fantasy leagues all came along after Thurman's career, but in James's *Historical Baseball Abstract,* updated in 2001, he ranked Thurman as the fourteenth-best catcher in history, behind Yogi Berra, Johnny Bench, Roy Campanella, Mickey Cochrane, Mike Piazza, Carlton Fisk, Bill Dickey, Gary Carter, Gabby Hartnett, Ted Simmons, Joe Torre, Bill Freehan, and Ivan Rodriguez, with Elston Howard fifteenth.

At the time of his death, Thurman owned apartments and an office building in Canton, and real estate estimated to be worth about $1.5 million, according to Jerry Anderson. Diana completed one of his transactions after he died, and later sold most of his holdings, including his piece of the Belden Village mall property. She held on to the office building, which provided a cash flow for her, as well as property in Boca Raton, Florida.

Would Thurman have managed the Yankees? There can hardly be any doubt that the offer would have come. Steinbrenner absolutely respected him as a leader, as a "true Yankee," and as a great baseball mind. While he was running through Dick Howser, Gene Michael, Bob Lemon, Michael again, Clyde King, Billy Martin (again), Yogi Berra, Billy Martin (again), Lou Piniella, Billy Martin (again), Lou Piniella (again), Dallas Green, Bucky Dent, Stump Merrill, Buck Showalter, Joe Torre, and Joe Girardi, it seems clear that Thurman's turn would have come up. Unless, of course, he was managing elsewhere (Cleveland?), or making so much money outside baseball that his desire to resume the travel would have made him say no.

It was reported that Steinbrenner told Munson, during spring training of 1979, "Learn everything you can, because you're going to be my manager someday."

"Thurman would've been thrilled with that because no matter what anyone else said, he really loved the Yankees," says Diana.

If he was among those who returned each year for Old-Timers' Day, you can be sure he would have been right there with all the beloved Yankee immortals, getting the biggest ovations. One can almost see him, probably a little overweight, chugging out to the first base line to slap hands with old buddies like Murcer and Nettles, Piniella, Randolph, Rivers, Chambliss, Guidry, White, Lyle, Gossage, and yes, Reggie Jackson. And someone would have taken a photo of him with Derek Jeter—Yankee captains, then and now—Jeter, respectful, calling him Mr. Munson, and Thurman, playfully tapping Jeter on the back of his neck, the symbols of two very different dynasties, one succeeding by overcoming conflict to rise to the top, the other succeeding in an era of peace and harmony in the clubhouse of Joe Torre. Jeter's locker is next to Munson's.

Or perhaps some poor Yankee publicist would scramble to get a photo of Yankee captains Munson, Nettles, Guidry, Randolph, Mattingly, and Jeter . . . only to find Munson in the TV lounge watching the Three Stooges.

THURMAN MUNSON'S CAREER STATISTICS

Year	Club	AVG	G	AB	R	H	2B	3B	HR	RBI	BB	SO	SB	CS	OBP	SLG	SH	SF	DP	HBP
1968	Binghamton	.301	71	226	28	68	12	3	6	37	36	27	4	6	.469	.540	0	2	n/a	2
1969	Syracuse	.363	28	102	13	37	9	1	2	17	13	11	1	1	.435	.529	0	0	n/a	0
1969	New York	.256	26	86	6	22	1	2	1	9	10	10	0	1	.333	.349	0	1	5	0
1970	New York	.302	132	423	59	137	25	4	6	53	57	56	5	7	.389	.415	5	1	13	7
1971	New York	.251	125	451	71	113	15	4	10	42	52	65	6	5	.337	.368	4	3	10	7
1972	New York	.280	140	511	54	143	16	3	7	46	47	58	6	7	.344	.364	4	2	13	3
1973	New York	.301	147	519	80	156	29	4	20	74	48	64	5	6	.364	.487	1	4	13	4
1974	New York	.261	144	517	64	135	19	2	13	60	44	66	2	0	.320	.381	1	8	12	4
1975	New York	.318	157	597	83	190	24	3	12	102	45	51	3	2	.372	.429	3	10	14	1
1976	New York	.302	152	616	79	186	27	1	17	105	29	37	14	11	.343	.432	1	10	23	6
1977	New York	.308	149	595	85	183	28	5	18	100	39	55	5	6	.352	.462	0	2	17	9
1978	New York	.297	154	617	73	183	27	1	6	71	35	70	2	3	.337	.373	1	10	18	2
1979	New York	.288	97	382	42	110	18	3	3	39	32	37	1	2	.343	.374	1	4	15	0
Major League Totals		**.292**	**1423**	**5344**	**696**	**1558**	**229**	**32**	**113**	**701**	**438**	**571**	**48**	**50**	**.350**	**.410**	**21**	**58**	**160**	**42**
AL Championship Series																				
1976	vs. KC	.435	5	23	3	10	2	0	0	3	0	1	0	1	.435	.522	0	0	1	0
1977	vs. KC	.286	5	21	3	6	1	0	1	5	0	2	0	0	.273	.476	0	1	0	0
1978	vs. KC	.278	4	18	2	5	1	0	1	2	0	0	0	0	.278	.500	0	0	1	0
Totals		**.339**	**14**	**62**	**8**	**21**	**4**	**0**	**2**	**10**	**0**	**3**	**0**	**1**	**.333**	**.500**	**0**	**1**	**2**	**0**
World Series																				
1976	vs. Cin	.529	4	17	2	9	0	0	0	2	0	1	0	0	.529	.529	0	0	0	0
1977	vs. LA	.320	6	25	4	8	2	0	1	3	2	8	0	0	.370	.600	0	0	1	0
1978	vs. LA	.320	6	25	5	8	3	0	0	7	3	7	1	0	.393	.560	0	0	1	0
Totals		**.373**	**16**	**67**	**11**	**25**	**5**	**0**	**1**	**12**	**5**	**16**	**1**	**0**	**.417**	**.567**	**0**	**0**	**2**	**0**

Acknowledgments

For assistance and support in completing this book, I would like to thank Brian Appel, Deborah Appel, Irv Appel, Katie Appel, Norm Appel, Steve Berman, Rob Bloom, Terry Cashman, Gloria Coleman, David Corcoron, Pearl Davis, Mike DeMarco, Paul Doherty, Mark Durand, Joe Fosina, John Frew, Dick Friedman, Terry Fudin, Joe Grippo, David Hall, Jane Hamilton, Dr. Stuart Hershon, Erik Jensen, Doubleday's fine editor Jason Kaufman, Mark Kriegel, Bowie Kuhn, Dr. Judith Kuriansky, Jane Leavy, Jeffrey Lyons, Lourdes Magbanua, Rich Marazzi, Matt Merola, Juliet Papa, Dale Petroskey, Jorge Posada, Sy Preston, Pete Quagliarini, Louis Requena, Frank Russo, Al Santasiere, Dom Scala, Steve Schanwald, Art Shamsky, David Smith, Mark Stamas, Rusty Staub, Arthur Toretzky, Lonn Trost, Dewey Wigod, my agent Rob Wilson, Paul Winfield, and Jason Zillo.

Notes on Sources

I joined the Yankee front office in 1968, the year Thurman Munson was drafted out of Kent State, and I then had the privilege of enjoying a front-row seat for most of his career. When I left the Yankees early in 1977, I remained close to Thurman, collaborating with him on his autobiography, and keeping in touch with the teammates from the teams now identified as from *The Bronx Zoo* and *The Bronx Is Burning* years.

Many of the scenes here were re-created from my memory. When you have such remarkable access to the team you grew up rooting for, you pay attention. Whether I was in the clubhouse, in George Steinbrenner's office, or on a team flight, it all stayed in my mind in great detail.

It took some hunting, but we were able to go beyond the subjects Thurman wanted to cover in his autobiography, and thanks to able researchers at the *Daily News* in New York, we found his brother Duane Munson in Georgia and then his sister Darla Day in Canton, whose cooperation opened the doors to the period of Thurman's life he chose to skim over in that book. Darla graciously provided a guided tour to all the homes, schools, and landmarks in Canton that were part of Thurman's life.

In addition, many classmates from his early years and on through his college years came forward with stories that helped paint the picture of the future star in development. These included Ed Baird, Bob Belden, Randy Benson, Randy Board, Billy Bor, Robert Forshione, John Frobose, Steve Greenberg, George Greer, Bob Henderson, Susan Hines Leanues, Joe Kociubes, Glen Lautzenhiser, Tim Lewis, Jim Lurie, Lenny May, Tom Palbu, Jerome Pruett, Ken Rhyne, Earl Rodd, Steve Saradnik, Gregg Schorsten, Bill Shearer, Bonnie Eyessen Steenrod, Steve Stone, Bobby Valentine, Susie Wilson, and Tom Wilson.

While Diana Munson did not play an active interview role in this, she and I have shared stories for nearly forty years, and through her close friend Joanne Murray a number of facts related to years, addresses, and the like were able to be double-checked.

Among Thurman's professional teammates, some have told their stories in other books, as shown in the bibliography, and others were freshly interviewed for this project, including Ron Blomberg, Chris Chambliss, Ed Figueroa, Ron Guidry, Fran Healy, Ken Holtzman, Reggie Jackson, Jim Kaat, Sparky Lyle, Tippy Martinez, Gene Michael, trainer Gene Monahan, Bobby Murcer, Graig Nettles, Fritz Peterson, Lou Piniella, Willie Randolph, Mickey Rivers, Mickey Scott, Mel Stottlemyre, Ron Swoboda, and Roy White. Some player wives who were very helpful included Gretchen Randolph, Audra Chambliss, Kay Murcer, and Mara Blomberg Young. Billy Joe Martin shared memories of his father, Billy.

Baseball officials and media who had interesting reflections included Seth Abraham, Maury Allen, Jimmy Bank, Peter Bavasi, Sy Berger, Howard Berk, Art Berke, Ira Berkow, Hal Bock, Rick Cerrone, Jim Charlton, Murray Chass, Wayne Coffey, Dennis

D'Agostino, Joe D'Ambrosio, David Fisher, Rob Franklin, Joe Garagiola Jr., Joe Garagiola Sr., Rick Gentile, Pat Gillick, Ross Greenburg, Michael Grossbardt, Bill Guilfoile, Henry Hecht, Jeff Idelson, Steve Jacobson, Dave Kaplan, Jerry Kirshenbaum, Dennis Lewin, Lee Lowenfish, Bruce Lowitt, Lee MacPhail, Bill Madden, Loren Mathews, Jack McKeon, Leigh Montville, Mickey Morabito, Tony Morante, Gerry Murphy, Herschel Nissenson, Marty Noble, Keith Olbermann, Phil Pepe, Arthur Pincus, Gary Pomerantz, Jay Rosenstein, Spencer Ross, Bill Shannon, Corky Simpson, Tal Smith, Ted Spencer, Tom Villante, Larry Wahl, Michael Weissman, Bill White, and Pat Williams.

There were "off the field" friends in addition to his long-running friendships with the Canton residents he maintained contact with, including Phil Castinetti, Jack Danzis, Carmine DeNoia, Elliott Pollak, Bob Solomon, and the sons of Nat Tarnopol—Mark Solomon and Paul Tarnopol—who remembered the years Thurman lived with them.

The coverage of the accident and its aftermath in the *New York Times,* New York's *Daily News,* the *New York Post, Newsday,* the *Canton Repository,* the *Cleveland Plain Dealer,* WCBS-TV, WNBC-TV, WABC-TV, WNEW-TV, WPIX-TV, and WINS radio was extensive and valuable, along with wire service coverage from the Associated Press and United Press International. We filled in some gaps with stories from the *Washington Post* and *Chicago Tribune,* and the *Tucson Citizen* reported on Thurman's father a few weeks after the accident. The YES Network's *Yankeeography* about Munson and ESPN's twenty-fifth-anniversary coverage were valuable, as was ABC Sports' coverage of the game the night of the funeral.

Statistics, cross-references, and assorted facts were found all over the Internet, but these sites were especially useful: Wikipedia.com, Retrosheet.org, Baseball-reference.com, Baseball-almanac.com, VoteThurmanIn.com, thedeadballera.com, and Aviation-safety.net.

Sports Illustrated and *Sport* magazine were also consulted.

Craig Hunter of the *New York Times,* a pilot, graciously gave me an afternoon to go through the accident report of the National Transportation Safety Board, and simulate, as I sat on his right, what the cockpit experience would have been like. Jerry Anderson, who was aboard the actual flight, gave me a great deal of time and guidance, and his ESPN interview from 2004 was provided to me by producer Willie Weinbaum, with Jerry's blessing. Don Armen, Marion Rossi, and Adam Rossi, Jr., aided in compiling the facts in this portion of the book.

In addition, we went to the many hours of tapes that Thurman recorded for the autobiography project in 1977 to hear him tell his story in his own voice.

Bibliography

BOOKS

Appel, Marty. *Now Pitching for the Yankees*. Total Sports Illustrated, Kingston, NY, 2001.

Cairns, Bob. *Pen Men*. St. Martin's, New York, 1992.

Devine, Christopher. *Thurman Munson*. McFarland, Jefferson, NC, 2001.

Eig, Jonathan. *Luckiest Man*. Simon and Schuster, New York, 2005.

Figueroa, Ed, and Dorothy Harshman. *Yankee Stranger*. Exposition Press, Smithtown, NY, 1982.

Guidry, Ron, and Peter Golenbock. *Guidry*. Prentice Hall, Englewood Cliffs, NJ, 1980.

Hunter, Jim "Catfish," and Armen Keteyian. *Catfish: My Life in Baseball*. Berkeley Publishing, New York, 1989.

Jackson, Reggie, with Mike Lupica. *Reggie*. Ballantine, New York, 1985.

Jacobson, Steve. *The Best Team Money Could Buy*. Atheneum, New York, 1978.

James, Bill. *The New Bill James Historical Baseball Abstract*. Revised edition. Free Press, New York, 2001.

Kahn, Roger. *October Men*. Harcourt, New York, 2003.

Lee, Bill, with Dick Lally. *The Wrong Stuff*. Penguin, New York, 1985.

Linn, Ed. *Inside the Yankees: The Championship Year*. Ballantine, New York, 1978.

MacPhail, Lee, with Marty Appel. *My Nine Innings.* Meckler, Westport, CT, 1989.

Madden, Bill. *Pride of October.* Warner Books, New York, 2003.

Madden, Bill, and Moss Klein. *Damned Yankees.* Warner Books, New York, 1990.

Martin, Billy, and Peter Golenbock. *Number One.* Dell, New York, 1980.

Munson, Thurman, and Marty Appel. *Thurman Munson: An Autobiography.* Revised edition. Coward, McCann and Geoghegan, New York, 1979.

Murcer, Bobby, with Glen Waggoner. *Yankee for Life.* HarperCollins, New York, 2008.

Nettles, Graig, and Peter Golenbock. *Balls.* Pocket Books, New York, 1985.

New York Yankees. *Media Guides,* 1969–1980, 2007.

Piniella, Lou, and Maury Allen. *Sweet Lou.* Bantam, New York, 1987.

Rivers, Mickey, and Michael DeMarco. *Ain't No Sense Worryin': The Wisdom of "Mick the Quick" Rivers.* Sport Publishing, Toronto, Canada, 2003.

Robinson, Ray. *Iron Horse.* Norton, New York, 1990.

Society for American Baseball Research. *The SABR Baseball List & Record Book.* Scribner, New York, 2007.

Sporting News. *Official Baseball Guide,* 1969–1980.

Ward, Ettie, editor. *Courting the Yankees: Legal Essays on the Bronx Bombers.* Carolina Academic Press, Durham, NC, 2003.

GOVERNMENT REPORT

National Transportation Safety Board. Aircraft Accident Report 80-2, Thurman L. Munson, Cessna Citation 501, N15NY Near Canton, Ohio, August 2, 1979. United States Government, Washington, DC. 1979.

ARTICLES OF SPECIAL NOTE

Coffey, Wayne. "Thurman Munson's Final Hour." *Daily News* (New York), July 3, 2004.

Paterniti, Michael. "The House That Thurman Munson Built." *Esquire,* September 1999.

SPECIAL THANKS

Transcript of 2004 Jerry Anderson interview for ESPN's *Outside the Lines,* courtesy of producer Willie Weinbaum and ESPN.

Permissions

Index

Ackley, George, 224
Adams, Glenn, 39
Albert, Marv, 289, 317
Albohn, Frankie, 290
Albu, Tom, 27–28
Alexander, Doyle, 128
Ali, Muhammad, 313
Allen, Maury, 136, 157, 175, 217, 264
Alomar, Sandy, 103, 115
Alston, Dell, 309, 317
Althouse, Jim, 316
Anderson, Dave, 279, 291, 311
Anderson, Jeff, 329
Anderson, Jerry, 117–18, 169, 181, 182,
    222–27, 229–30, 257–58, 329,
    338–39, 353
  Munson plane crash, account of,
    230–31, 234–56
  Munson's relationship with, 221–22,
    229, 231–34, 249
Anderson, Sparky, 128, 129–31
Appel, Marty, 5, 54, 80–81, 85, 100–101,
    106, 111, 114, 116, 122–23, 132, 141,
    150–51, 204–5, 208, 230, 268–70,
    271–72, 303–6, 308, 317, 319, 326,
    331–32, 346–47, 348, 349, 353

last conversation with Munson,
    186–89
Munson's autobiography, 144–47
Munson's relationship with, 7, 8–9
Arbus, Diane, 66
Armen, Don, 183, 258–59
Association for the Help of Retarded
    Children, 331–32

Bahnsen, Stan, 51, 58
Baird, Ed, 39, 40
Bando, Sal, 196
Barlow, Mike, 184, 185
Barr, Jim, 190
Beattie, Jim, 310
Beene, Fred, 97, 101, 102
Belanger, Mark, 322
Beldon, Bob, 30–31
Bell, Buddy, 309
Bench, Johnny, 5, 60, 126, 129–30,
    344
Beniquez, Juan, 209, 210, 310
Bergesh, Bill, 261, 288
Berk, Howard, 9

Berra, Yogi, 60, 123, 139, 195, 290, 297, 309, 324, 338
Beutel, Bill, 283
Bird, Doug, 166
Biskup, John, 316
Blair, Paul, 76, 309, 317
Blomberg, Ron, 64–65, 66, 67, 88
Blyleven, Bert, 76
Board, Randy, 27
Bonds, Bobby, 105, 106, 109, 111, 114–15, 204, 205, 309
Bor, Billy, 41
Bosh, Steve, 281, 282–83
Bouton, Jim, 171, 173–74, 313
Bowa, Larry, 49
Boyer, Cloyd, 47, 48
Brett, George, 132, 166
Brett, Ken, 115
Broberg, Pete, 44
Brooks, Larry, 207
Brown, Bobby, 207, 289, 310
Burke, Michael, 69–70, 83, 84
Burris, Ray, 310
Buskey, Tom, 97, 101
Byrne, Brendan, 289

Cairns, Bob, 159
Caldwell, Mike, 196–97
Campanella, Roy, 60, 285
Carey, Hugh, 289
Carney, Don, 294, 296
Castinetti, Phil, 163–64
Cerone, Rick, 335
Cerrone, Rick, 288
Cey, Ron, 168
Chambliss, Audra, 319, 335
Chambliss, Chris, 101, 102, 105, 111, 127, 165, 185, 190, 265, 292, 310, 322, 335, 352
Chass, Murray, 118, 120, 134–35, 149, 152, 190, 278
Claassen, Harold, 279
Clark, Jim, 277
Clarke, Horace, 115
Clay, Ken, 310
Clemente, Roberto, 53, 75, 314, 344

Cmich, Stanley, 307, 312
Coffey, Wayne, 327
Cohen, Arnold, 269
Coleman, J. Robert, 50, 312, 313–14, 318
Collins, Richard L., 182
Cooke, Terence Cardinal, 297
Cooper, Cecil, 196, 198, 199
Cosell, Howard, 322, 325
Cott, Marty, 44–45
Crocker, Bill, 316
Cronin, Joe, 93
Cuccinello, Al, 41
Curtis, John, 43–44

D'Agostino, Dennis, 276–77
D'Ambrosio, Joe, 124–25
Danzis, Jack, 72–73
Davis, Ron, 198, 210, 268, 310
Davis, Scott, 157
Dempsey, Rick, 95–96, 104, 309
Dent, Bucky, 165–66, 177, 185, 265–66, 310, 323, 329
Dickey, Bill, 60, 112, 123, 310
Dillon, Gene, 221
DiMaggio, Joe, 111
Dobson, Pat, 87, 97, 103
Dockery, John, 171–74
Dole, Jack, 182–83
Dominick, Pauline, 305, 312
Dominick, Tony "Tote," 73–74, 137, 169, 201–2, 220, 221, 258, 259, 263, 318, 340
Downing, Al, 49, 51, 52
Doyle, Brian, 62, 159, 210
Doyle, Jack, 260
Drago, Dick, 164
Drury, Bob, 281
Duca, Frank, 291

Eddins, Don, 18, 28–29, 33, 284
Ellis, Dock, 115, 261
Ellis, John, 54–55, 77, 85, 309
Etchebarren, Andy, 76–77
Evans, William, 257

Fernandez, Frank, 51
Ferraro, Mike, 201, 296, 309
Ferrer, Christy, 281
Figueroa, Ed, 115, 125, 192–93, 196, 210,
    289, 292, 296, 310
Finley, Charley, 92, 93, 106
Fishel, Bob, 8, 9, 54, 58, 89, 129, 303, 308
Fisk, Carlton, 88–89, 122, 126, 151, 270,
    344
  Munson's relationship with, 60, 61–63,
    343
Fisk, Linda, 343
Flynn, Pat, 278
Foli, Tim, 44
Ford, Whitey, 111
Fosina, Joe, 287–88
Foster, Roy, 59
Fowler, Art, 297, 309
Franklin, Rob, 86
Franz, Art, 77
Frobose, John, 40–41, 177
Fudin, Terry, 346
Fulz, Joanne. See Murray, Joanne Fulz

Gallo, Bill, 279–80
Gamble, Oscar, 207–8, 209, 218, 310
Gantner, Jim, 201
Garagiola, Joe, Jr., 141
Garagiola, Joe, Sr., 171, 190
Garcia, Mike, 24
Garcia, Rich, 309
Garland, Wayne, 309
Gehrig, Eleanor, 54–55, 90, 294, 313
Gehrig, Lou, 116, 269, 310
Gelal, Chuck, 284
Gentile, Rick, 136
Gibbs, Jake, 53, 54
Gilhousen, Joe, 31
Gillick, Pat, 44, 45
Girard, Jerry, 281, 282, 283
Girardi, Joe, 352
Goldstein, Joe, 289
Golenbock, Peter, 158, 177, 180, 185,
    264, 334
Gossage, Goose, 158, 165, 166, 168, 177,
    199, 217, 265, 310

Munson's relationship with, 159–60
Gothot, Denny, 30
Gowdy, Curt, 61–62
Greenberg, Steve, 40
Greer, George, 39–40
Grich, Bobby, 133, 138
Grossbardt, Michael, 8, 69–72, 123
Guidry, Ron, 158–59, 160, 164, 165,
    167–68, 189, 190, 207, 217, 264, 287,
    310, 321, 323, 329, 343–44
Guilfoile, Bill, 8, 54
Gulden, Brad, 190, 289, 296, 310
Gullett, Don, 133, 138, 163, 310

Hall, Dave, 222–27, 230, 235–47, 249,
    256, 257, 330
Haller, Bill, 309
Hamilton, Steve, 51, 57
Hargrove, Mike, 309
Harrah, Toby, 309
Hartnett, Gabby, 60
Healy, Fran, 49, 142, 143, 148, 151, 295,
    299, 310, 326
Heath, Mike, 160, 207, 304, 309
Hecht, Henry, 167
Hegan, Jim, 309
Hegan, Mike, 102
Henderson, Bob, 27, 170
Herzog, Whitey, 166
Hesse, Harry, 41–42
Hisle, Larry, 34
Holtzman, Ken, 128, 163
Honig, Gary, 278–79
Hood, Don, 218, 310
Houk, Ralph, 49, 55, 58, 64, 85, 87, 88,
    89–90
  Munson's relationship with, 74
Howard, Elston, 52, 66, 78, 122, 123, 139,
    309
Howser, Dick, 111, 149, 309, 335
Hunter, Billy, 76
Hunter, Catfish, 52, 98–99, 106–7, 108–9,
    165, 166, 168, 187, 188, 208, 263–64,
    283, 288, 310, 333
  Munson's relationship with, 109
Hutchinson, Ed, 257

Jackson, Reggie, 5, 10, 63, 149, 153, 159, 164, 166, 170, 176, 177, 178, 201, 207, 218, 219, 338
  brawl in Milwaukee, 196–98
  Martin and, 147–48, 161
  as Mr. October, 154
  Munson's death and funeral, 296, 299–300, 302, 308, 310, 313, 317
  Munson's relationship with, 142–43, 144, 148
  Sport interview, 141–44
  Yankees' acquisition of, 138–39
Jacobson, Steve, 149
James, Bill (baseball statistician), 345, 353
James, Bill (friend of Munson's), 284
Jensen, Erik, 349–51
Jensen, Jim, 289, 290
John, Tommy, 78, 172, 209, 210, 310
Johnson, Cliff, 160, 177, 309
Johnson, Johnny, 42, 45, 47
Johnstone, Jay, 309
Joyce, Dick, 277

Kaat, Jim, 168, 218, 310
Kane, Bill, 191, 261, 306, 310
Keith, Larry, 126
Kekich, Mike, 71, 86
Kenney, Jerry, 66, 75, 85
Kessinger, Don, 217
Keteyian, Armen, 18, 263
Klein, Moss, 302
Kline, Steve, 81, 97, 101
Klutz, Clyde, 187
Koch, Ed, 289
Kociubes, Joe, 31
Krausse, Lew, 52
Kravec, Ken, 218
Kubek, Tony, 4
Kucinich, Dennis, 307–8
Kuhn, Bowie, 62, 91, 114, 119, 207, 209, 218, 269, 270, 303–4, 308, 314, 317
Kuiper, Duane, 309
Kyriakides, A. H., 258

Lang, Jack, 132
Lau, Charley, 309
Lauck, Dan, 278
Lautzenhiser, Glen, 39
Layton, Eddie, 292
Lee, Bill, 61, 122
LeFlore, Ron, 324
Lemon, Bob, 158, 162, 165, 168, 171, 176–77, 307
Lewin, Dennis, 325
Lewis, Joe "Skip," 39, 41
Lidle, Cory, 347
Lindstrom, Jimmy, 271, 272, 273
Linn, Steve, 345
Littell, Mark, 127
Lolich, Mickey, 75
Lombardi, Dick, 316
Lupica, Mike, 143
Lurie, Jim, 29
Lyle, Sparky, 79–81, 97, 118, 137, 153, 158, 159, 160, 165, 207, 268, 309, 329

Macks, Ron, 42
MacPhail, Lee, 22, 44, 45–46, 49, 85, 87, 89, 92–93, 303, 308
Madden, Bill, 219, 344–45
Maddox, Elliott, 102–3, 112
Maddox, Gary, 273
Mahler, Jonathan, 158, 349
Malloy, Tim, 281
Manning, Rick, 96–97
Mantle, Mickey, 6–8, 82, 109, 167
Marazzi, Rich, 97
Marchiano, Sal, 289–90
Martin, Billy, 1, 10, 113, 115, 122, 128, 130, 149, 150, 152, 153, 158, 179, 184, 185–86, 190–91, 195–96, 197, 209, 210, 213, 218, 321, 323, 335, 338
  firing by Yankees in 1978, 161, 162
  flying with Munson, 180–81
  hiring by Yankees in 1975, 110, 111
  Jackson and, 147–48, 161
  Munson's death and funeral, 267–68, 292, 309, 317

Munson's naming as Yankee captain, 116, 119

rehiring by Yankees in 1979, 177

Martin, Billy Joe, 267–68

Martinez, Dennis, 322

Martinez, Tippy, 96, 105, 288, 299, 323–24

Mashburn, Jeff, 257, 258

Mason, Jim, 105

May, Carlos, 150–51

May, Lenny, 24–25, 30

Mayberry, John, 105

Mazer, Bill, 290

McAvoy, Edward, 181, 335, 336, 337

McCarthy, Joe, 116, 310

McCarthy, John, 338

McCarver, Tim, 273

McDaniel, Lindy, 51, 59

McDowell, Sam, 87, 97

McGregor, Scott, 93, 105, 299, 309

McKeon, Jack, 105

McKinney, Rich, 44

Medich, George "Doc," 97, 103, 115

Melvin, Doug, 310

Merola, Matt, 141, 296

Merrill, Robert, 297

Messer, Frank, 186, 211–16, 281, 282, 294, 299, 310, 320

Messersmith, Andy, 118, 209

Michael, Gene, 35–36, 49, 52, 55, 63, 76, 77, 88–89, 305, 309, 331, 332, 335, 345, 347

Molitor, Paul, 199

Monahan, Gene, 94–95, 185, 196, 306, 310

Money, Don, 199

Morabito, Mickey, 124, 141, 161, 261, 267, 268, 277, 291, 300, 310, 318

Moses, Gerry, 85

Moss, Dick, 170–71

Munson, Darla (sister), 12, 15–16, 18, 19, 21, 33, 44, 46, 50, 85–86, 271, 307, 311, 334–35, 340

Munson, Darrell (father), 4, 15–16, 17–18, 19–20, 46, 50, 271, 305, 311, 318, 333–34, 339

Munson's relationship with, 18, 20–23, 106

Munson, Diana (Diane) Dominick (wife), 4, 9, 10, 18, 21, 55, 73, 85–86, 117, 118, 126, 147, 152, 179–80, 205, 206, 217, 325, 326, 331–32, 337, 346, 347, 348, 352, 353–54

life after Munson's death, 327–29

Munson's childhood infatuation with, 32–33

Munson's death and funeral, 251, 258, 259, 262, 268, 272, 286, 294, 302, 303, 304–5, 308, 309, 313, 316, 318

wedding, 49–50

Munson, Duane (brother), 2, 12, 13, 15, 16–18, 24, 25, 31, 33, 46, 50, 271, 307, 318, 340

Munson, Janice (sister), 12, 19, 21, 33, 50, 86, 271, 307, 340

Munson, Kelly (daughter), 73, 117, 258, 302, 305, 308, 332

Munson, Michael (son), 4, 69, 112, 117–18, 202, 258, 305, 308, 312, 329, 332–33, 343

Munson, Ruth Smylie (mother), 15–16, 17, 50, 73, 271, 305, 307, 339

Munson's relationship with, 18–19

Munson, Thurman

athleticism of, 16–17, 21, 25, 26–28

autobiography of, 9–10, 144–47, 189, 230, 353

as baseball fan, 24

betting on dog races, 163

childhood difficulties, overcoming of, 339–41

childhood family life, 12–23

children's affection for, 72

education vs. athletics issue, 31

everyman persona, 6–7, 26

as family man, 71–72, 117–18

flying by, 1–4, 69, 147, 157–58, 175–76, 177–83, 189, 201–2, 217–19, 222–28, 235–48, 251–52

as gun enthusiast, 98–99

handball playing, 231

humor of, 122, 136, 147, 157, 232–33

injuries to, 24–25, 76–77, 94–95, 156, 164, 185–86, 188, 193, 218

insecurities of, 18

intense approach to life, 252–53

interviews in 1979, 171–74, 211–16

maturity of, 68

memorials to, 341–43

military service, 36, 48–50, 51

off-season activities, 169–70

real estate ventures, 73, 83, 117, 222, 232, 233–34, 353–54

self-confidence of, 38

surliness of, 67, 86, 126, 135, 137

television commercials, 156–57

walk of, 183–84

See also Munson, Thurman, baseball career of; Munson, Thurman, plane crash and death of; *specific persons*

Munson, Thurman, baseball career of

All-Star Games, 75, 125, 151

amateur play, 30–31, 38, 39

autographing for fans, 24, 67, 72, 163–64, 349

batting skills and stats, 13, 15, 16, 29, 30, 38, 39, 40, 42, 49, 51–52, 53, 55, 56–57, 59, 74, 75–76, 81, 90, 104, 112, 121, 125, 127, 128–29, 153, 160–61, 166–67, 183–84, 200, 210

Binghamton Triplets, 7–9, 21, 47–49

calling the game and working the dynamics, 96, 113

catching position, adoption of, 29–30

Chatham A's, 39–41, 43–44

childhood play, 13, 26

Cleveland, interest in playing for, 118, 224, 233, 292, 327

clutch hitting, 13, 112

college, 21–22, 33, 34, 36–39, 42

competitiveness in play, 29

Darrell Munson's views on, 20–22

error incident in 1971, 76–77

fan relations, 56, 57–58, 122, 190, 345–46

fielding skills and stats, 20–21, 38–39, 52, 60, 75, 76–78, 79–80, 94, 99, 187–88, 200, 201, 210

final game as catcher, 195–200

free agency issue, 118

Gold Glove awards, 94

"greatest catcher" issue, 60, 353

Hall of Fame issue, 344–47

high school, 16–18, 26–27, 28–30, 34

home run of 1978, 166–67

injuries, playing with, 62, 94–95, 160, 195–96, 207

managing position had he lived, 354

media relations, 99–101, 134–37, 172–73, 211, 218, 282, 313, 327

memorabilia, market for, 348–49

missing games due to knee problems, 186–88, 190, 200

Most Valuable Player Award, 131–33

Pittsburgh Pirates tryout, 31

potential earnings had he lived, 330–31

Rookie of the Year Award, 59–60

rookies, treatment of, 96–97

San Juan Crabbers, 53

Syracuse Chiefs, 50–51, 52

talking while catching, 40, 63, 97

television programs about, 326, 349–51, 352

uncertainty about future in 1979, 211–16

Yankee Stadium debut, 7–9, 49

See also New York Yankees

Munson, Thurman, plane crash and death of

Anderson's account of crash, 230–31, 234–56

coroner's report, 250–51, 258

crash site today, 351–52

emergency rescue response, 257–58

fans' reaction, 273, 281–82, 292, 298, 299, 300

funeral service, 272–73, 300, 301–11, 312–19

grave site, 341

lawsuits resulting from, 337–38

media coverage of, 258, 269–70, 273–85, 288, 289–93, 294–96

Munson's handling of plane, 222–28, 251–52

notification of family and teammates, 258–66, 267–69, 271–72, 273

NTSB report, 251, 335–37

training of pilots, effect on, 338–39

Yankees' response, 286–93, 294–300, 302

Munson, Tracy Lynn (daughter), 56, 117, 258, 302, 305, 308, 332

Murcer, Bobby, 1, 2–3, 48, 50, 52, 57, 72, 73, 75, 76, 81, 87, 102, 103, 104, 105, 176, 190, 208, 209, 210, 217, 218, 219, 347, 348

Munson's death and funeral, 271–73, 292, 296, 304, 310, 315–16

Munson's relationship with, 203–4, 205

"Murcer Game" following Munson's funeral, 321, 322–23, 324, 325

return to Yankees in 1979, 203, 206

trade to San Francisco, 105–6, 204–5

Murcer, Kay, 1, 3, 205, 206, 219, 272, 304, 319

Murphy, Gerry, 259–60, 261, 262–63, 310, 319

Murray, Joanne Fulz, 303, 328, 343

Nachman, Jerry, 290–91

Narron, Jerry, 185, 190, 216, 218, 268, 296, 297, 298–99, 310

Naughton, Jim, 279

Nederlander, Jimmy, 66

Nettles, Graig, 41, 85–86, 110, 122, 135, 158, 160, 165, 166, 177–78, 191, 219, 263, 264, 283, 288, 310–11, 318, 320, 334, 338

New York Yankees

American League Championship Series (1976), 127–28

American League Championship Series (1977), 153

American League Championship Series (1978), 166–67

attendance situation, 82, 127

Diana Munson's payment following Munson's death, 326–27

haircut policy, 87

lawsuit related to Munson's death, 338

Munson beard episode, 151–52

Munson contract's no-fly provision, 170–71

Munson memorials, 341–42

Munson's death, response to, 286–93, 294–300, 302

Munson's debut with, 51–52

Munson's drafting by, 8, 41–43, 44–46

Munson's leadership role, 57, 58, 108, 122–24, 125–26, 148, 150

Munson's naming as captain, 114, 116–17, 119, 121

Munson's number 15, 51, 294

Munson's salary, 22, 103, 104, 120–21, 133, 139–40, 157, 170

Munson trade, consideration of, 104–5

1969 season, 51–53

1970 season, 54–59

1971 season, 64–65, 74–78

1972 season, 79, 81–82

1973 season, 87–91

1974 season, 92–104

1975 season, 107–12

1976 season, 119–33

1977 season, 147–55

1978 season, 158–68

1979 season, 176–77, 183–86, 189–201, 206–11, 216–18, 299–300, 320–25, 333

1980 roster changes, 335

Red Sox playoff game of 1978, 165–66

Red Sox rivalry, 60–61, 88–89, 108, 122, 149, 163, 164

Steinbrenner's purchase of, 84–85

trading youth for veterans, 87

World Series (1976), 128–31

World Series (1977), 153–55

World Series (1978), 167–68

Nissenson, Herschel, 99–101

Noble, Marty, 136, 302, 317, 320

Nottebart, Don, 51

O'Connell, Tim, 50

O'Day, Joe, 139

Ogle, Jim, 101

Olbermann, Keith, 273–76

Olen, Bob, 70

Palermo, Steve, 97

Palmer, Jim, 49

Papa, Juliet, 299

Paskert, Moose, 29, 37, 43

Patek, Fred, 105

Paterniti, Michael, 98, 318, 327–28
Paul, Gabe, 66, 84, 85, 92–93, 101, 102,
    103, 104, 105–7, 110, 114, 120, 133,
    139, 204–5, 270, 284, 292, 307–8,
    327, 338
Pepe, Phil, 108, 121, 136–37, 179, 279
Pepitone, Joe, 52
Peterson, Fritz, 51, 55, 58, 59, 77–78,
    97–98, 101, 102, 309
  wife-swapping incident, 71, 86–87
Pincus, Arthur, 278–79
Piniella, Lou, 2, 50, 110, 122, 150, 152,
    157, 158, 163, 164, 165, 175–76, 201,
    206, 207, 209, 210, 217, 218, 219,
    322, 323, 324, 342
  Munson's death and funeral, 264–65,
    275, 286, 287, 290, 304, 310, 313,
    314–15
  Munson's relationship with, 94
  talking about hitting, 208
  Yankees' acquisition of, 93–94
Pollack, Elliott, 139–40
Posada, Jorge, 343–44, 352
Preston, Sy, 142
Priore, Nick, 287, 310
Pruett, Jerome, 19–20, 25, 26–27, 28–30,
    169

Rajsich, Dave, 309
Randle, Lenny, 289, 310
Randolph, Willie, 115, 125, 149, 159,
    164, 185, 190, 198, 209–10, 265,
    297–98, 310, 322, 323, 352
Redmond, Jimmy, 34
Requena, Louis, 70, 72
Rhodes, James, 284
Richardson, Bobby, 271–72
Richman, Arthur, 273
Righetti, Dave, 207
Rinaldi, Tom, 234–56
Ripple, Terry, 29
Rivers, Mickey, 115, 125, 132, 160, 163, 166,
    190, 198, 199, 206–7, 208, 273, 309, 317
Rizzuto, Phil, 66, 196, 211, 295, 299, 300,
    310, 320–21
Rodd, Earl, 27

Roden, Bill, 314
Rose, Pete, 128, 217, 270
Rosen, Al, 112, 161, 307
Ross, Don, 152
Rossetti, Diana, 277
Rossi, Marion, 302
Rossiter, Bob, 277
Russo, Frank, 346

Sacknoff, Larry, 288
Samuel, Marsh, 310
Santilli, Carl, 28
Saradnik, Steve, 40
Scala, Dom, 192, 310
Scamardella, Roseanne, 283
Scarbery, Randy, 216
Schneck, Dave, 94
Schneider, Herman, 142
Schorsten, Gregg, 50
Schreiber, LeAnn, 279
Score, Herb, 307
Scott, Mickey, 48
Scurre, Paul, 316
Seghi, Phil, 307
Shannon, Bill, 77
Shearer, Bill, 182–83
Sheehy, Pete, 51, 85, 123, 124, 195, 287,
    288, 310
Sheppard, Bob, 297, 298
Shulock, John, 197, 198
Simpson, Carole, 290
Simpson, Corky, 20, 23, 333–34
Sims, Duke, 91
Singleton, Ken, 322
Skinner, Tom, 302
Smith, Tal, 44–45, 93, 105, 106
Solomon, Bob, 68
Solomon, Mark (stepson of Nat
    Tarnopol), 66–67, 68
Spencer, Jim, 190, 199, 216, 218, 310
Spikes, Charlie, 85
Sprowl, Bobby, 163
Stanley, Bob, 166
Stanley, Fred, 192, 288, 310
Steinbrenner, George, 10, 69, 86–87, 89,
    92, 105, 107, 115, 119, 120, 128, 130,

133, 138, 139, 148, 153, 156, 160, 171, 177, 185–86, 206, 321–22, 326, 327, 354
letter of appreciation to Munson, 131–32
Martin's hiring in 1975, 110, 111
Martin's rehiring in 1979, 177
Munson's death and funeral, 259–61, 263, 264, 265, 269, 291–93, 300, 309, 317
Munson's naming as Yankee captain, 114, 116–17, 121
Munson's relationship with, 87, 140–41, 291–92
purchase of Yankees, 84–85
suspension from baseball, 91, 114, 115
Yankee turbulence of 1977, 149–52
Stewart, Bob, 277–78
Stone, Steve, 34, 37–39, 42, 44
Stoneham, Horace, 105
Stottlemyre, Jean, 107
Stottlemyre, Mel, 51, 57, 58, 78, 81, 97, 101, 107, 352
Sudakis, Bill, 100, 104
Sutton, Don, 153
Swoboda, Ron, 64, 75–76

Talbot, Fred, 51
Tallis, Cedric, 105, 207, 261, 263, 268, 310
Tarnopol, Nat, 65–66, 92–93, 140, 270
Munson's relationship with, 67–69
Tarnopol, Paul, 68–69, 270
Tebbetts, Birdie, 110
Teitel, Dave, 316
Tenace, Gene, 34
Tiant, Luis, 172, 218, 296, 310, 322
Tidrow, Dick, 101, 102, 310
Torborg, Jeff, 191, 309
Toretzky, Art, 279
Torre, Joe, 309
Torres, Rusty, 85
Torrez, Mike, 153, 165
Tresh, Tom, 51
Tucker, Jess, 117, 232, 259
Tuite, Jim, 278, 279

Valentine, Bobby, 39–40, 44
Vecchione, Joe, 278, 279
Velez, Otto, 93
Verdi, Frank, 64
Villante, Tom, 284–85
Virdon, Bill, 93, 102, 103, 104, 109–11

Wahl, Larry, 124, 261–62, 263, 310, 319
Ward, Ettie, 336–37
Ward, Robert, 141, 142, 143
Weaver, Earl, 270, 322
Weber, Jim, 277
Weinbaum, Willie, 230, 234, 255–56
Weinberg, Barry, 174–75, 310
White, Bill, 14–15, 66, 112, 155, 166, 211, 281, 282, 294–95, 296, 299, 326
White, Roy, 41, 57, 66, 139, 149, 163, 165, 170, 275, 279, 286–87, 310, 317
Wigod, Dewey, 346
Williams, Chee Chee, 283, 317
Williams, Dick, 66, 92–93
Wilson, Susie, 25, 26, 31–32
Wilson, Tom, 25–26
Winfield, Dave, 330–31
Winfield, Paul, 279
Wohlford, Jim, 93, 201
Wolf, Warner, 283–84
Woolf, Bob, 307
Wood, Wilbur, 153
Woodling, Gene, 22, 42–43, 44, 45, 52, 182
Wortham, Rich, 209, 210
Wright, Mel, 111
Wright, Toby, 80

Yankee Stadium, 82–83, 84, 90, 121
Yastrzemski, Carl, 49, 166, 269–70
Yoder, Harry, 257
Young, Dick, 327
Young, Mara Blomberg, 73, 112

THE BILLION DOLLAR GAME
by Allen St. John

Think the Super Bowl is only about two teams of titans clashing on the field? Think again. The Super Bowl is about fans, hundreds of millions of fans. It's about money, more money than the GDP of twenty-five sovereign nations. It's about precision, the timing of everything from the notorious commercials to the epic halftime show. And it's about the vision and skill of designing a state-of-the-art stadium to house the great show. Here, Allen St. John reveals how America's biggest sporting event is more than just a couple hours on a Sunday: it's a high stakes, real-life dramatic story, with millions of participants all hoping for the same thing—the greatest game ever.

Sports/Football/978-07679-2815-1

THE CATCHER WAS A SPY
by Nicholas Dawidoff

The only Major League ballplayer whose baseball card is on display at the headquarters of the CIA, Moe Berg has the singular distinction of having both a 15-year career as a catcher for such teams as the New York Robins and the Chicago White Sox and that of a spy for the OSS during World War II. As Dawidoff follows Berg from his claustrophobic childhood through his glamorous (though equivocal) careers in sports and espionage and into the long, nomadic years during which he lived on the hospitality of such scattered acquaintances as Joe DiMaggio and Albert Einstein, he succeeds in establishing who Berg was beneath his layers of carefully constructed cover.

Biography/978-0-679-76289-8

THE COMPLETE GAME
by Ron Darling

World Series champion, former All-Star, and award-winning television analyst Ron Darling gives readers a inside look at one of the most demanding and strategic positions in all of sports: the pitcher. Drawing on vivid situations from his playing days for the New York Mets and the Oakland Athletics, and from moments he has observed as a broadcaster, Darling offers an engaging look at the art, strategy, and psychology of pitching. No other book examines the position in such compelling depth—*The Complete Game* will be an essential book for every fan and aspiring player.

Sports/978-0-307-39058-5

THE ECHOING GREEN
by Joshua Prager

At 3:58 p.m. on October 3, 1951, Bobby Thomson hit a home run off Ralph Branca. The ball sailed over the left field wall and into history. The Giants won the pennant. That moment—the Shot Heard Round the World—reverberated from the West Wing of the White House to the Sing Sing death house to the Polo Grounds clubhouse, where hitter and pitcher forever turned into hero and goat. It was also in that centerfield block of concrete that, after the home run, a Giants coach tucked away a Wollensak telescope. *The Echoing Green* places that revelation at the heart of a larger story, re-creating in extravagant detail and illuminating as never before the impact of both a moment and a long-guarded secret on the lives of Bobby Thomson and Ralph Branca.

Sports/History/978-0-375-71307-1

THE YANKEE YEARS
by Joe Torre and Tom Verducci

When Joe Torre took over as manager of the Yankees in 1996, they had not won a World Series title in eighteen years. In that time seventeen others had tried to take the helm of America's most famous baseball team. Each one was fired by George Steinbrenner. After twelve triumphant seasons—with twelve straight playoff appearances, six pennants, and four World Series titles—Torre left the Yankees as the most beloved manager in baseball. But dealing with players like Jason Giambi, A-Rod, Derek Jeter, Mariano Rivera, Roger Clemens, and Randy Johnson is what managing is all about. Here, for the first time, Joe Torre and Tom Verducci take readers inside the dugout, the clubhouse, and the front office, showing what it took to keep the Yankees on top of the baseball world.

Sports/978-0-7679-93052-0

VINTAGE BOOKS AND ANCHOR BOOKS
Available at your local bookstore, or visit
www.randomhouse.com